AF556383

INTEGRATED NUTRIENT MANAGEMENT IN CHICKPEA

INTEGRATED
NUTRIENT MANAGEMENT
IN CHICKPEA

Editors

Dr. Virendra Kumar

Plant Protection Officer (PP)
Government of India
Ministry of Agriculture & Farmers Welfare
Department of Agriculture, Cooperation & Farmers Welfare
Directorate of Plant Protection, Quarantine & Storage
Regional Pesticides Testing Laboratory
Kanpur - 208 022, U.P. (INDIA)

&

Dr. Nirmal Kumar Katiyar

Assistant Plant Protection Officer (Chemistry)
Government of India
Ministry of Agriculture and Farmers Welfare
Department of Agriculture, Cooperation and Farmers Welfare
Directorate of Plant Protection, Quarantine and Storage
Regional Pesticides Testing Laboratory
Kanpur - 208 022, U.P. (INDIA)

DISCOVERY PUBLISHING HOUSE PVT. LTD.

INDIA

Published by:

Namit Wasan

DISCOVERY PUBLISHING HOUSE PVT. LTD.
4383/4B, Ansari Road, Darya Ganj
New Delhi-110 002 (India)
Phone : +91-11-23279245, 43596064-65
Fax : +91-11-23253475
E-mail : discoverypublishinghouse@gmail.com
namitwasan9@gmail.com
sales@discoverypublishinggroup.com

website: www.discoverypublishinggroup.com

***First Edition:* 2017**

ISBN: 978-93-5056-872-9

Integrated Nutrient Management in Chickpea

Printed at:
Infinity Imaging Systems
Delhi

Acknowledgement

Behind every success there is certainly an unseen power of Almighty GOD, but aim is the external condition of success which is attainable at perfection in everything by who preserve with the association for giving me this unique opportunity to express my heartfelt gratitude to all those who have given me help to make this success.

Space does not allow to set fourth my desired extent; words fail to express our feelings of deep gratitude and indebtedness to Dr. U.S. Mishra, Associate Professor (Soil Science), Dr. Pawan Sirothia, Head, Department of Natural Resource Management, Dr. H.S. Kushwaha Associate Professor (Agronomy) and Professor Aroop Kumar Gupta, Dean Faculty of Agriculture M.G.C.G.V.V. Chitrakoot, Satna (M.P.), India, whose blessings, guidance, constant inspiration, conservative criticism and encouragement enabled me to prepare this book.

We are also indebted and express our heartful regards to Dr. K.K. Pandey, Principal Scientist, (Plant Pathology), Crop Protection Division, Indian Institute of Vegetable Research (IIVR), Varanasi and our Officer-in-charge, Mr. S.K. Gupta, Assistant Director (Chemistry), Regional Pesticides Testing Laboratory, Kanpur for their Constant moral support.

Most cordial thanks are also expressed to all our respected teachers, Dr. S.K. Bansal, Director IPRI, Gurgaon (Haryana) and Dr. Arvind K. Shukla, Project Co-ordinator (MSN), I.I.S.S., Bhopal, (M.P.), Ex. Professor and Head Dr. R.K. Pathak, Dr. B.R. Gupta, Dr. D.D. Tiwari Pesticide Chemist, Dr. R.C. Nigam Professor and Head/Residue Analyst, Dr. R.K. Pathak and Dr. A.K. Sachan Assistant Professor, Mr. Rajesh Saxena and Mr. Yogesh Mishra (Technical Assistant) Department of Soil Science and Agricultural Chemistry, C.S.A.U.A. & T., Kanpur. Dr. Ashok Kumar (Assistant Professor, National Sugar Institute, Kanpur), Dr. Jagmohan Singh Katiyar, Mr. Ramasare Yadav and Mr. Akhilesh Kulahade and Dr. R.P. Singh, Professor, Department of

Botany, Udai pratap autonomous College, Varanasi, thanks are also due to my rendered their valuable assistance in complication of this book for their help, fruitful suggestions and generous advice.

We are extremely grateful to Mrs. Aarti Saraswat and Mr. Ajai Kumar, Plant Protection Officer (Chemistry), Mr. P.K. Vats, Mr. Ali Ahmed, Mr. Ratnesh Kumar Mall, APPO (Chem.) and Mr. S.M.H. Jafri, Mrs. Angoori Devi, Mr. Mahendra Kumar, Mr. Rajendra Prasad and Mr. Jai Singh of Regional Pesticides Testing Laboratory, Kanpur for their kind moral support and encouragement.

Special thanks also goes to our life partner Mrs. Nandini Devi W/O Dr. Virendra Kumar and Mrs. Sarika Katiyar W/O Dr. Nirmal Katiyar and our children Master Abhinav Kumar and Baby Nivedita Katiyar whose love cannot be denied and also their constant support at each and every moments of life.

Last but not the least, we are indeed grateful to our respected and beloved parents, who inspired us at every step and gave us steadfast and unflinching moral support, encouragement and showered packet of selfless love at each and every moments, we would have not achieved this goal without their blessings and support and my heartful thanks goes to whose encouragement enabled me to achieve this lofty goal.

'Act with knowledge, Knowledge is truth,
The path of action is the truth; the path of truth is action'

कर्म करो तुम ज्ञान से, श्रेष्ठ ज्ञान है धर्म ।
कर्मयोग ही धर्म है, धर्मयोग ही कर्म ।।

Virendra Kumar
Nirmal Kumar Katiyar

Preface

Soil is the wonderful gift of the nature it is the best culture media which nourish to all living beings on the globe. Most soil conditions in different agro-climatic region in India can provide plants adapted to that climate and soil with sufficient nutrition for a complete life cycle, without the addition of nutrients as fertilizer. Nutrient Management is an inter-disciplinary aspect of biological science concerned to deficiency diseases problems and production in agriculture. The importance of micronutrients realised during the past three decades when widespread micronutrient deficiencies were observed in most of the soils in our country, where intensive agriculture is practiced. The distribution of micronutrient minerals is not uniform in a soil and the spatial variation is very high. The natural resources of micronutrient in soil vary considerably from soil to soil. Soil amendments and fertilizers are frequently using by farmers to enhance the plant growth and maximum yield and deficiency disease free plants.

As we know that 17 plant food nutrients are essential for proper crop development. Each is cruelly important to the plant, yet each is required in vastly different amounts. These differences have led to the grouping of these essential elements into three categories primary (macro) nutrients, secondary nutrients and micronutrient plant respond to an inadequate supply of an essential element by forming characteristic deficiency symptoms. Such visually observed symptoms include: stunted growth of roots, stems or leaves and chlorosis of necrosis of various organs. Characteristic symptoms often help to determine the necessary function of elements in the plants and knowledge of symptoms helps agriculturist and forests determine how and when to fertilize crops.

Plants, animals and human beings require several micronutrients (Fe, Mn, Cu, Zn and Cl) in less than 100 mg kg^{-1} in dietary food. In India, about 6.73 Mha are lying barren or produces very low and uneconomical yields of various crops due to excessive accumulation of salts. The critical role that the secondary and micronutrients will play in enhancing food grain production in the country in addition to major nutrients is now a very well recognized fact. To achieve the required massive increase in food production, application of micronutrient is indispensable along with major nutrients not only for meeting the huge demands of food production but also for sustain soil health and reducing malnutrition in animal and human beings.

Chickpea is one of the major pulse crop grown in the *Rabi* season of India. Chickpea is a rich source of highly digestible protein (17-21%) and 62 per cent carbohydrate. It is also rich source of calcium, iron, niacin, vitamin C and vitamin B. Therefore nutrient management enhances the production of chickpea. A literature reveals that application of Zn, B and Mo play a very significant role of basal/foliar growth of chickpea. Zn increased productivity when, B deficiency may causes yield losses up to 100 per cent.

So, this book gives us great pleasure to present before our readers, researchers on *Integrated Nutrient Management (INM)* specially in chickpea crop because it cover a great collections of researches which were conducted by different researchers from the world. This book also provides comprehensive knowledge especially fundamental principle, experimental field applications, Current practices and trends in the field of nutrient management in chickpea. This book consists of various researches which were conducted across the world and latest information has been given in this book on nutrient management aspects in chickpea. It is also extremely important to develop skill the correct soil application of micronutrient in the management of chickpea, micronutrient recommendations to mitigate micronutrient deficiencies and sustaining agricultural production system. This book will be highly useful for extension agencies, farmers, researchers including students and other stakeholders.

Particularly thanks are due to all contributors and publisher also for their contribution and assistance. We hope this book will provide a multidisciplinary forum to explore emerging areas in the field of '*Integrated Nutrient Management in Chickpea*'.

Virendra Kumar

Nirmal Kumar Katiyar

Contents

Pages 1-5

INTEGRATED NUTRIENT MANAGEMENT IN CHICKPEA
***Edited by* : Dr. Virendra Kumar and Dr. Nirmal Kumar Katiyar**
***Edition* : 2017**
ISBN : 978-93-5056-872-9
***Published by* : Discovery Publishing House Pvt. Ltd., New Delhi (India)**

Influence of Zinc, Boron and Molybdenum Application on Biochemical Composition of Chickpea Grain Grown under Rainfed Conditions of Madhya Pradesh

Nirmal Kumar Katiyar[1]
U.S. Mishra[2]
R.K. Pathak[3]

ABSTRACT

The effect of application of micro-nutrients viz; zinc, boron and molybdenum on the biochemical and nutritional quality of chickpea variety Avarodhi was studied during 2012-13 and 2013-14. The application of zinc @ 5.0kg ha^{-1} increased grain protein to 21.21 per cent and protein yield to 470.69kg ha^{-1}. Tryptophan of grain increased significantly on application of zinc, whereas methionine was not affected on zinc application either at 2.5 or 5.0kg ha^{-1}. Similarly, the application of boron @ 2.0kg ha^{-1} gave the highest values of protein (20.65%), protein yield (450.35kg ha^{-1}), tryptophan (0.75g/100g protein) and ash content (2.99%), whereas methionine and lipid content were not affected. Application of molybdenum @ 400g ha^{-1} increased the protein content of grain as well as total protein yield and tryptophan contents significantly. The carbohydrate decreased significantly with increasing levels of zinc, boron and molybdenum. Zinc application @ 5.0kg ha^{-1} increased potassium, sulphur and zinc contents of grain significantly. Boron when applied @ 2.0kg ha^{-1} and molybdenum @ 400g ha^{-1} increased phosphorus, potassium, sulphur, boron and molybdenum contents of grain significantly.

Keywords: Chickpea, Rainfed Condition, Protein, Methionine, Tryptophan, Ash, Minerals.

1. E-mail: nirmalkatiyar83@gmail.com.
2. Department of Natural Resource Management, Faculty of Agriculture, Mahatma Gandhi Chitrakoot Gramodaya Vishwavidyalaya, Chitrakoot, Satna - 485 334 (MP) India.
3. C.S. Azad University of Agriculture and Technology, Kanpur - 208 002, India.

Chickpea is a premier pulse crop of Madhya Pradesh. It occupies the highest area and production among the pulse crops at the national level. Madhya Pradesh produces 5042 thousand tonnes chickpea from 5327 thousand hectares and shares 28.6 per cent and 22.3 per cent of national production and area, respectively (1). It is an important source of food and has distinction of providing important food components like: carbohydrate, protein, lipids and minerals. Plant foods don't have cholesterol. Among the ten essential amino acids methionine and tryptophan are most limiting amino acids in pulses (2). Carbohydrates are present in chickpea in considerable amounts, which contribute for bulk of energy supply in our diet (3). Ash contains several macro and micro-nutrients. Comparatively lesser reports are available regarding the nutritional improvement in food components due to balanced fertilization of mineral nutrients, specially the micro-nutrients such as: zinc, boron and molybdenum. These nutrients are well known to play significant role in the growth, yield and metabolism of crop resulting in improvement in crop quality (4, 5, 6). In the present study, an attempt was made to work out information in the food value of chickpea in terms of biochemical composition of the crop grown under rainfed conditions of Chitrakoot. Soils were deficient in zinc, boron and molybdenum. Influence of Zn, B and Molybdenum Application on Biochemical Composition of Chickpea under Rainfed Conditions.

A field experiment was conducted during the rabi seasons of 2012-13 and 2013-14 at Agricultural Research Farm, Rajaula of Mahatma Gandhi Chitrakoot Gramodaya Vishwavidyalaya, Chitrakoot, Satna (MP). The soil of experimental field was sandy loam deficient in zinc, boron and molybdenum besides macronutrients N, P and S. Three levels of each of zinc (0, 2.5 and 5.0kg ha^{-1}) and boron (0, 1.0 and 2.0kg ha^{-1}), and two levels of molybdenum (0 and 400g ha^{-1}) were applied as zinc sulphate, borax and ammonium molybdate, respectively. The experiment was laid out in factorial randomized block design with three replications on variety Avarodhi. Basal uniform doses of nitrogen 20kg, phosphorus 40kg, potassium 20kg and sulphur 30kg ha^{-1} were applied as urea, diammonium phosphate, muriate of potash and elemental sulphur, respectively.

Protein content in grain of chickpea was estimated by Lowry's method (7). The yield of protein (kg ha^{-1}) was calculated by grain protein content and its yield. Methionine content was analyzed by the method as described by the Horn *et al.* (8). Tryptophan content was estimated by the method as described by Spice and Chamber (9). Ash content was estimated by incineration of dried sample in a muffle furnace for six hours at 550°C (10). The total carbohydrate was calculated by difference. Total extractable lipid was determined by Soxhlet method (10). Samples were wet digested in di-acid mixture (HNO3: HClO4) as described by Jackson (11). In this extract, phosphorus was estimated colorimetrically using vanadomolybdate (11). Sulphur was also estimated in the same digest turbidimetrically (12) and zinc was estimated by Atomic Absorption Spectrophotometer. Boron in grain was extracted by diacid mixture and estimated colorimetrically by method of Wolf (13). Molybdenum was estimated colorimetrically by thiocyanate method from diacid extracts (11).

The biochemical parameters *viz;* protein, total protein yield, methionine and tryptophan, ash content, total lipids and total carbohydrate of chickpea grain as influenced by application of various levels of zinc, boron and molybdenum are presented in Table 1.1. Application of zinc from 0 to 5.0kg ha^{-1} influenced protein content of grain from 18.70 to 21.21 per cent. Application of 5.0kg ha^{-1} of zinc yielded highest protein in grain. Similarly, boron influenced protein content of the grain from 19.09 to 20.65 per cent on application of 0 to 2.0kg ha^{-1} of boron in soil. The increase in protein content was significant. Molybdenum application also increased the protein content of grain, but the increase was non-significant. Protein yield also increased significantly on application of zinc in soil and highest yield of 470.69kg ha^{-1} of protein was recorded in case of zinc application of 5.0kg ha^{-1}. A linear and significant increase in protein yield was also observed from 386.74 to 450.35kg ha^{-1} on application of boron in soil. The protein yield was also significantly increased from 422.66 to 445.62kg ha^{-1} on applicat ion of molybdenum. The increase in protein content due to zinc, boron and molybdenum application has also been reported by other investigators (4, 5, 6, 14). The influence of zinc, boron and molybdenum on limiting essential amino acid of pulses (methionine and tryptophan) is reported in Table 1.1. The methionine of grain was not affected due to zinc, boron and molybdenum application. However, an increase in methionine contents has been reported on application of zinc (15). The tryptophan content significantly increased on application of zinc @ 2.5 and 5.0kg ha^{-1} as compared to no application of zinc. Similar, results were observed in case of boron and molybdenum application.

Ash content increased on application of zinc @ 2.5 and 5.0kg ha^{-1} from 2.80 to 2.97 and 3.15 per cent, respectively. The differences among all the three levels of zinc were significant. The boron application @ 1.0 or 2.0kg ha^{-1} increased ash content of grain significantly. The effect of molybdenum application was not significant on ash content of grain. The lipid content was not affected on application of zinc, boron and molybdenum. The carbohydrate content of grain decreased with increasing levels of zinc, boron and molybdenum. There was a continuous decrease in carbohydrate content on application of higher doses of zinc, boron and molybdenum. This decrease was due to higher biosynthesis of protein in the grain on application of zinc, boron and molybdenum.

Table 1.1: Effect of zinc, boron and molybdenum on biochemical parameters of chickpea grain

Treatment	Protein (%)	Protein Yield (kg ha^{-1})	Methionine (g/100g protein)	Tryptophan (g/100g protein)	Ash Content (%)	Lipid (%)	Carbo-hydrate (%)
Zinc (kg ha^{-1})							
0	18.70±0.21	361.77	1.07±0.07	0.68±0.06	2.80±0.20	6.22±0.04	72.28±1.13
2.5	19.71±0.02	436.58	0.95±0.06	0.73±0.05	2.97±0.07	6.24±0.06	71.08±1.14
5.0	21.21±0.03	470.69	0.93±0.08	0.74±0.05	3.15±0.05	6.24±0.04	69.40±1.61
CD (P=0.05)	0.62	31.50	NS	0.04	0.14	NS	0.82
Boron (kg ha^{-1})							
0	19.09±0.08	386.74	1.08±0.07	0.67±0.04	2.78±0.06	6.21±0.04	71.92±1.14
1.0	19.88±0.04	429.80	0.96±0.05	0.74±0.06	2.95±0.10	6.24±0.05	70.93±1.16
2.0	20.65±0.04	450.35	0.94±0.07	0.75±0.06	2.99±0.07	6.24±0.05	70.12±1.27
CD (P=0.05)	0.62	17.50	NS	0.05	0.12	NS	1.72
Molybd-enum (g ha^{-1})							
0	19.87±0.03	422.66	1.05±0.06	0.65±0.70	2.82±0.07	5.98±0.08	71.33±1.15
400	20.01±0.06	445.62	0.98±0.06	0.74±0.71	2.88±0.07	6.23±0.03	70.88±1.20
CD (P=0.05)	NS	19.55	NS	0.07	NS	NS	1.65

Table 1.2: Effect of zinc, boron and molybdenum on mineral contents of chickpea grain

Treatment	mg g^{-1}			mg kg^{-1}		
	Phosphorus	Potassium	Sulphur	Zinc	Boron	Molybdenum
Zinc (kg ha^{-1})						
0	3.5	4.9	6.8	39.74	52.50	3.43
2.5	3.6	5.2	6.9	42.21	53.21	3.47
5.0	3.3	5.3	7.0	45.04	53.76	3.49
CD (P=0.05)	N.S.	0.11	0.14	0.64	NS	NS
Boron (kg ha^{-1})						
0	3.3	5.0	6.8	42.73	52.22	3.28
1.0	3.6	5.2	7.0	42.75	54.77	3.54
2.0	3.6	5.3	7.0	42.52	55.48	3.71
CD (P=0.05)	0.12	0.11	0.14	NS	0.73	0.07
Molybdenum (g ha^{-1})						
0	3.5	5.1	6.9	42.34	54.16	3.51
400	3.7	5.3	7.1	42.25	55.47	3.79
CD (P=0.05)	0.10	0.09	0.12	NS	0.60	0.06

Application of zinc, boron and molybdenum increased phosphorous, potassium, sulphur, zinc, boron and molybdenum content of grain in chickpea (Table 1.2). The variability in P, K and S was recorded from 3.3 to 3.7 mg g^{-1}, 4.9 to 5.3 mg g^{-1} and 6.8 to 7.1 mg g^{-1} respectively. The zinc content of the grain increased from 39.74 to 45.04 mg kg^{-1} on application of zinc @ 5.0kg ha^{-1}, whereas application of boron and molybdenum had no significant effect on zinc content of grain. Boron and molybdenum application had increased boron content of grain significantly, whereas zinc had no significant effect. Boron and molybdenum also had similar effect on molybdenum content of grain. Similar results were eelier reported in chickpea and black gram (5, 6, 16,17).

REFERENCES

1. Government of Madhya Pradesh, *Agriculture Economic Survey* (2014), Bhopal, India.
2. Trehan K. (1990). *Biochemistry*, 2nd edn, New Age International Private Limited, New Delhi, 165.
3. Sharma A., Sharma S., Singh G. and Gill B.S. (2014). *Indian J. Agric Biochem*, 27 (2), 223.
4. Ceyhan E., Onder M., Harmankaya M., Hamurcu M. and Gezgin S. (2007). *Communications in Soil Sci Plant Anal*, 38 (17/18), 2381.
5. Singh M., Chaudhary S.R., Sharma S.R. and Rathore M.S. (2004) *Agric Sci Digest*, 24 (4), 268.
6. Singh R.P., Bisen J.S., Yadav P.K., Singh S.N., Singh R.K. and Singh J. (2008). *Legume Res*, 31 (3), 214.
7. Lowery O.H., Rosebrough N.J., Farr A.L. and Randal R.J. (1951). *J. Biol Chem*, 193, 265.
8. Horn J.M., Jones D.B. and Blum A.E. (1946) *J. Biol Chem*, 166, 313.
9. Spice J.T. and Chamber DC (1949). *Anal Chem*, 21 (3), 1249.
10. AOAC (1970). *Official Methods of Analysis* 11th edn. Association of Official Agriculture Chemists, Washington DC, USA.
11. Jackson ML (1973). *Soil Chemical Analysis*, Prentice Hall Inc. Englewood eliffs, New Jersey. 68.
12. Chesnin L and Yien CH (1951). *Proc Soil Soc Amer*, 14,149.
13. Wolf B (1974). *Comm Soil Sci Plant Anal*, 5, 39.
14. Thiyagarajan TM, Backiyavathyand MR and Savithri P (2003). *Agric Rev*, 24 (1), 40.
15. Tripathi H.C., Singh R.S. and Pathak R.K. (1999). *Indian J. Agric Biochem*, 12 (2), 88.
16. Singh D. and Singh H. (2012) *Ann Pl Soil Res*, 14 (1), 71.
17. Poongothai S., Savithri P. and Chitdeshwari T. (2004). *Agril Sci Digest*, 24 (1), 67.

Pages 6-24

INTEGRATED NUTRIENT MANAGEMENT IN CHICKPEA

Edited by **: Dr. Virendra Kumar** and **Dr. Nirmal Kumar Katiyar**

Edition **: 2017**

ISBN : 978-93-5056-872-9

Published by **: Discovery Publishing House Pvt. Ltd., New Delhi (India)**

Potential Role of Bio-inoculants and Organic Matter for the Management of Root-Knot Nematode Infesting Chickpea

Mohammad Akram[1], Rose Rizvi[1]
Aisha Sumbul[1]*, Rizwan Ali Ansari[1]
Irshad Mahmood[1]

ABSTRACT

A pot experiment was conducted during 2013-14 to observe the potential role of some organics and bio-organics such as: Calotropis procera, Glomus fasciculatum, and Azotobacter chroococcum on some growth attributes of chickpea and sub-sequently on the root-knot development caused by Meloidogyne incognita. Individual and conjoint treatments significantly enhanced the plant growth parameters as compared to unamended control. Physiological parameter such as: chlorophyll content also exhibited significant improvement in all the treatments over non-amended control. The highest improvement in growth parameters of chickpea was observed in combined application of G. fasciculatum and A. chroococcum in pots amended with C. procera. Moreover, combined treatments of both bio-inoculants and C. procera markedly reduced the multiplication and reproduction rate of root-knot nematodes in terms of number of root galls and nematode population. Per cent mycorrhization in terms of external and internal colonizations was increased significantly in plant amended with organic and bio-organics conjointly. The regression studies revealed significant relationship between number of galls and some plant growth variables. Present findings may promote organic-based farm products and eco-friendly management of M. incognita as this is a safer and cost-effective option.

Keywords: Azotobacter; Glomus Fasciculatum, *Root-knot Nematode, Mycorrhization, Organic Matter.*

1* Section of Plant Pathology and Nematology, Department of Botany, Aligarh Muslim University, Aligarh 202 002, India. E-mail: aishasumbul92amu@gmail.com.

INTRODUCTION

Chickpea (*Cicer arietinum*) is one of the most important pulse crops in India, occupying about 6.67 × 10^6 ha and producing 5.3 × 10^6 t annually (Singh, 2012). Its economic importance renders to its high protein content as well as its ability to fix atmospheric nitrogen. Chickpea is a major source of human food and livestock because of high content of protein (Jiménez-Díaz, Castillo, Jiménez- Gasco, Landa, and Navas-Cortés, in press). Among all plant parasitic nematodes, *Meloidogyne spp.*, are the most serious ones (Hussain, Mukhtar, and Kayani, 2011; Mukhtar *et al.* 2013). They are considered among the top five major plant enemies and ranked first among the ten economically important genera of phytonematodes globally (Jones *et al.* 2013; Kayani, Mukhtar, and Hussain, 2012). *Meloidogyne incognita,* one of the most economically important species of root-knot nematodes, adversely affects plant growth and yield causing an estimated $100 billion loss per year (Mukhtar, Hussain, Kayani, and Aslam, 2014). *M. incognita* is found to be constantly associated with chickpea (Sumbul *et al.* 2015) and several other agricultural crops (Ansari and Khan, 2012a and, b) and is of considerable importance, both in terms of qualitative as well as quantitative loss. Occurrence of root-knot in chickpea has been reported from various states in India (Jamal, 1976; Khan and Siddiqui, 2005). In order to meet the increasing requirement for chickpea, there is an urgent need to manage the constraints over its production (Ansari *et al.* 2015; Rizvi, Ansari, Zehra, and Mahmood, 2015; Rizvi, Singh, Ansari, Tiyagi, and Mahmood, 2015).

A variety of management strategies are being adopted to manage root-knot nematode, *Meloidogyne incognita,* one of the most difficult pests of agricultural crops. Although, the most effective and commonly used practice of combating this problem is use of chemical nematicides, they cause a huge damage to ecosystem. Indiscriminate use of chemical nematicides causes environmental degradation, which gives an impetus to search the alternative means (Collange, Navarrete, Peyre, Mateille, and Tchamitchian, 2011; Hallmann, Davies, and Sikora, 2009; Huang *et al.* 2009; Nico, Jiménez-D1az, and Castillo, 2004; Siddiqui, Qureshi, and Akhtar, 2009).

Organic farming has emerged as an important priority area in view of the growing demand for safe and healthy food and long-term sustainability that concern on environmental pollution associated with indiscriminate use of agrochemicals. Amending soil with pesticides of botanical origin such as: oil-cakes, chopped plant parts, and seed dressing with plant parts, which are safe, ecofriendly, and bio-degradable in nature, has now become the prime means to protect crops (Muller and Gooch, 1982; Tiyagi and Ajaz, 2004). *Calotropis procera*, a common weed is found in various parts of the country and is reported to possess some nematicidal properties (Hussain *et al.* 2011;

Walia and Gupta, 1995). Plant parts of *C. procera*, have been reported to contain pesticidal properties that inhibit the larval penetration of *M. incognita* and consequently reduction in root-knot development (Mahmood, Tiyagi, and Azam, 2007; Tiyagi, Mahmood, Rizvi, and Dev, 2009). In addition, due to presence of some alkaloids, *C. procera* has been reported to cause juvenile mortality of *M. incognita* (Nelaballe and Mukkara, 2013).

Rhizosphere supports a large and active microbial population capable of exerting beneficial, neutral, and detrimental effects on plant growth. The micro-organisms, which can grow in the rhizosphere are ideal for use as biocontrol agents, since rhizosphere provides the initial barrier against pathogen attack of the root system (Weller, 1988). Biological nitrogen fixers help to enhance productivity by biological nitrogen fixation, producing hormones, vitamins, and other growth factors required for plant growth and development, solubilizing phosphorus, and suppression of growth of plant pathogens (Verma, Yadav, and Tiwari, 2010) on several crops. *Azotobacter* is a free-living nitrogen-fixing, plant growth promoting rhizobacteria (PGPR), that enhance emergence, colonize roots, and stimulate overall plant growth and can also suppress disease of plants. The manipulation of crop rhizosphere by inoculation with *Azotobacter* for bio-control of root-knot nematode has shown considerable promise (Siddiqui and Mahmood, 2001). Arbuscular Mycorrhizal (AM) fungi colonize the roots of many crop plants (Ozgonen, Bicici, and Erkilic, 1999) and are of immense value in enhancing the uptake of phosphorus, minor elements, and water, and thus improving the plant growth and yield (Allen, 1996; Rizvi, Singh, *et al.* 2015; Siddiqui and Mahmood, 1999). These fungi induce changes in the host root exudation pattern following host colonization with altered microbial microflora in the mycorrhizosphere (Akhtar and Siddiqui, 2008) and are also reported to reduce the severity of several plant diseases (Akkopru and Demir, 2005; Barea, Azcón, and Azcón-Aguilar, 2002; Khan *et al.* 2015; Linderman, 2000; Rizvi, Singh, *et al.* 2015). They have also widely been reported as biocontrol agents against plant parasitic nematodes (Khan *et al.* 2008; Siddiqui and Mahmood, 1999; Tian, Yang, and Zhang, 2007).

Present study was conducted to monitor the effects of *A. chroococcum* and *G. fasciulatum* either solely or conjointly on some plant growth parameters and root-knot development on chickpea amended with or without *C. procera*.

Materials and Methods

The root-knot nematode, *M. incognita* (Kofoid and White) Chitwood was selected as a test pathogen and chickpea (*Cicer arietinun* L.) var. Avrodhi as a test plant. PGPR, *A. chroococcum*, VAM fungi, *G. fasciulatum* and organic matter like: chopped leaves of *C. procera* were used alone and in various combinations for the management of chickpea root-knot disease.

Preparation and Sterilization of Soil Mixture

Appropriate amount of sandy loam soil was collected from the field of Department of Botany, A.M.U. Aligarh and allowed to pass through 20-mesh sieve. The soil, river sand, and organic manure was mixed in the ratio of 3:1:1, respectively, and the mixture were filled in the clay pots of 15 cm diameter at the rate of 1 kg soil per pot. Before transferring to the autoclave for sterilization at 20 lb pressure for 20 min, a little water was poured in each pot just to wet the soil. These sterilized pots were kept to cool down at room temperature before use for further experiments.

Growth and Maintenance of Test Plant

Seeds of chickpea, var. Avrodhi were surface sterilized with 0.01 per cent mercuric chloride (H_gCl_2) for two minutes and washed three times with distilled water. Five seeds per pot were sown and thinning was done after germination to maintain one plant per pot. Pots were watered depending on the requirement. One week old, healthy, and well-established seedlings were used for experimental purpose.

Preparation of Nematode Inoculum

A number of egg masses were handpicked with the help of sterilized forceps from heavily infested eggplant roots on which pure culture of *M. incognita* was maintained. These egg masses, after washing thoroughly in distilled water were placed in a coarse sieve (10 cm diameter) mounted with cross double-layered tissue paper. The sieves were placed in Petri dishes containing water that were incubated at 25°C in the laboratory. Three days later, when the majority of the eggs hatched, the second stage juveniles (J2) of the nematode were collected by rinsing the Petri dishes with distilled water.

The identification of the species was confirmed by the morphology according to the perineal pattern (Hartman and Sasser, 1985). The concentration of second-stage juveniles of *M. incognita* in the water suspension was adjusted so that 2,000 freshly hatched juveniles could be added as initial inoculum level in 10 ml., of water suspension to each pot containing a chickpea seedling.

Preparation of Organic Matter

Leaves of *C. procera* were collected from the AMU campus and brought to laboratory, rinsed with distilled water, and chopped with a sharp sterile knife. These chopped leaves were incorporated in soil at the rate of 20 g/kg leaves per pot and the pots were immediately watered for decomposition to prepare the compost of *C. procera*.

Preparation of Inoculum of Biocontrol Agents

Mycorrhizal spores were isolated by a modified wet sieving and decanting method (Gerdemann and Nicolson, 1963). For this aspect, a sample of 100 g dry soil was mixed in 1,000 ml water, and the heavier particles were allowed to settle for few seconds. The lumps were broken and heavier particles were removed. The suspension was poured through a coarse sieve to remove large pieces of organic matter. The liquid passed through this sieve was collected and again passed through sieves of 80, 100, 150, 250, and 400 meshes. Spores obtained on sieves were collected with water in separate beakers and counted in 1 ml of the suspension in counting dish under the stereoscopic microscope. The final number of spores/100g of soil was calculated accordingly for each treatment.

Charcoal-based commercial culture of free-living nitrogen-fixing bacteria *Azotobacter chroococcum* was obtained from Quarsi Agriculture Farm, Aligarh, India. For inoculation, 100 gram culture was mixed separately in 1,000 ml distilled water which means 10 ml (equivalent to 2 g culture) was added around each seedling. Commercially standardized culture of *A. chroococcum* having 1.2 × 108 cfu/g was used in the experiment.

Inoculation Technique

For inoculation of *M. incognita, A. chroococcum, and G. fasciculatum,* soil around the root was carefully removed in order to avoid the damage. Inoculum suspensions of these micro-organisms were poured around the roots uniformly and soil was replaced to cover the roots. Equal amount of water was poured in the pot that served as control.

Experimental Design

The 14 treatments each with 5 replicates were arranged in a completely randomized block design and maintained in a glasshouse with air temperature ranging from 22 ± 3°C. All the plants were watered up to the soil capacity. Following combinations were used during the experimentation:

- Control (C).
- *Calotropis procera* (CP).
- *Meloidogyne incognita* (MI).
- *Azotobacter chroococcum* (Azo).
- *Glomus fasciculatum* (GF).
- CP + MI.
- CP + AC.
- CP + AC + MI.
- CP + GF.

- CP + GF + MI.
- AC + MI.
- GF + MI.
- CP + AC + GF.
- CP + AC + GF + MI.

Observations

Per cent pollen fertility was estimated at the flowering stage by the method suggested by Brown (1949), using 1 per cent acetocarmine solution to stain the pollen grains. Plants were harvested 90 days after nematode inoculation. Root systems were gently washed with tap water taking care to avoid losses and injury during the entire operation. Data were recorded on plant length (cm), plant fresh weight (g), plant dry weight (g), chlorophyll content (mg g^{-1} fresh leaves), nematode population (both in soil and root), number of gall/root system, number of egg masses/root system, fecundity in terms of number of egg/egg masses.

Chlorophyll Estimation

Chlorophyll content was estimated per gram of fresh leaf weight by the technique of Arnon (1949). 1 g finely cut fresh leaves was pulverized with the help of mortar and pestle using sufficient quantity of 80 per cent acetone. The leaf homogenate thus obtained, was filtered through filter paper, and supernatant was collected in the volumetric flask. The final volume of the supernatant was made up to 10 ml with 80 per cent acetone. 5-ml chlorophyll solvent was transferred to a clean cuvette and the absorption values were noted at 645 and 663 nm in a spectrophotometer against the solvent (80% acetone) blank. The calculation of the total chlorophyll content per gram fresh leaves was done by the following formula:

$$\text{Total chlorophyll content (mg g}^{-1}) = 20.2(A645) + 8.02(A663) \times \frac{V}{1000} \times W$$

where $A663$ = solution absorbance at 663 nm, $A645$ = solution absorption at 645 nm, V = volume of solution (taken in cuvette), W = weight of leaf tissue used for extraction of pigments *i.e.* 1 g.

Extraction of Nematode Population

For extraction of nematodes from the soil, 250 g sub-sample of well-mixed soil from each treatment was processed by Cobb's sieving and decanting method followed by Baermann funnel method (Southey, 1986). Nematode suspension was collected after 24 h and number of nematodes was counted in counting dish taking five replicates of 1 ml suspension from each sample. Mean of five such counting was obtained and a population of nematodes per kg soil was calculated. For estimation of larvae, eggs, and females inside the roots, each root system was cut into small pieces and mixed. One-gram root sample was taken and macerated for 30-40 s in Waring blender to recover nematode eggs, females, and larvae. Counting was done from the suspensions thus obtained. Total number of nematodes present in the roots was calculated by multiplying the number of nematodes present in one gram root with the weight of the root.

Assessment of Root Mycorrhizal Colonization (Phillips and Hayman, 1970)

Roots were washed with tap water and cut into 1-cm long segments and then boiled in 10 per cent KOH solution at 90°C for 45 min. KOH solution was then poured off and roots were rinsed well in a beaker until no brown color appeared in the rinsed water. Alkaline H_2O_2 which was used to bleach the roots was made by adding 3 ml of NH_4OH to 30 ml of 10 per cent H_2O_2 and 567 ml of tap water. The roots were rinsed thoroughly at least three times using tap water to remove the H_2O_2. Roots were then treated with 0.05 per cent trypan blue (in lactophenol) and were kept for an hour. The specimens were then removed from trypan blue and kept for overnight in a destaining solution, prepared with acetic acid (laboratory grade) – 875 ml, glycerine – 63 ml and distilled water – 63 ml. The cellular contents were removed by this method and the AM fungal structures stained dark blue. These stained root segments were used for determining the root colonization by AM fungi. The percentage/proportion of root colonization by AM fungi was determined by the grid line intersecting method (Giovannetti and Mosse, 1980). The root segments were selected at random from the stained sample and mounted on microscopic slides in group of 10. One hundred to one hundred and fifty root segments from each sample were used for the assessment. The presence or absence of colonization in each root segment was recorded and the per cent root colonization (mycorrhizal infection in the roots) was calculated as follows:

$$\% \text{ Root colonization} = \frac{\text{Number of AM positive segments}}{\text{Total number of segments screened}} \times 100$$

Statistical Analysis

All data collected were analyzed statistically and least significant differences were calculated at $p < 0.05$. Duncan's multiple range test was employed to denote significant differences. Both the analyses were carried out using 'R' software (R i3863.2.3 version).

Results

The effects of individual as well as concomitant treatments were recorded in relation to different growth parameters of chickpea like plant length, fresh as well as dry weights, number of pods and branches per plant, per cent pollen fertility, and chlorophyll content (Fig. 2.1, Tables 2.1 and 2.2).

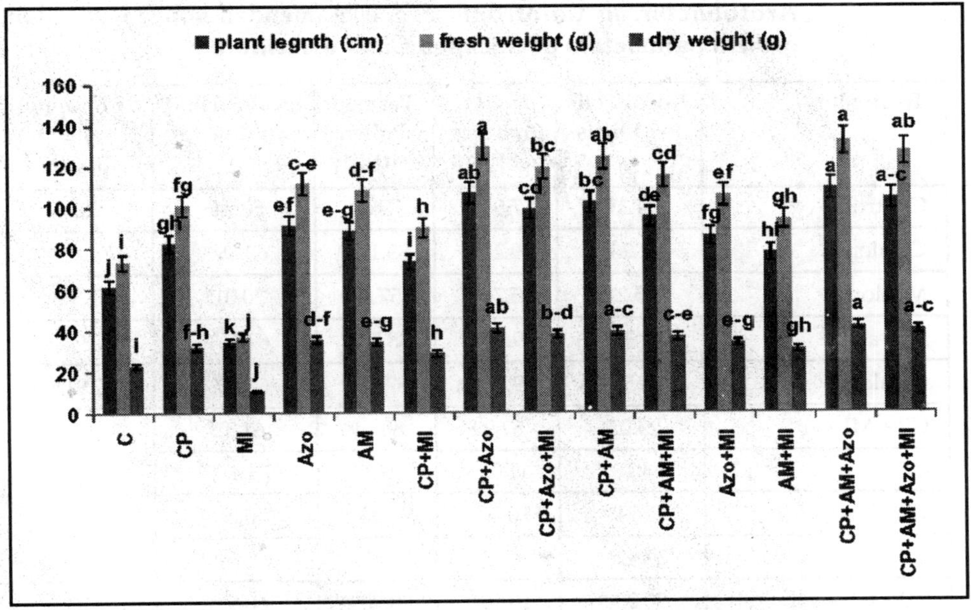

Fig. 2.1: Interactive effects of *Meloidogyne incognita, Glomus fasciculatum, Azotobacter*, in *Calotropis procera*-amended soil on the plant length, fresh and dry weight of chickpea *Cicer arietinum*

Plant treated with *C. procera, G. fasciculatum,* and *A. chroococcum* alone and in combination significantly increased plant dry weight over uninoculated control (Fig. 2.2). *A. chroococcum* increased plant dry weight more than *G. fasciculatum*. Further enhancement in dry weight was observed when soil was amended with *C. procera*. Similar increase in dry weight was shown in plants treated with *C. procera* + *G. fasciculatum, C. procera* + *A. chroococcum* and those inoculated in combination with *C. procera* + *G. fasciculatum* + *A. chroococcum* (Fig. 2.2). Inoculation of plants with *M. incognita* caused a significant reduction of plant dry weight compared to untreated control (Fig. 2.2). Application of *C. procera/G. fasciculatum/A. chroococcum* alone or in combination caused a significant increase in plant dry weight even in pathogeninoculated plants. Inoculation of *A. chroococcum/G. fasciculatum* resulted in a significantly greater increase in plant dry weight of pathogen inoculated plants than that caused by *C. procera*. Plants raised in *C. procera*-amended soil and inoculated with *A. chroococcum* and *G. fasciculatum* caused significant and similar improvement in plant dry weight even if inoculated with test pathogen (Fig. 2.1).

Table 2.1: Interactive effects of *Meloidogyne incognita*, AM fungus, *Azotobacter*, in *Calotropis procera*-amended soil on the plant-growth parameters of chickpea *Cicer arietinum*

Treatments	No. of Pods per Plants	No. of Branches per Plant	Per cent Pollen Fertility	Fresh Weight of Fruits (g)	Chlorophyll content (mg/g)
Control	24.33[h]	7.56[d]	79.62[e]	50.24[g]	2.24[f]
CP alone	31.24[fg]	9.28[c]	85.19d[e]	63.38[eg]	2.81[e]
MI alone	15.21[i]	5.74[e]	57.07[f]	30.01[h]	1.36[g]
Azo alone	34.34[d-f]	9.93[b]	88.50[b-d]	67.56[b-f]	2.96[cd]
GF alone	33.51[d-f]	9.75[b]	87.16[c-e]	66.26[c-f]	2.91[de]
CP + MI	29.27[g]	8.89[c]	80.64[e]	61.52[f]	2.70[e]
CP + Azo	38.78[ab]	11.07[a]	96.33[a]	73.47[ab]	3.27[ab]
CP + Azo + MI	35.94[b-d]	10.40[a]	91.94[a-d]	70.2[a-d]	3.08[a-c]
CP + GF	37.42[a-b]	10.62[a]	93.62[a-c]	71.16[a-c]	3.15[a-c]
CP + GF + MI	35.23[c-e]	10.19[b]	89.90[a-d]	68.9[b-e]	3.04[bc]
Azo + MI	32.34[e-g]	9.51[b]	86.73[c-e]	65.09[d-f]	2.86[e]
GF + MI	30.45[g]	9.07[e]	84.77[de]	62.65[f]	2.73[e]
CP + GF + Azo	39.82[a]	11.43[a]	97.52[a]	75.18[a]	3.34[a]
CP + Azo + GF + MI	38.00[a-c]	10.83[a]	95.00[a]	72.41[a-c]	3.21[a-c]
C.D ($p = 0.05$)	3.32	0.79	7.70	6.23	0.259

Notes: CP = *Calotropis procera*, MI = *Meloidogyne incognita*, Azo = *Azotobacter*, GF = *Glomus fasciculatum*. Letters are meant for comparison within columns and different letters depict values that are significantly different at $p = 0.05$.

* Each value is an average of 5 replicates.

The number of pods was significantly reduced in plants inoculated with *M. incognita* (Table 2.1). Application of *C. procera*/*G. fasciculatum*/*A. chroococcum* alone or in combination significantly increased the number of pods per plant both in pathogen inoculated and uninoculated plants. Highest improvement was found in case of plants treated in combination with *C. procera*, *G. fasciculatum*, and *A. chroococcum* in the absence of pathogen, and the inoculation with *M. incognita* resulted in not much significant change (Table 2.1).

Table 2.2: Interactive effects of *Meloidogyne incognita*, *Glomus fasciculatum*, *Azotobacter chroococcum* in *Calotropis procera* amended soil on the plant-growth parameters of chickpea *Cicer arietinum* in relation to myrorrhization, root-knot development, and nematode multiplication

Treatments	Root-galls	Nematode Population	Rf = (Pf/Pi)	Rootnodule/ Plants	Mycorrhizal Colonization(%)	
					External	Internal
Control	0.00	0.00	0.00	18.58^{h}	0.00	0.00
CP alone	0.00	0.00	0.00	24.08^{fg}	0.00	0.00
MI alone	158.50^{a}	14674^{a}	7.33^{a}	11.77^{i}	0.00	0.00
Azo alone	0.00	0.00	0.00	25.54$^{c\text{-}f}$	0.00	0.00
GF alone	0.00	0.00	0.00	25.19$^{d\text{-}g}$	40.19^{c}	45.80^{d}
CP + MI	120.20^{b}	11580^{b}	5.79^{b}	23.16^{g}	0.00	0.00
CP + Azo	0.00	0.00	0.00	27.90^{ab}	0.00	0.00
CP + Azo + MI	50.23^{d}	04612^{f}	2.30^{e}	26.67$^{a\text{-}d}$	0.00	0.00
CP + GF	0.00	0.00	0.00	27.06$^{a\text{-}d}$	46.48^{b}	49.62^{c}
CP + GF + MI	57.16^{d}	06257^{e}	3.12^{de}	26.03$^{b\text{-}e}$	24.00^{d}	33.93^{e}
Azo + MI	80.23^{c}	07586^{d}	3.79^{d}	24.82$^{e\text{-}g}$	0.00	0.00
GF + MI	110.73^{b}	09365^{c}	4.68^{c}	23.70^{g}	19.37^{e}	25.77^{fs}
CP + GF + Azo	0.00	0.00	0.00	28.45^{a}	56.62^{a}	63.56^{a}
CP + Azo + GF + MI	37.19^{e}	01264^{g}	0.63^{f}	27.59^{abc}	49.50^{b}	55.30^{b}
C.D ($p = 0.05$)	9.67	22.62	0.85	2.20	3.11	3.21

Notes: CP = *Calotropis procera*, MI = *Meloidogyne incognita*, Azo = *Azotobacter*, G F = *Glomus fasciculatum*. Letters are meant for comparison within columns and different letters depict values that are significantly different at $p = 0.05$.

* Each value is an average of five replicates.

Number of branches per plant decreased significantly in plants inoculated with *M. incognita* as compared to control. Treatment of plants with *C. procera*/ *G. fasciculatum* / *A. chroococcum* alone or in combination significantly increased the number of branches per plant both in pathogen-inoculated and uninoculated plants. Highest and similar increase was found in plants treated with *C. procera* + *G. fasciculatum* + *A. chroococcum*, *C. procera* + *G. fasciculatum* + *A. chroococcum* + *M. incognita*, *C. procera* + *A. chroococcum*, *C. procera* + *G. fasciculatum*, *and C. procera* + *A. chroococcum* + *M. incognita* (Table 2.1). Pollen fertility of the plants was significantly lowered by the inoculation of plants with *M. incognita* as compared to control. Application of *C. procera*/

G. fasciculatum/A. chroococcum alone and in combination significantly increased the pollen fertility in both pathogen-inoculated and uninoculated plants. Highest and similar increase in pollen fertility was observed in plants treated combinely with *C. procera* + *G. fasciculatum* + *A. chroococcum*, *C. procera* + *A. chroococcum*, and *C. procera* + *G. fasciculatum* + *A. chroococcum* + *M. incognita*. Increase in pollen fertility of pathogeninoculated plants treated with *A. chroococcum* was similar to pathogen-uninoculated plants treated with only *G. fasciculatum*. Treatment of pathogen-inoculated plants with *C. procera/ G. fasciculatum* gave similar increase in pollen fertility as that of control plants (Table 2.1). Inoculation of plants with *M. incognita* also caused a significant decrease in fresh weight of fruits as compared to control and again the application of *C. procera/G. fasciculatum/A. chroococcum* alone and in combination significantly increased the fresh weight of fruits. Highest increase was observed in pathogen-uninoculated plants treated with combination of *C. procera*, *G. fasciculatum*, and *A. chroococcum* followed by those inoculated with *C. procera* and *A. chroococcum*. Application of both the inoculants along with *C. procera* in the presence of *M. incognita* increased fresh weight of fruits similarly as in case of those treated with *C. procera* and *G. fasciculatum*. Chlorophyll content of the uninoculated plants increased greatly when *C. procera*, *G. fasciculatum*, and *A. chroococcum* were applied concomitantly (Table 2.1). Inoculation of plants with *M. incognita* significantly decreased the chlorophyll content. Combine application of *C. procera*, *G. fasciculatum*, and *A. chroococcum* caused a significant improvement in chlorophyll content of pathogen-inoculated plants. The increase was similar in case of inoculated plants treated with either *C. procera* plus *A. chroococcum* or *C. procera* plus *G. fasciculatum* (Table 2.1). Number of nodules per root system was significantly higher in plants treated with *C. procera/G. fasciculatum/A. chroococcum* alone or in combination. Combine application of *C. procera* and *A. chroococcum* was most effective in enhancing the root nodulation in both pathogen-inoculated and uninoculated plants (Table 2.2). External and internal colonization of root by *G. fasciculatum* was high when inoculated in the presence of *C. procera* and *A. chroococcum*, while presence of pathogen reduced its colonization. Highest root colonization was observed in plants combinely inoculated with *G. fasciculatum* and *A. chroococcum* in *C. procera*-amended soil in pathogen-free plants followed by pathogen-inoculated plants (Table 2.2).

The number of galls per root system and nematode multiplication was high in plants inoculated with *M. incognita* alone. Reduction in root galling was significantly higher and similar in plants treated with *C. procera* and *G. fasciculatum* followed by *A. chroococcum*. Amending soil with *C. procera* caused maximum reduction in nematode multiplication followed by *G. fasciculatum* and *A. chroococcum*. Combine inoculation of plants with

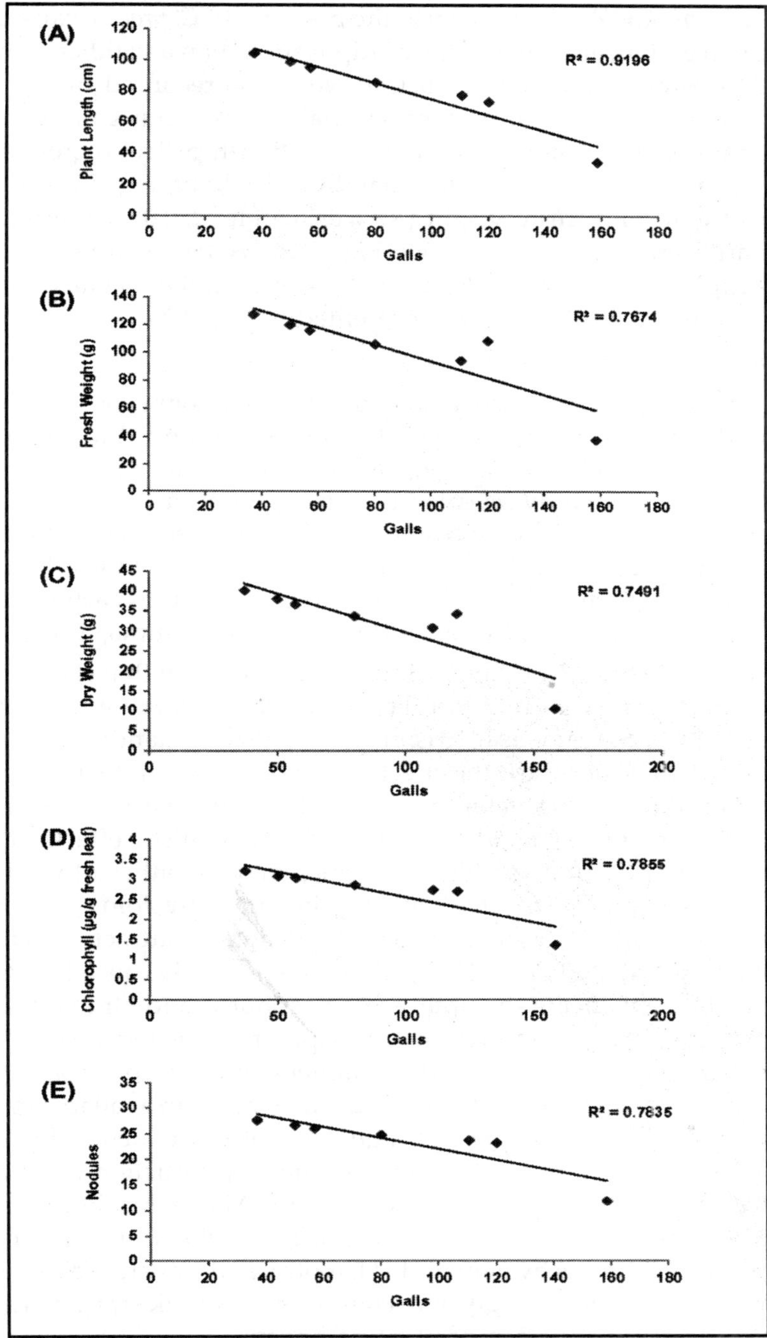

Fig. 2.2: Regression analysis (plot) between galls vs. (A) plant length, (B) fresh weight (C), dry weight, (D) chlorophyll, and (E) nodules of chickpea, *Cicer arietinum*

G. fasciculatum plus *A. chroococcum* in the presence of *C. procera* caused highest reduction in galling and nematode multiplication than any other combination (Table 2.2). Similar trends of reduction were also recorded in reproduction factor (Table 2.2). Besides, regression analysis between galls and various growth parameters exhibited significant relationship. The regression values between number of galls and plant length (R^2 = 0.919; Fig. 2.2(A)), between number of galls and fresh weight (R^2 = 0.767; Fig. 2.2(B)), between number of galls and dry weight (R^2 = 0.749; Fig. 2. 2(C)), between number of galls and chlorophyll (R^2 = 0.785; Fig. 2.2(D)), between number of galls and nodules (R^2 = 0.783; Fig. 2.2(E)) which are presented in Fig. 2.2.

Discussion

Application of biofertilizers in various combinations constantly improved the growth of plant in comparison to the control and those treated with *M. incognita* alone. Our results are in conformity with Singh, Kumar, and Rana (2000). Present study revealed that the application of *A. chroococcum*, *G. fasciculatum*, and *C. procera* concomitantly decreased the disease intensity in the nematode-infested chickpea. The detrimental effect of these biofertilizers against root-knot nematodes was also observed by various earlier researchers (Khan, Mohiddin, Ejaz, and Khan, 2012; Kumar and Gupta, 2010).

Effectiveness of AM fungi for increased plant growth has been reported by many workers (Jothi and Sundarababu, 2000; Oruru and Njeru, 2016; Rizvi *et al.* 2015; Shreenivasa, Krishnappa, and Ravichandra, 2007). Akhtar and Siddiqui (2008) observed the effect of *G. intraradices* on chickpea in relation to their plant growth parameters and found that it was surprisingly increased over control. The mechanisms to explain the antagonistic effects of AMF on nematode multiplication and their activities may be either physiological or physical in nature. *G. fasciculatum* can alter the physiology of the roots, including the root exudates responsible for chemotactic attraction of nematode (Mc Guidwin, Bird, and Safir, 1985). Yield loss normally caused by nematode is mitigated by enhancing the uptake of phosphorus and other nutrients due to AM fungi leading to improvement of plant vigor and growth (Hussey and Roncadori, 1982). Nematode development and reproduction might have retarded in mycorrhiza-treated plants due to decrease in available food (Saleh and Sikora, 1984). Physiological changes in root inoculated with AM fungi may result in development of resistance due to production of antagonistic substances (Suresh, Bagyaraj, and Reddy, 1985). Mycorrhizal fungi may alter the microbial activity in the rhizosphere affecting the survival of nematode and penetration of roots by nematode (Timothy and Robert, 1992). The above mechanisms may operate singly or in combination to make mycorrhizal plants resistant against the invasion of plant pathogens.

Similarly, inoculation of *Azotobacter spp.*, significantly improved the plant growth parameters and nutrient status (Abdel-Monaim, Abdel-Gaid, and El-Morsi, 2012) resulting in reduced population of *M. incognita* and its pathogenicity. Khan *et al.* (2012) observed the effect of *A. chroococcum* in combination with organic matters on the population of plant parasitic nematodes on chili plants and found significant reduction in the multiplication of nematodes as well as number of root galls. Being soil bacteria, *Azotobacter* is reported to produce growth promoting substances as auxins, cytokinins, and gibberellins and these materials are the primary substances controlling the enhanced growth. These substances, which originate from the root surface, affect the growth of the closely associated higher plants (Wani, Chand, and Ali, 2013). The inoculation of *Azotobacter* along with oil cake increased the internal as well as external colonization of mycorrhiza which increased the phosphorus contents of the soil rhizosphere. This productiveness of the rhizosphere for AM fungi may be attributed to favorable impact exerted by root exudates (Bais, Weir, Perry, Gilroy, and Vivanco, 2006), which contain amino acids, carbohydrates, organic acids and growth-promoting substances, and phytohormones produced by *A. chroococcum.*

Organic matter acts as nutrient reservoir and it also provides suitable substrate for growth of micro-organisms. Thus, addition of oil seed cake of *C. procera* resulted in enhanced proliferation of biofertilizers, in turn improving the plant-growth parameters and reducing nematode multiplication. The rate of reproduction and multiplication got checked due to the presence of some nematicidal properties (Hussain *et al.* 2011). Chedekal (2013) also reported reduction in galling and fecundity of nematode larvae on chickpea over control when plant was provided with *C. procera*. Chlorophyll contents were also increased in plants inoculated with *G. fasciculatum* and *A. chroococcum* individually as well as concomitantly in soil amended with *C. procera*. Similar results were recorded against root-rot disease of chickpea by Akhtar and Siddiqui (2008). The improvement in these parameters might be due to improvement in soil physical properties like: porocity, water holding capacity, and tendency of soil toward neutral pH which in turn increased the microbial biomass pool in the soil rhizosphere. The increase in chlorophyll contents in leaves in the presence of decomposed organic wastes (Siddiqui and Akhtar, 2008), due to increase in N uptake by the addition of organic compounds resulted in increased photosynthetic efficiency, translocation of nutrients, and other metabolites toward formation of fruits. The chickpea plants also showed significant improvement in growth parameters with the addition of *G. fasciculatum* (Bagyaraj, Manjunath, and Patil, 1979).

Conclusion

The findings of our study showed that combined application of both bioagents along with the organic matter, *C. procera,* surrogate to chemical nematicides, may be helpful to the growers of chickpea suffering from root-knot disease. This approach will also minimize the environmental perturbations, preserve the biota, and keep the management module more economic.

REFERENCES

Abdel-Monaim, M.F., Abdel-Gaid, M.A., and El-Morsi, M.E.A. (2012). Efficacy of rhizobacteria and Humic Acid for Controlling Fusarium wilt Disease and Improvement of Plant Frowth, Quantitative and Qualitative Parameters in Tomato. *eSci Journal of Plant Pathology*, 1, 39-48.

Akhtar, M.S., and Siddiqui, Z.A. (2008). Arbuscular mycorrhizal Fungi as Potential Biprotectants against Plant Pathogens. In Z.A. Siddiqui, M.S. Akhtar, and K. Futai (Eds.), Mycorrhizae: Sustainable agriculture and forestry (pp. 61-97). Dordrecht: Springer.10.1007/978-1-4020-8770-7.

Akkopru, A., and Demir, S. (2005). Biological Control of Fusarium wilt in Tomato caused by Fusarium Oxysporum f. *sp.* lycopersici by AMF Glomus Intraradices and some rhizobacteria. *Journal of Phytopathology*, 153, 544-550.10.1111/jph.2005.153.issue-9.

Allen, M.F. (1996). The Ecology of arbuscular mycorrhizas: A look back into 20th Century and a Peak into the 21st Century. Mycorrhizal Research, 100, 769-782..

Ansari, R.A., and Khan, T.A. (2012a). Diversity and Community Structure of phytonematodes Associated with Guava in and Around Aligarh, Uttar Pradesh, India. Trends in Biosciences, 5, 202-204.

Ansari, R.A., and Khan, T.A. (2012b). Parasitic Association of Root-knot Nematode, Meloidogyne Incognita on Guava. *e-Journal of Science and Technology* (e-JST), 5, 65-67.

Ansari, R.A., Rizvi, R., Safiuddin Agrawal, P., Sumbul, A., Tiyagi, S.A., and Mahmood, I. (2015). Effect of some Organic Fertilizers and Bioinoculant on Growth Attributes of Tomato in Relation to Sustainable Management of Root-knot Nematode. *The Journal of Plant Pathology*, Photon 115, 206-215.

Arnon, D.I. (1949). Copper Enzymes in Isolated chloroplasts. Polyphenoloxidase in Beta vulgaris. Plant Physiology, 24, 1-15.10.1104/pp.24.1.1.

Bagyaraj, D.J., Manjunath, A., and Patil, R.B. (1979). Occurrence of Vesicular – Arbuscular mycorrhizas in some Tropical Aquatic Plants. Transactions of the British Mycological Society, 72, 164–167.10.1016/S0007-1536(79)80023-6

Bais, H.P., Weir, T.L., Perry, L.G., Gilroy, S., and Vivanco, J.M. (2006). The Role of Root Exudates in rhizosphere Interactions with Plants and other organisms. *Annual Review of Plant Biology*, 57, 233-266.10.1146/annurev.arplant.57.032905.105159.

Barea, J. M., Azcón, R., and Azcón-Aguilar, C. (2002). Mycorhizosphere Interactions to Improve Plant Fitness and Soil Quality. Antonie van Leeuwenhoek, 81, 343–351.10.1023/A:1020588701325.

Brown, G.T. (1949). Pollen-slide Studies. Springfield, IL: Charles C. Thomas.

Chedekal, A.N. (2013). Effect of four Leaf Extracts on Egg Hatching and Juvenile Mortality of Root-knot Nematode Meloidogyne incognita. *International Journal of Advance Life Sciences*, 6, 68-74.

Collange, B., Navarrete, M., Peyre, G., Mateille, T., and Tchamitchian, M. (2011). Root-knot Nematode (Meloidogyne) Management in Vegetable Crop Production: The Challenge of an Agronomic System Analysis. Crop Protection, 30, 1251-1262.10.1016/j.cropro.2011.04.016.

Gerdemann, J.W., and Nicolson, T.W. (1963). Spores of Mycorrhizal Endogone Species Extracted from Soil by Wet-sieving and Decanting Method. Transaction of British Mycological Society, 46, 235-245.

Giovannetti, M., and Mosse, B. (1980). An Evaluation of Techniques for Measuring Vesicular Arbuscular Mycorrhizal Infection in Roots. New Phytologist, 84, 489-500.10.1111/j.1469-8137.1980.tb04556.x

Hallmann, J., Davies, K.G., and Sikora, R. (2009). Biological Control using Microbial Pathogens, Endophytes and Antagonists. In R.N. Perry, M. Moens, and J.L. Starr (Eds.), Root-knot Nematodes (pp. 380-411). Wallingford: CABI.10.1079/9781845934927.0000.

Hartman, K., and Sasser, J.N. (1985). Identification of Meloidogyne Species on the basis of differential Hosts test and Perineal Pattern Morphology. In K.R. Barker, C.C. Carter, and J.N. Sasser (Eds.), An Advanced Treatise on Meloidogyne (Vol. II, pp. 69-77). North Carolina State University Graphics. Raleigh, NC: Methodology. A Co-operative Publication of the Department of Plant Pathology and the United States Agency for International Development.

Huang, Y., Xu, C. K., Ma, L., Zhang, K.Q., Duan, C.Q., and Mo, M.H. (2009). Characterization of volatiles Produced from Baccillus megateriumYFM 3.25 and their Nematicidal Activity against Meloidogyne incognita. *European Journal of Plant Pathology*, 126, 417-422.

Hussain, A., Mukhtar, T., and Kayani, M.Z. (2011). Special Issue, (Medicinal Plants: Conservation and Sustainable use) Efficacy Evaluation of Azadirachta indica, Calotropis procera, Datura Stramonium and Tagetes erecta against root-knot nematodes Meloidogyne incognita. Pakistan Journal of Botany, 43, 197–204.

Hussey, R.S., and Roncadori, R. W. (1982). Vesiculararbuscular Mycorrhizae may Limit Nematode Activity and Improve Plant Growth. *Plant Disease*, 66, 9-14.

Jamal, A. (1976). Studies on the Relationship between Meloidogyne incognita and Galling Behaviour of Cicer arietinum Roots. *Current Science*, 45, 230-231.

Jiménez-Díaz, R.M., Castillo, P., Jiménez-Gasco, M.M., Landa, B.B., and Navas-Cortés, J.A. (in press). Fusarium wilt of chickpeas: Biology, Ecology and Management. Crop Protection. doi:10.1016/j.cropro.2015.02.023.

Jones, J.T., Haegeman, A., Danchin, E.G. J., Gaur, H. S., Helder, J., Jones, M. G.K., ... Perry, R.N. (2013). Top 10 Plant-parasitic Nematodes in Molecular Plant Pathology. Molecular Plant Pathology, 14, 946-961.10.1111/mpp.2013.14.issue-9.

Jothi, G., and Sundarababu, R. (2000). Interaction of Four Glomus *spp.* with Meloidogyne Incognita on Brinjal (Solanum melongena L.). *International Journal of Tropical Plant Disease*, 18, 147-156.

Kayani, M.Z., Mukhtar, T., and Hussain, M.A. (2012). Evaluation of Nematicidal Effects of Cannabis *sativa L.* and Zanthoxylum alatum Roxb., against root-knot nematodes, Meloidogyne incognita. Crop Protection, 39, 52-56.10.1016/j.cropro.2012.04.005.

Khan, A.A., and Siddiqui, M.A. (2005). Status of Root-knot nematodes in U.P. India. In S. Nehra (Ed.), *Plant Microbes and Biotechnology* (pp. 209-226). Jaipur: Pointer.

Khan, Z., Kim, S.G., Jeon, Y.H., Khan, H.U., Son, S.H., and Kim, Y.H. (2008). A Plant Growth Promoting rhizobacterium, Paenibacillus polymyxa strain GBR-1, suppresses root-knot nematode. Bioresource Technology, 99, 3016-3023.10.1016/j.biortech.2007.06.031.

Khan, M.R., Mohiddin, F.A., Ejaz, M.N., and Khan, M. M. (2012). Management of Root-knot Disease in Eggplant through the Application of Biocontrol Fungi and Dry Neem Leaves. *Turkish Journal of Biology*, 36, 161-169.

Khan, N., Safiuddin Rizvi, R., Ansari, R. A., Mahmood, I., Sumbul, A., and Tiyagi, S.A. (2015). Efficacy of Organic Matter and some bio-inoculants for the Management of Root-knot Nematode Infesting Tomato. *International Journal of Environment*, 4, 206-220.

Kumar, V., and Gupta, P. (2010). Studies of Shelf life of Fly ash based Azotobacter chroococcum and their after effects on Succeeding maize (Zea mays) in wheat Maize Cropping System. *Indian Journal of Agricultural Sciences*, 76, 465-468.

Linderman, R.G. (2000). Effects of mycorrhizas on Plant Tolerance to Disease. In Y. Kapulnik (Ed.), Arbuscular Mycorrhizas: Physiology and Function (pp. 345-367). Dordrecht: Kluwer Academic.

Mahmood, I., Tiyagi, S.A., and Azam, M.F. (2007). Efficacy of Latex Bearing Plants for the Management of Plant Parasitic nematodes and Soil-inhabiting Fungi on Chickpea and Mungbean. *Environmental and Biological Conservation*, 12, 23-37.

Mc Guidwin, F.A., Bird, G.W., and Safir, G.R. (1985). Influence of Glomus fasciculatum on Meloidogyne hapla Infecting Allium cepa. *Journal of Nematology*, 17, 389-395.

Mukhtar, T., Arshad, I., Kayani, M.Z., Hussain, M.A., Kayani, S.B., Rahoo, A.M., and Ashfaq, M. (2013). Estimation of Damage to okra (Abelmoschus esculentus) by Root-knot Disease Incited by Meloidogyne incognita. *Pakistan Journal of Botany*, 45, 1023-1027.

Mukhtar, T., Hussain, M.A., Kayani, M. Z., and Aslam, M.N. (2014). Evaluation of Resistance to Root-knot nematode (Meloidogyne incognita) in okra cultivars. Crop Protection, 56, 25-30.10.1016/j.cropro.2013.10.019.

Muller, R., and Gooch, P.S. (1982). Organic Amendment in Nematode Control. An Examination of the Literature. *Nematropica*, 12, 319-326.

Nelaballe, V.K., and Mukkara, L.D. (2013). A Pre-liminary Study on the Nematicidal Effect of some Local Flora on Meloidogyne Incognita chitwood infesting mulberry. *International Journal of Chemical, Environmental and Biotechnological Sciences*, 1, 475-477.

Nico, A.I., Jiménez-Di´az, R.M., and Castillo, P. (2004). Control of Root-knot Nematodes by Composted Agro-industrial Wastes in Potting Mixtures. Crop Protection, 23, 581-587.10.1016/j.cropro.2003.11.005.

Oruru, M.B., and Njeru, E.M. (2016). Upscaling Arbuscular Mycorrhizal Symbiosis and Related Agro-ecosystems Services in Small-holder Farming Systems. BioMed Research International, 4376240, 12 p. doi:10.1155/2016/4376240.

Ozgonen, H., Bicici, M., and Erkilic, A. (1999). The Effect of Salicylic Acid and Endomycorrhizal Fungus G. Intraradices on Plant Development of Tomato and Fusarium wilt caused by Fusarium oxysporum f. *spp.* Lycopersici. *Turkish Journal of Agriculture and Forestry*, 25, 25-29.

Phillips, J. M., and Hayman, D. S. (1970). Improved Procedures for Clearing Roots and Staining Parasitic and Vesicular-arbuscul ar Mycorrhizal Fungi for Rapid Assessment of Infection. Transactions of the British Mycological Society, 55, 158–IN18.10.1016/S0007-1536(70)80110-3.

Rizvi, R., Ansari, R. A., Iqbal, A., Ansari, S., Sumbul, A., Mahmood, I., and Tiyagi, S. A. (2015). Dynamic Role of Organic matter and Bioagent for the Management of Meloidogyne Incognita–Rhizoctonia Solani Disease Complex on Tomato in Relation to some Growth Attributes. Cogent Food and Agriculture, 1, 1068523. doi: 10.1080/23311932.2015.1068523.

Rizvi, R., Ansari, R.A., Zehra, G., and Mahmood, I. (2015). A Farmer Friendly and Economic IPM Strategy to Combat root-knot nematodes infesting lentil. Cogent Food and Agriculture, 1, 1053214. doi:10.1080/23311932.2015.1008859.

Rizvi, R., Singh, G., Safiuddin Ansari, R.A., Tiyagi, S.A., and Mahmood, I. (2015). Sustainable Management of Root-knot Disease of Tomato by neem cake and Glomus fasciculatum. Cogent Food and Agriculture, 1, 1008859. doi: 10.1080/23311932.2015.1008859.

Shreenivasa, K. R., Krishnappa, K., and Ravichandra, N.G. (2007). Interaction effects of AM Fungus Glomus Fasciculatum and Root-knot nematode, M. incognita on growth and phosphorous uptake of Tomato. *Karnataka Journal of Agriculture Science*, 20, 57-61.

Siddiqui, Z.A., and Akhtar, M.S. (2008). Effects of Organic Wastes,Glomus Intraradices and Pseudomonas Putida on the Growth of Tomato and on the Reproduction of the Root-knot Nematode Meloidogyne incognita. Phytoparasitica, 36, 460–471.10.1007/BF03020292.

Siddiqui, Z.A., and Mahmood, I. (1999). Role of Bacteria in the Management of Plant Parasitic Nematodes: A Review. Bioresource Technology, 69, 167–179.10.1016/S0960-8524(98)00122-9

Siddiqui, Z.A., and Mahmood, I. (2001). Effects of rhizobacteria and Root Symbionts on the Reproduction of Meloidogyne Javanica and Growth of chickpea. Bioresource Technology, 79, 41–45.10.1016/S0960-8524(01)00036-0.

Siddiqui, Z.A., Qureshi, A., and Akhtar, M. S. (2009). Biocontrol of Root-knot Nematode Meloidogyne Incognita by Pseudomonas and Bacillus isolates on Pisum Sativum. Archives of Phytopathology and Plant Protection, 42, 1154-1164.10.1080/03235400701650890.

Singh, N.P. (2012). All India Co-ordinated Research Project on Pulses: A Profile. Kanpur: Indian Institute of Pulses Research.

Singh, R., Kumar, N., and Rana, N.S. (2000). Response of Rainfed Guinea grass (Panicum maximum) to bio-fertilizer Inoculation and Nitrogen. *Indian Journal of Agronomy*, 45, 205-209.

Southey, J.F. (1986). Laboratory Methods for Work with Plant and Soil Nematodes (p. 402). London: Ministry of Agriculture.

Sumbul, A., Rizvi, R., Salah, M., Tiyagi, S.A., Ansari, R.A., and Safiuddin Mahmood, I. (2015). Role of different Sawdusts and Bioinoculant in the Management of Root-knot Nematode Infesting chickpea. *Asian Journal of Crop Science*, 7, 197-206. doi:10.3923/ajcs.2015.

Suresh, C.K., Bagyaraj, D.J., and Reddy, D. D. R. (1985). Effect of Vesicular-Arbuscular Mycorrhiza on Survival, Penetration and Development of Root-knot Nematode in Tomato. *Plant and Soil*, 87, 305–308.10.1007/BF02181869.

Tian, B., Yang, J., and Zhang, K. (2007). Bacteria used in the Biological Control of Plant-parasitic Nematodes: Populations, Mechanisms of Action, and Future Prospects. FEMS Microbiology Ecology, 61, 197–213.10.1111/fem.2007.61.issue-2.

Timothy, C.P., and Robert, G.L. (1992). Mycorrhizal Interaction with Soil Organisms. In K. Dilip Arora, Bharat Rai, K. G. Mukhergee, and R.K. Guy(Eds.), Handbook of Applied Mycology Soil and Plants (Vol. I, pp. 77-130). New York, NY: Marcel Dekker.

Tiyagi, S. A., and Ajaz, S. (2004). Biological Control of Plant-parasitic Nematodes Associated with chickpea using Oil-cakes and Paecilomyces lilacinus. *Indian Journal of Nematology*, 34, 44-48.

Tiyagi, S. A., Mahmood, I., Rizvi, R., and Dev, R. T. (2009). Utilization of Medicinal Plants for the Management of Root-knot and Reniform Nematodes Infecting Tomato and Chilli. Trends in Biosciences, 2, 47-49.

Verma, J. P., Yadav, J., and Tiwari, K. N. (2010). Application of Rhizobium *spp.* BHURC01 and Plant Growth Promoting rhizobactria on Nodulation, Plant Biomass and Yields of Chickpea (Cicer arietinum L.). *International Journal of Agricultural Research*, 5, 148-156.

Walia, K.K., and Gupta, D.C. (1995). Neem - An Effective Biocide against Meloidogyne javanica Attacking Vegetable Crops. *Plant Disease Research*, 10, 59-61.

Wani, S.A., Chand, S., and Ali, T. (2013). Potential use of Azotobacter chroococcum in crop production: *An Overview. Current Agriculture Research Journal*, 1, 35-38.

Weller, D.M. (1988). Biological Control of Soilborne Plant Pathogens in the rhizosphere with Bacteria. *Annual Review of Phytopathology*, 26, 379–407.10.1146/annurev.py.26.090188.002115.

Pages 25-32

INTEGRATED NUTRIENT MANAGEMENT IN CHICKPEA
Edited by : **Dr. Virendra Kumar** and **Dr. Nirmal Kumar Katiyar**
Edition : **2017**
ISBN : 978-93-5056-872-9
Published by : **Discovery Publishing House Pvt. Ltd., New Delhi (India)**

3

Integrated Wilt Management in Chickpea (*Cicer aritinum L.*) in Bundelkhand Region

Anil Kumar Singh[1], R.K.S. Tomar[2]
B.S. Kasana[3], Y.C. Rikhari[4]
Pradeep Kushwaha[5]

ABSTRACT

Chickpea wilt incited by Fusarium oxysporum f. sp., ciceris is one of the severe diseases causes heavy losses (20-100%) depending upon stage of infection and wilting. Minimizing this disease can only be accomplished by careful crop management. On-farm demonstration on use of resistant variety JG-16, summer deep ploughing, Trichoderma viride, PSB, Rhizobium and fungicides was conducted during Rabi (Oct-February) 2011-12 and 2012-13 in two villages of Datia district (M.P.) in Bundelkhand region. The field experiments comprised of four treatments module. In treatments module 1 (T1), where summer deep ploughing (SDP) + resistant variety (JG-16), wilt incidence was recorded 8.7 per cent at village Sitapur and 9.04 per cent at village Kakraua. In treatments module 2 (T2), where treatments module 1 (T1) + seed treatment with the combination of Carbendazim (1.0g) + Thiram (2.0g) per kg seed followed by Trichoderma viride @ 5.0 gram/kg were applied as seed treatment, wilt incidence was 5.2 per cent at village Sitapur and 5.46 per cent at village Kakraua. In treatments module 3 (T3), where treatments module 1 (T1) was applied followed by seed were treated with PSB and Rhizobium, wilt

1. Scientist, Krishi Vigyan Kendra Datia (M.P.) E-mail: aksingh_kvk@rediffmail.com
2. Senior Scientist, Krishi Vigyan Kendra Datia (M.P.)
3. Scientist, Krishi Vigyan Kendra Datia (M.P.)
4. P.A, Krishi Vigyan Kendra Datia (M.P.)
5. SRF, Krishi Vigyan Kendra Datia (M.P.)

incidence was 7.7 per cent at village Sitapur and 8.10 per cent at village Kakraua. Highest seed germination per cent (87.22), 100 seed weight (17.65g), yield (22.35q/ha), Benefit Cost ratio (3.61) and reduction in wilt incidence (69.26%) was found in treatments module 4 (T4) at village Sitapur where integration of the treatments module 1(T1), treatments module 2 (T2), and treatments module 3 (T3) followed by Trichoderma viride 4.0 kg/ha with 200kg farm yard manure (FYM) was applied as basal application at the time of field preparation.

Keywords: Resistant Variety, Wilt Incidence, IPM, INM, BCR.

Chickpea, *Cicer aritinum* L., is the world third most important pulse crop. India rank first in terms of chickpea production and consumption in the world. Low yield of chickpea is attributed to its susceptibility to several fungal, bacterial and viral diseases. Chickpea wilt incited by *Fusarium oxysporum f. sp. ciceris* is one of the serious diseases causes annual loss at 10 per cent in yield (*Dubey et al.* 2007). It is an important pest in chickpea growing areas of the world particularly in United State, India, Mexico and in the Mediterranean region (*Andrabi et al. 2011; Harveson 2011; Arvayo-Ortiz et al. 2012*). The pathogen of chickpea wilt disease is seed-borne (*Pande et al.* 2007) as well as soil borne (*Jiménez-Fernández et al. 2011*). The spores of fungus enter in the plants passing through the roots. When the spore reaches in the vascular system they produce certain enzymes that disgrace the cell walls and obstruct the plant's transport system. Discoloration occurs inside tissues from the root to the aerial parts. Yellowing and wilting of the foliage occur and finally there is necrosis (*Leslie and Summerell, 2006*). *F. oxysporum* survive as mycelium and chlamydospores in seed and soil, and also on infected crop residues, roots and stem tissue buried in the soil for up to 6 years and yield losses of up to 72.16 per cent may occur under favourable condition (*Kumar, S. and V.A. Bourai*, 2012). Chemical management of its infection by systemic fungicides is extravagant but also cause ecological problem. Hence, scientists are steadily looking out for non-perilous and eco-friendly measures for plant disease management. Integrated management strategies should include solution to maintain plant health. These strategies should include minimum use of chemicals for checking the pathogen population, encouragement of beneficial biological agents to reduce pathogen inoculums, modification of cultural practices and use of resistance varieties (*Moradi et al. 2012*).

The aim of present investigation to minimize the wilt incidence and develop an economically justified and sustainable system of crop protection that leads to maximum productivity of chickpea.

Methodology

In order to evaluate the efficacy of integrated use of cultural, biological, and chemical practices for the effective management of wilt disease in chickpea. The experiment was conducted during the post rainy season at farmers' field at Sitapur and Kakraua villages in Datia district (M.P.) of Bundelkhand region during Rabi 2011-12 and 2012-13. Chickpea wilt resistant variety JG-16 was used during the experiments with a seed rate of 75kg/ha. The crop was sown during the third week of October at a spacing of 30×10 cm. Fertilizer NPKS @ 20, 60, 20 and 30 kg/ha in the form of Urea, SSP and Muriate of potash respectively were applied as basal at the time of sowing seed. The experiment was conducted completely randomized block design (RBD) replicated three times.

The field experiments comprised of 4 treatments module and control (untreated check). The IDM treatment modules *viz;*

T1–Summer ploughing + certified seed of resistant variety (JG-16).

T2–T1 + seed treatment with the combination of Carbendazim (1.0g) + Thiram (2.0g) per kg seed followed by *Trichoderma viride* (Jawahar Trichoderma, JNKVV, Jabalpur) @ 5.0 gram/kg seed.

T3–T1 + Phosphate Solubilizing Bacteria (Jawahar PSB, JNKVV, Jabalpur) and Rhizobium culture (Jawahar Rhizobium, JNKVV, Jabalpur) @ 5.0g each/kg seed as a seed treatment.

T4–T2 + T3 + *Trichoderma viride* @ 4.0 kg/ha with 200 kg farm yard manure (FYM) was applied as basal application at the time of field preparation.

Control–Untreated check where seed was sown with imbalanced fertilizer (9.0 kg N and 23 kg P2O5).

The per cent field emergence was calculated based on following formula:

$$\frac{\text{No. of seed germinated}}{\text{No. of seed sown}} \times 100$$

The wilt incidence was recorded at 30 days intervals till harvest. In each plot, three rows, each 10 m long, were chosen arbitrarily. Plants in each row were examined and the number of plants showing symptoms of yellowing or wilting vascular noted. Disease incidence is expressed as the percentage of affected plants, counted in three rows by the total number of plants. Per cent disease incidence in each treatment was calculated using the following formula.

$$\text{Wilt incidence (\%)} = \frac{\text{No. of plants wilted}}{\text{No. of plants examined}} \times 100$$

The benefit cost ratio was calculated on the basis of prevailing market prices of chickpea and other inputs. Benefit cost ratio was calculated as follows:

$$BCR \quad \frac{\textit{Gross return}}{\textit{Total cost}}$$

Results and Discussion

In the present study, seed treatment with chemical fungicide, PSB, *Rhizobium* and *Trichoderma viride* followed by soil application of *Trichoderma viride* and recommended dose of inorganic Nitrogen, Phosphorus, Potash and Sulfur were used to control wilt incidence effectively and increased chickpea yield significantly over other treatments. To find out the best disease management module by this study the result showed (Table 3.1) that at village Sitapur, T1, T2 and T3 individually gave 41.22, 64.86 and 47.97 per cent management of disease over the unprotected field, respectively. However, their integrated effects resulted in 69.26 per cent management of disease thereby given 47.70, 12.5 and 40.90 per cent additional management of disease over T1, T2 and T3, respectively. In the same way, results produce by the experiment at village Kakraua showed the best disease management in T4 (68.62%) fallowed by T2 (64.68%), T3 (47.61%) and T1 (41.52%) whereas, the lowest disease incidence was recorded at village Sitapur by T4 (4.55%).

The highest field emergence of 87.22 and 87.08 per cent were observed in T4 from both locations (Sitapur and Kakraua) where integrated application of all the treatments. Whereas, combined application of chemical and bio-agents (T2) were used and showed 86.56 and 86.36 per cent seedling emergence. In T3, 85.46 and 85.36 per cent seed germination were observed where variety JG-16, summer ploughing and bio-inputs were applied. 84.60 and 84.0 per cent seed germination were found in T1 and the lowest germination per cent (78.20 and 77.82) was noted from village Sitapur and Kakraua in untreated check of T5 (Table 3.2). The present finding is partially supported by the observation made by *Amalraj et al.* (2012). They recorded the highest seedling emergence in carbendazim treated seeds and it was on a par with a combination of chemical and bio-agents.

With regard to effect of all the 4 treatments on the 100 grain weight (g), Table 3.2 shows that the highest 100 grain weight (17.65g) was recorded in treatment 4 at village Sitapur and 17.59g at village Kakraua followed by treatment 3 (17.59g and 17.51g), treatment 2 (17.48g and 17.40g), treatment 1 (17.42g and 17.38g) and control at both village Sitapur and Kakraua experiment locations. The differences in these results were significant in each location and this indicates a significant effect of treatment in 100 seed weight. However, at both locations Treatment 4 was effective but significantly at par with treatment 3.

Table 3.1: Detail of wilt incidence in chick pea field (Pooled data of 2011-12 and 2012-13)

Treatment	Village Sitapur					Village Kakraua				
	Wilt Incidence (%)				Reduction disease in (%)	Wilt Incidence (%)				Reduction disease in (%)
	After 30 days of sowing	After 60 days of sowing	After 90 days of sowing	Harvesting time		After 30 days of sowing	After 60 days of sowing	After 90 days of sowing	Harvesting time	
T1	0.60 (4.44)	4.60 (12.38)	7.47 (15.86)	8.7 (17.15)	41.22 (4.52)	0.62 (13.05)	5.10 (10.08)	7.67 (17.50)	9.04	41.52
T2	0.37 (3.49)	3.53 (10.83)	4.77 (12.62)	5.2 (13.18)	64.86 (3.63)	0.40 (11.24)	3.80 (12.83)	4.93 (13.51)	5.46	64.68
T3	0.47 (3.93)	3.87 (11.35)	6.07 (14.26)	7.7 (16.11)	47.97 (4.01)	0.49 (12.15)	4.43 (14.38)	6.17 (16.54)	8.10	47.61
T4	0.22 (2.69)	3.13 (10.19)	3.77 (11.20)	4.55 (12.32)	69.26 (2.87)	0.25 (10.74)	3.47 (11.49)	3.97 (12.72)	4.85	68.62
Control	0.67 (4.70)	5.37 (13.40)	12.07 (20.33)	14.8 (22.63)	00 (4.90)	0.73 (16.50)	8.07 (20.68)	12.47 (23.15)	15.46	00
SE(m) ± C.D. at 5%	0.19 0.60	0.095 0.311	0.14 0.48	0.09 0.31	0.23 0.76	0.18 0.60	0.12 0.40	0.12 0.39		

Figures in parenthesis represent angular transformed value.

Table 3.2: Detail of per cent seed germination, seed weight and yield of chick pea (Pooled data of 2011-12 and 2012-13)

Treatment	Village Sitapur				Village Kakraua			
	Germin-ation (%)	100 grain weight (g)	Yield (q/ha)	Increase in yield (%)	Germin-ation (%)	100 grain weight (g)	Yield (q/ha)	Increase in yield (%)
T1	84.60(66.89)	17.42	18.5	27.06	84.00(66.42)	17.38	18.10	26.04
T2	86.56(68.49)	17.48	20.22	38.87	86.36(68.33)	17.4	19.98	39.14
T3	17.59	20.12	38.19	85.36(67.50)	17.51	19.94	38,86	
T4	87.22(69.05)	17.65	22.35	53.50	87.08(68.93)	17.59	21.85	52.16
Control	78.20(62.17)	17.18	14.56	—	77.82(61.90)	17.12	14.36	—
SE(m) ±	0.23	0.018	0.07		0.09	0.03	0.03	
C.D. at 5%	0.76	0.07	0.22	0.29	0.09	0.11		

Figures in parenthesis represent angular transformed value.

Data presented in Table 3.2 reveal that the highest mean yield of chickpea per field was recorded in T4 (22.35q/ha) at farmer's field from village Sitapur which is 53.50 per cent more than untreated field followed by T2 (20.22 q/ha), T3 (20.12q/ha), T1 (18.50q/ha) and the lowest yield was observed with control (14.46q/ha).

Table 3.3: Detail of economics of treatments (Pooled data of 2011-12 and 2012-13)

Treatment	Village Sitapur			Village Kakraua			
	Cost of treatment (Rs.)	Gross return	Net Return (Rs.)	BCR	Gross return	Net Return (Rs.)	BCR
T1	3490	61050	41440	3.11	59730	40120	3.05
T2	3690	66726	46916	3.37	65934	46124	3.33
T3	3736	66396	46540	3.34	65802	45946	3.31
T4	4320	73755	53315	3.61	72105	51665	3.53
Control	00	48048	31928	2.98	47388	31268	2.94

Similar results obtained from Kakraua village whereas, the highest mean yield recorded in treatment 4 (21.85 q/ha) fallowed by T2 (19.98 q/ha), T3 (19.94 q/ha) and T1 (18.10q/ha).

Treatment 4 (T2 + T3 + *Trichoderma viride* 4.0 kg/ha with 200 kg farm yard manure) provided the highest gross returns (Rs. 73755/ha) in village Sitapur. Remaining other treatments provided identical gross return. The lowest gross returns (Rs. 47388/ha) was computed from untreated field at village Kakraua. The highest benefit cost ratio (3.61) with the highest net return (Rs. 53315) was obtained from T4 at village Sitapur. Similarly, results found in other location at Kakraua followed by T2, T3 and T1at both locations. (Table 3.3)

Fusarium oxysporum f. spp. ciceris is one of the yield limiting factors of chickpea across the world. Use of bio-agents in combination with reduced doses of chemical fungicide has recently been emphasised for sustainable agriculture (*Someya et al. 2007; Andrabi et al. 2011*). Due to the soil borne nature of the disease, use of chemicals in controlling the chickpea wilt is hardly successful. Hence, the economical and feasible approach would be either to search for resistant source or resort of biological control. *T viride* was found most effective which is in accordant with report of *Pandey and Upadhyay (1999)* and the possible suppression of wilt incidence in chickpea is due to antagonistic activity by *T. viride* by producing various extracellular enzymes which play an important role in biological control (*Kredics et al.* 2003). *Ainmisha et al. (2011)* found that wilt of chickpea incited by *Fusarium oxysporum f. sp. ciceris* could be minimize by use of Carbendazim and *Trichoderma viride. Andrabi et al. 2011* also found that seed treatment with Carbendazim increased the disease reduction percentage 86.66 over control. *Kolte et al. (1998)* effectively controlled chickpea wilt with seed treatment by Rhizobium and T. *viride. De et al. (1996)* found that coating of chickpea seed with Carbendazim was more effective in reducing wilt and increasing seed yield by 25.9 to 42.65 per cent. Due to synergistic effects of both the chemicals seed treatment with Thiram (0.15%) + Carbendazim (0.1%) were found most effective against *F. oxysporum* f. sp. *ciceris* (*Gupta et al. 1997*).

Conclusion

It can be concluded from the present study that chemical seed dressing along with mixture of bacteria and fungi may be beneficial in reducing the intensity of wilt disease and enhancing seed germination percentage as well as productivity of chickpea.

REFERENCES

Ainmisha and Zacharia, S. (2011). Effect of Carbendazim, Neem Cake and Trichoderma viride on wilt of Chickpea. *J. Mycol. Plant Pathol.* 41 (4):550-553.

Amalraj, ELD, Praveen Kumar G., Mir Hassan Ahmed S.K., Desai S. (2012). On-farm Evaluation of Integrated Nutrient and Pest Management in Cicer arietinum L. *J. Phytol* 4:48-51.

Andrabi, M., Vaid, A. and Razdan, V.K. (2011). Evaluation of different Measures to Control wilt causing Pathogen in Chickpea. *J. Plant Prot.Res.* 51(1):55-59.

Arvayo-Ortiz, R.M., Esqueda, M. Acedo-Felix, Gonzalez-Rios, E.H. and Vargas-Rosales G. (2012). New lines of Chickpea against Fusarium Oxysporum f. sp. ciceris wilt. *Am. J. Appl. Sci.* 9(5):686-693.

De, R.K., Chaudhry, R.G. and Naimuddin (1996). Comparative efficacy of Biocontrol agent and Fungicides for Controlling Chickpea wilt caused by Fusarium Oxysporum *f. sp. ciceris. Indian J. Agri. Sci.*, 66: 370-373.

Dubey, S.C., Suresh, M. and Singh, B. (2007). Evaluation of Trichoderma Species against Fusarium Oxysporum *f. sp. ciceris* for Integrated Management of Chickpea *wilt. Biol Con.* 40:118-27.

Gupta, S.K., Upadhyay, J.P. and Ojha, K.H. (1997). Effect of Fungicidal Seed Treatment on the Incidence of Chickpea wilt Complex. *Ann. Plant Prot. Sci;* 5: 184-187.

Harveson, R.M. (2011). Soil Borne Diseases of Chickpea in Nebraska. http://extension.unl.edu/publication.

Jiménez-Fernández, D., Montes-Borrego, M. Jiménez-Díaz, R.M. Navas-Cortés, J.A. Landa, B.B. (2011). In Planta and Soil Quantification of Fusarium Oxysporum *f. sp. ciceris* and Evaluation of Fusarium wilt Resistance in Chickpea with a Newly Developed Quantitative Polymerase chain Reaction Assay. *Phytopathol.* 1(2):250-62.

Kolte, S.O., Thakre, K.G., Gupta M. and Lokhande, V.V. (1998). Biocontrol of Fusarium wilt of Chickpea (*Cicer arietinum*) under wilt sick Field Condition. Proceeding of the ISOPP National Symposium on Management of Soil and Soil borne Diseases, February 9-10, 1998, ISOPP, pp. 22.

Kredics, L., Anta, Z., Manczinger, L., Szekeres, A., Kevei, F. and E. Nagy. (2003). Influence of Environmental Parameters on Trichoderma Strains with Biocontrol Potential. *Food Tech Biotech.* 41(1): 37-42.

Kumar, S. and Bourai, V.A. (2012). Economic Analysis of Pulses Production their Benefits and Constraints" (A Case Study of Sample Villages of Assan valley of Uttarakhand, India). *J. Hu. Social Sci.* 4(1):41-53.

Leslie, J.F. and Summerell, B. A. (2006). The Fusarium Laboratory manual. Blackwell Publishing, State Avenue, ames, Lawa, USA.

Moradi H., Bahramnejad, B., Amini J., Siosemardeh A., Allahverdipoor K. (2012). Suppression of Chickpea (*Cicer arietinum L.*) Fusarium wilt by Bacillus subtillis and Trichoderma harzianum. *Plant Omics J.* 5:68-74.

Pande, S., Rao, J.N. and Sharma, M. (2007). Establishment of the Chickpea wilt pathogen *Fusarium Oxysporum* f. sp. *ciceris* in the Soil through Seed Transmission. *Plant Pathol*, 23 (1):3-6.

Pandey K.K. and Upadhyay, J.P. (1999). Comparative Studies of Chemical, Biological and Integrated Apprach for Management of Fusarium wilt of Pigeon pea. J. Mycol. *Plant Pathol*; 29: 214-216.

Someya N., Tsuchiya K., Yoshida T., Tsujimoto-noguchi M, Sawada H (2007). Combined Application of Pseudomonas fluorescens strain LRB3W1 with a low dosage of benomyl for control of cabbage yellows caused by Fusarium oxysporum f. sp. conglutinans. *Biocontrol Sci Technol*, 17:21-31.

Pages 33-45

INTEGRATED NUTRIENT MANAGEMENT IN CHICKPEA
***Edited by* : Dr. Virendra Kumar** and **Dr. Nirmal Kumar Katiyar**
***Edition* : 2017**
ISBN : 978-93-5056-872-9
***Published by* : Discovery Publishing House Pvt. Ltd., New Delhi (India)**

Effect of Supplemental Application of Nitrogen, Irrigation and Hormone on the Yield and Yield Components of Chickpea

Indrajit Roy[1], Parimal Kanti Biswas[1]
Md. Hazrat Ali[1], Md. Nazmul Haque[1]
Md. Shafiqul Islam[2]
Abdul Kabir Khan Achakzai[3]

ABSTRACT

In order to study the response of chickpea varieties to supplementary nitrogen, irrigation and hormones on the yield and yield attributes, a field experiment was conducted in December, 2012 to March, 2013 at Sher-e-Bangla Agricultural University, Dhaka, Bangladesh. The different supplementary treatments showed significant effect on number of pods plant^{-1}, seeds pod^{-1}, 1000-seed weight, shelling percentage, seed yield, stover yield, biological yield and harvest index of chickpea varieties. Among the varieties, the highest pods plant^{-1} (27.58), seeds pod^{-1} (1.65), 1000-seed weight (263.36 g), shelling percentage (0.69), seed yield (1702 kg ha^{-1}), stover yield (2727 kg ha^{-1}), biological yield (4429 kg ha^{-1}) and harvest index (38.28%) were recorded from BARI chola 9. The maximum pods plant1 (28.52), seeds pod^{-1} (1.67), 1000-seed weight (274.00 g), highest shelling percentage (0.73), seed yield (1851 kg ha^{-1}), stover yield (2830 kg ha^{-1}), biological yield (4681 kg ha^{-1}) and harvest index (39.48%) were obtained from supplemental irrigation along with aqueous N before flowering. In case of treatment combinations, BARI chola 9 cultivation with applying supplemental irrigation before flowering + aqueous N before flowering

1. Department of Agronomy, Faculty of Agriculture, Sher-e-Bangla Agricultural University, Sher-e-Bangla Nagar, Dhaka - 1207, Bangladesh.
2. Programme Co-ordinator, NUSRA.
3. Department of Botany, University of Balochistan, Quetta, Pakistan.

revealed maximum yield and yield contributing characters. It would suggest that both the yield and the yield parameters seem to be favorably affected by supplementary nitrogen, irrigation and hormone application.

Keywords: Biological yield, Chickpea, Harvest index, Seed yield, Shelling %, Stover yield.

INTRODUCTION

Chickpea (*Cicer arietinum* L.) is the third most widely grown grain legume in the world after bean and soybean. The agronomical importance of chickpea is based on its high protein concentration (approx. 19.3-25.4%) for the human and animal diet, being used more and more as an alternative protein source. Moreover, it is also widely used as fodder and green manure [1, 2, 3, 4].

Nitrogen (N) deficiency is frequently a major limiting factor for high yielding crops all over the world [4, 5]. Therefore, adequate supply of N is necessary to achieve high yield potential in crops. In general, N deficiency causes a reduction in growth rate, general chlorosis, often accompanied by early senescence of older leaves and reduced yield [3, 6]. Mckenzie and Hill [7] and Achakzai [8] reported that the increase of N rate significantly enhanced seed and dry matter yield, harvest index, number of pods plant^{-1} and 1000-seed weight.

Water deficiency has adverse effects on plant growth, average yield and crude protein in legume crops. The flowering stage is the most vulnerable stage for water stress and chickpea is somewhat tolerant to deficit water but susceptible to excess water [9]. Adequate supply of irrigation water along with chemical fertilizer is essential for normal growth and yield of a crop [10, 11]. On the other hand, chickpea is grown in rabi season when lack of water becomes a serious restriction specially after flowerings. Saraf *et al.* [12] stated that excess and deficient moisture conditions both are detrimental and reduce yield of chickpea. Irrigation is frequently used to supplement rainfall to increase crop productivity in chickpea [13].

Plant growth regulators (PGR's) are organic compounds, which in small amounts, somehow modify a given physiological plant process. It plays an essential role in many aspects of plant growth and development [14, 15]. PRH is an organic product of Natural Bio Agro Tech Co. (Pvt.) Ltd. (NBAT) is a Japan-Bangladesh joint venture agro based company. The product is a hormone made from fruits vinegar and other natural ingredients. The composition of the product is their patent. As per NBAT, the PRH is used in cereal crops, vegetables, fruit crops, cash crops, pulses and oil crops, fisheries, poultry and livestock (www.nbatbd.com). Application of PGR caused an increase of seed yield and pod diameter of an early sown chickpea crop [16].

This indicates that PGR may have the potential to control vegetative growth of chickpea during reproductive stage and to increase the partition of assimilates toward pod development which would be critical under the growing conditions. However, information on this aspect is lacking. This study was designed to evaluate the effects of supplementary N, irrigation and hormone application on performance of seed yield and yield attributes of chickpea.

Materials and Methods

Experimental Site, Soil and Climate

The experiment was conducted at the Sher-e-Bangla Agricultural University, Dhaka, Bangladesh during the period from December 11, 2012 to March 30, 2013 which was situated at 23°46° 'N latitude and 90°23°E longitude at an altitude of 8.45 meter above the sea level. The soil of the experimental site was sandy loam with pH and cation exchange capacity 5.6 and 2.64 meq/100 g soil, respectively. The experimental site is under subtropical humid climatic conditions and the detailed mean maximum, minimum temperature and rainfall is presented here in Fig. 4.1.

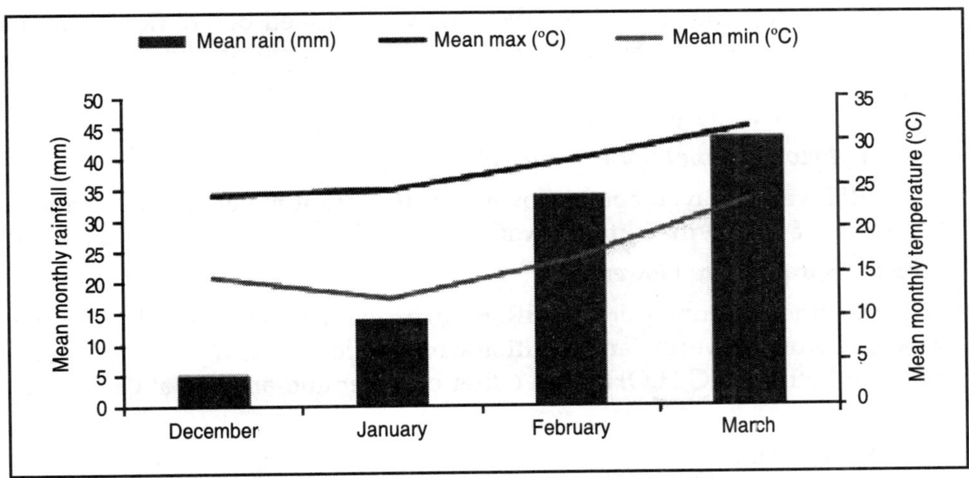

Fig. 4.1: Mean monthly rainfall and temperature during the experimental period

Experimental Treatments

The experiment consists of two chickpea varieties *viz;* BARI chola 8 (V_1), BARI chola 9 (V_2) and five supplementary treatments *i.e.* Control (no spray at flowering and afterwards) (T_1), supplemental irrigation before flowering (T_2), supplemental irrigation + aqueous N before flowering (T_3), PRH (a phytohormone) spray before flowering (T_4) and Kinetine spray before flowering (T_5).

Planting Materials, Design and Plot Size

The variety BARI chola 8 and BARI chola 9 were used as the test crops. The two factors experiment was laid out in split-plot design with three replications each. An area of 22.7 × 22 m was divided into blocks. The two varieties were assigned in the main plot and five supplementary treatments in sub-plot. The size of each unit plot was 4.0 × 3.2 m. The space between two blocks and two plots were 1.0 and 0.5 m, respectively.

Fertilizer Application

Urea, Triple Super Phosphate (TSP), Muriate of Potash (MoP), gypsum, zinc sulphate and boric acid were used as a source of N, P, K, Ca, S and B, respectively were applied @ 50, 90, 40, 110, 7 and 10 kg ha $^{-1}$, respectively. All of the fertilizers except urea were applied during final land preparation.

Supplemental Irrigation before Flowering (SIBF)

Supplementary irrigation was applied before flowering and it was done at 15 February at 65 Days after Sowing (DAS). Selected 6 plots were provided with flood irrigation.

SIBF + Aqueous N before Flowering

SIBF + Aqueous N before flowering was applied before flowering and done at 05 February at 55 DAS. Selected 6 plots were provided with flood irrigation and aqueous N. For aqueous nitrogen 153.6 g urea were mixed with 6 liter of water and sprayed in the plots.

PRH (a phytohormone) Spray before Flowering

PRH were sprayed before flowering and solution were made by adding 12 spoons of PRH with 6 liter of water and applied at 05 February at 55 DAS.

Kinetine Spray before Flowering

Kinetine (kinetine puriss CHR: 6-Furfurylaminopurine, $C_{10}H_5OH$) were sprayed before flowering and solution were made by adding 150 mg kinetene and 10 ml ethanol (C_6H_5OH) with 6 liter of water and applied at 05 February at 55 DAS.

Shelling Percentage

The mass of seeds obtained from the pods that were randomly drawn from a bulk sample and calculated the shelling percentage by using the following formula:

$$\text{Shelling percentage} = \frac{\text{Seed mass}}{\text{Pod mass}} \times 100$$

Biological Yield

The biological yield was calculated with the following formula:

$$\text{Biological yield} = \text{Seed yield} + \text{Stover yield}$$

Harvest Index

Harvest index is the relationship between seed yield and biological yield [17]. It was calculated by using the following formula:

$$HI\,(\%) = \frac{\text{Seed yield}}{\text{Biological yield}} \times 100$$

Statistical Analysis

Collected data were statistically analyzed by using MSTAT-C [18] programme and mean differences among the treatments were compared by least significant difference (LSD) test at 5 per cent level of probability.

Results and Discussion

Number of Pods Plant^{-1}

Number of pods plant^{-1} varied significantly ($p<0.05$) in chickpea varieties (Table 4.1). The maximum number of pods plant^{-1} (27.58) was found from BARI chola 9, while the minimum (26.03) was observed from BARI chola 8. Pods plant^{-1} varied for different varieties might be due to genetical and environmental influences as well as management practices. Mirzakhani *et al.* [19] reported that the number of pods plant^{-1} had non-significant differences between the different cultivar. Variability in chickpea varieties for number of pods plant^{-1} had been reported by Sadeghipour and Aghaei [20].

The effect of different supplementary treatments was statistically significant ($p<0.05$) on number of pods plant^{-1} in chickpea (Table 4.1). The maximum number of pods plant^{-1} (28.52) was observed from supplemental irrigation along with aqueous N before flowering, which was statistically similar with supplemental irrigation before flowering, PRH spray before flowering and kinetine spray before flowering, whereas the minimum (25.00) was recorded from control treatment *i.e.,* no spray at flowering and afterwards. Bicer *et al.* [13] reported that number of pods plant^{-1} was higher under irrigated than rainfed conditions.

Significant ($p<0.05$) variation was observed due to the interaction effect of chickpea varieties and different supplementary treatments on number of pods plant^{-1} (Table 4.1). The maximum pods plant^{-1} (28.80) was found from BARI chola 9 with supplemental irrigation along with aqueous N before flowering and the minimum (24.57) was obtained from BARI chola 8 with control treatment.

Number of Seeds Pod^{-1}

Statistically significant ($p<0.05$) difference was observed in terms of number of seeds pod^{-1} of chickpea varieties (Table 4.1). Different varieties responded differently for number of seeds pods^{-1} to input supply and the prevailing environment during the growing season. The maximum seeds pod^{-1} (1.65) was recorded from BARI chola 9 and the minimum (1.54) was recorded from BARI chola 8. Variability in chickpea varieties for number of seeds pod^{-1} had been reported by Sadeghipour and Aghaei [20].

Table 4.1: Effect of variety and/or supplemental nitrogen, irrigation and hormone spray on number of pods $plant^{-1}$, seeds pod^{-1}, 1000-seed weight, shelling percentage of chickpea

Treatments	Number of Pods $Plant^{-1}$	Number of Seeds Pod^{-1}	1000-Seed Weight(g)	Shelling Percentage (%)
Variety				
V_1	26.03 b	1.54 b	250.99 b	0.67 b
V_2	27.58 a	1.65 a	263.36 a	0.69 a
LSD (0.05)	1.412	0.08	8.511	0.016
Supplementary treatment				
T_1	25.00 c	1.51 c	234.89 c	0.64 c
T_2	27.57 ab	1.64 ab	268.52 a	0.70 ab
T3	28.52 a	1.67 a	274.00 a	0.73 a
T_4	26.75 a-c	1.59 bc	248.84 bc	0.66 bc
T_5	26.17 bc	1.56 bc	259.63 ab	0.69 a-c
LSD (0.05)	1.897	0.077	14.79	0.055
Treatment combination				
$V_1 T_1$	24.57 e	1.47 d	234.08 c	0.58 c
$V_1 T_2$	26.68 a-e	1.58 cd	261.63 ab	0.73 ab
V1 T3	28.24 a-c	1.60 bc	272.46 ab	0.71 ab
V1 T4	25.53 b-e	1.56 cd	236.54 c	0.67 ab
$V_1 T_5$	25.13 de	1.51 cd	250.27 bc	0.67 ab
$V_2 T_1$	25.43 c-e	1.56 cd	235.71 c	0.69 ab
$V_2 T_2$	28.46 ab	1.70 ab	275.42 a	0.67 ab
V2 T3	28.80 a	1.74 a	275.54 a	0.75 a
$V_2 T_4$	27.96 a-d	1.62 bc	261.14 ab	0.65 bc
$V_2 T_5$	27.22 a-e	1.62 bc	268.99 ab	0.71 ab
LSD (0.05)	2.683	0.110	20.92	0.077

**: significant at p 0.01, *: significant at $p<0.05$.

Means in a column followed by same letter(s) are not significantly different at 5 per cent level of least significant difference (LSD) test.

V_1: BARI chola 8; V_2: BARI chola 9; T_1: Control *i.e.,* no spray at flowering and afterwards; T_2: Supplemental irrigation before flowering; T_3: Supplemental irrigation + Aqueous N before flowering; T_4: PRH (a phytohormone) spray before flowering; T_5: Kinetine spray before flowering.

Number of seeds pod^{-1} was significantly ($p<0.01$) affected by supplemental application of nitrogen, irrigation and hormone (Table 4.1). The maximum seeds pod^{-1} (1.67) was found from supplemental irrigation along with aqueous N before flowering, which was statistically similar with supplemental irrigation before flowering and PRH spray before flowering and kinetine spray before flowering whereas, the minimum (1.51) was observed from control treatment. Bicer *et al.* [13] reported that number of seeds pods^{-1} was higher under irrigated than rainfed conditions.

Number of seeds pod^{-1} of chickpea showed significant ($p<0.01$) differences due to the interaction effect of chickpea varieties and different supplementary treatments (Table 4.1). The maximum seeds pod^{-1} (1.74) was recorded from BARI chola 9 with supplemental irrigation along with aqueous N before flowering, whereas the minimum (1.47) was obtained from BARI chola 8 with no spray at flowering and afterwards.

1000-Seed Weight

A significant ($p<0.05$) difference in 1000-seed weight was observed in studied chickpea varieties (Table 4.1). The highest 1000-seed weight (263.36g) was obtained from BARI chola 9, while the lowest (250.99 g) was attained from BARI chola 8. Mirzakhani *et al.* [19] found antagonistic result who reported that 1000-seed weight showed non-significant differences between the cultivars.

Different supplementary treatments significantly ($p<0.01$) affected the 1000-seed weight (Table 4.1). The maximum 1000-seed weight (274.00 g) was recorded from supplemental irrigation along with aqueous N before flowering, which was statistically at par with supplemental irrigation before flowering, kinetine spray before flowering and PRH spray before flowering, whereas the minimum (234.89 g) was found from control treatment.

The interaction effect between chickpea varieties and different supplementary treatments on 1000-seed weight was statistically significant ($p<0.05$) (Table 4.1). The highest 1000-seed weight (275.54 g) was observed from BARI chola 9 with supplemental irrigation along with aqueous N before flowering and the lowest (234.08 g) was obtained from BARI chola 8 with control treatment.

Shelling Percentage

Shelling percentage was significantly ($p<0.05$) influenced by various applied treatments (Table 4.1). The highest shelling percentage (0.69) was recorded for BARI chola 9 and the lowest (0.67) was found from BARI chola 8.

Significant variation ($p<0.05$) was recorded in terms of shelling percentage of chickpea for the supplementary application of nitrogen, irrigation and hormones (Table 4.1). The maximum shelling percentage (0.73%) was found from supplemental irrigation along with aqueous N before flowering, which was statistically similar with supplemental irrigation before flowering, kinetine spray before flowering and PRH spray before flowering.

The minimum shelling percentage (0.64) was observed from control *i.e.,* no spray at flowering and afterwards. Hafiz [21] reported that chickpea cultivars Giza 1, Giza 88 and Giza 195 and early soil application of nitrogen fertilizer up to 40 kg N ha^{-1} significantly increased shelling percentage.

Table 4.2: Effect of variety and/or supplemental nitrogen, irrigation and hormone spray on seed, stover, biological yield and harvest index of chickpea

Treatments	Seed Yield (kg ha^{-1})	Stover Yield (kg ha^{-1})	Biological Yield (kg ha^{-1})	Harvest Index (%)
Variety				
V_1	1438 b	2469 b	3907 b	36.67 b
V_2	1702 a	2727 a	4429 a	38.28 a
LSD (0.05)	47.62	16.88	58.06	0.4030
Supplementary treatment				
T_1	1269 d	2318 c	3587 c	35.35 c
T_2	1716 b	2777 a	4493 a	38.11 ab
T_3	1851 a	2830 a	4681 a	39.48 a
T4	1499 c	2464 bc	3963 b	37.72 ab
T_5	1516 c	2600 b	4116 b	36.72 bc
LSD (0.05)	134.7	166.9	241.0	2.274
Treatment combination				
V_1 T_1	1202 e	2110 e	3312 e	36.11 bc
V_1 T_2	1558 d	2651 c	4209 c	37.01 a-c
V_1 T_3	1758 a-c	2743 a-c	4502 bc	38.98 ab
V1 T4	1337 e	2318 de	3655 d	36.54 bc
V1 T5	1336 e	2520 cd	3856 d	34.70 c
V_2 T_1	1335 e	2527 cd	3862 d	34.59 c
V_2 T_2	1873 ab	2903 ab	4776 ab	39.21 ab
V_2 T_3	1944 a	2917 a	4860 a	39.98 a
V2 T4	1662 cd	2610 c	4272 c	38.89 ab
V_2 T_5	1695 b-d	2680 bc	4375 c	38.73 ab
LSD (0.05)	190.5	236.0	340.8	3.215

**: significant at p<0.01, *: significant at p<0.05.

Means in a column followed by same letter(s) are not significantly different at 5 per cent level of least significant difference (LSD) test.

V_1: BARI chola 8; V_2: BARI chola 9; T_1: Control *i.e.,* no spray at flowering and afterwards; T_2: Supplemental irrigation before flowering; T_3: Supplemental irrigation + Aqueous N before flowering; T_4: PRH (a phytohormone) spray before flowering; T_5: Kinetine spray before flowering.

Interaction of chickpea varieties and different supplementary treatments on shelling percentage exhibited a significant ($p<0.05$) effect (Table 4.1). The highest shelling percentage (0.75%) was recorded from BARI chola 9 with supplemental irrigation along with aqueous N before flowering, whereas the lowest (0.58%) was obtained from BARI chola 8 with control treatment.

Seed Yield

Varieties play an important role in producing high yield of chickpea. Significant ($p<0.01$) effect of varieties was found on the seed yield of chickpea (Table 4.2). The highest seed yield (1702 kg ha^{-1}) was observed from BARI chola 9, whereas the lowest (1438 kg ha^{-1}) was found from BARI chola 8. The variation in yield for different varieties might be due to genetical and environmental influences as well as management practices. Mukherjee and Singh [22] reported that chickpea genotypes differed significantly with respect to seed yield.

The results of this experiment showed that different supplementary treatments had significant ($p<0.01$) effect on seed yield of chickpea (Table 4.2). The highest seed yield (1851 kg ha^{-1}) was recorded from supplemental irrigation along with aqueous N before flowering and the lowest (1269 kg ha^{-1}) was attained from control treatment. It was revealed by other researchers that supplementary spraying of nitrogen, irrigation and hormones ensured favorable condition for the growth of mungbean plant with optimum vegetative growth and the ultimate results was the highest yield. Fallah *et al.* [23] reported that planting Greet palong with supplementary irrigation, may lead to a significant increase in grain yield under dry land conditions. Palta *et al.* [24] reported that the potential to increase yields of chickpea by application of foliar nitrogen near flowering in environments in which terminal droughts reduce yield. Hafiz [21] reported that late supplementary foliar spraying with aqueous solution of 1 per cent urea significantly increased yield and yield quality compared to the unsprayed control. Mohammadi *et al.* [25] reported that among phenological stages of chickpea, pod formation was the most sensitive to water deficit and that under water limitation conditions chickpea yield could be improved by irrigation at this stage.

Seed yield of chickpea significantly ($p<0.05$) varied due to interaction between varieties and different supplementary treatments (Table 4.2). The highest seed yield (1944 kg ha^{-1}) was found from BARI chola 9 with supplemental irrigation along with aqueous N before flowering which was statistically similar with BARI chola 9 with supplemental irrigation before flowering and BARI chola 8 with supplemental irrigation along with aqueous N before flowering. The lowest seed yield (1202 kg ha^{-1}) from BARI chola 8 with control treatment which was statistically at par with BARI chola 9 and control treatment, BARI chola 8 and kinetine spray before flowering, BARI chola 8 and PRH spray before flowering. Increased seed yield may be cumulative result of increased number of pods $plant^{-1}$ and 1000-seed weight.

Stover Yield

Significant ($p<0.01$) response of varieties was found on the stover yield of chickpea (Table 4.2). The highest stover yield (2727 kg ha^{-1}) was observed from BARI chola 9, while the lowest (2469 kg ha^{-1}) was recorded from BARI chola 8. Different supplementary treatments exerted significant ($p<0.01$) effect on stover yield of chickpea (Table 4.2). The highest stover yield (2830 kg ha^{-1}) was found from supplemental irrigation along with aqueous N before flowering, which was statistically similar with supplemental irrigation before flowering. Conversely, the lowest stover yield (2318 kg ha^{-1}) was found from control treatment which was statistically similar with PRH spray before flowering. Singh and Smita [26] reported that irrigation proved better in terms of straw yield.

Interaction effect of chickpea varieties and different supplementary treatments showed statistically significant ($p<0.05$) variation in terms of stover yield (Table 4.2). The highest stover yield (2917 kg ha^{-1}) was recorded from BARI chola 9 with supplemental irrigation along with aqueous N before flowering which was statistically similar with BARI chola 9 and supplemental irrigation before flowering, BARI chola 8 with supplemental irrigation along with aqueous N before flowering. The lowest stover yield (2110 kg ha^{-1}) was observed from BARI chola 8 with no spray at flowering and afterwards which was statistically at par with BARI chola 8 and PRH spray before flowering.

Biological Yield

Varieties exerted significant ($p<0.01$) effect on biological yield of chickpea (Table 4.2). The highest biological yield (4429 kg ha^{-1}) was recorded from BARI chola 9, while the lowest (3907 kg ha^{-1}) was found from BARI chola 8.

A significant ($p<0.01$) variation was recorded for biological yield of chickpea due to different supplementary treatments (Table 4.2). The highest biological yield (4681 kg ha^{-1}) was observed from supplemental irrigation along with aqueous N before flowering, which was statistically similar with supplemental irrigation before flowering, while, the lowest (3587 kg ha^{-1}) was recorded from no spray at flowering and afterwards.

Results showed that the highest biological yield (4860 kg ha^{-1}) was found from BARI chola 9 with supplemental irrigation along with aqueous N before flowering which was statistically at par with BARI chola 9 with supplemental irrigation before flowering, whereas the lowest (3312 kg ha^{-1}) was obtained from BARI chola 8 with control treatment (Table 4.2).

Harvest Index (%)

There was a significant ($p<0.05$) effect of varieties of chickpea on harvest index has been presented in Table 4.2. The maximum harvest index (38.28%) was found from BARI chola 9, while the minimum (36.67%) was recorded from BARI chola 8.

It is evident from Table 4.2 that different supplementary treatments were significantly ($p<0.05$) different in terms of harvest index. The maximum harvest index (39.48%) was found from supplemental irrigation along with aqueous N before flowering, which was statistically similar with supplemental irrigation before flowering and PRH spray before flowering, whereas the minimum (35.35%) was found from control treatment which was statistically similar with Kinetine spray before flowering.

Interaction effect of chickpea varieties and different supplementary treatments showed statistically significant ($p<0.05$) variation in terms of harvest index (Table 4.2). The maximum harvest index (39.98%)was recorded from BARI chola 9 with supplemental irrigation along with aqueous N before flowering, whereas the minimum (34.59%) was observed from BARI chola 9 and control treatment which was statistically similar with BARI chola 8 and kinetine spray before flowering.

Conclusions

Different variety of chickpea varied significantly for yield and yield attributes. Among the varieties, BARI chola 9 performed better in term of yield. Supplemental irrigation before flowering along with aqueous N increased the yield of chickpea. Considering the findings of the present experiment, it may be concluded that BARI chola 9 cultivated with applying supplemental irrigation along with aqueous N before flowering revealed maximum yield and yield contributing characters compared to others.

REFERENCES

1. Ali, H., M.A. Khan and Sh.A. Randhawa, (2004). Interactive Effect of Seed Inoculation and phosphorus Application on Growth and Yield of Chickpea (*Cicer arietinum* L.). *Int. J. Agric. Biol.*, 6(1): 110-112.

2. Togay, N., Y. Togay, K.M. Cimrin and M. Turan, (2008). Effect of Rhizobium Inoculation, Sulfur and phosphorus Application on Yield, Yield Components and Nutrient Uptake in Chick pea (*Cicer aretinum* L.). *African J. Biotechnol.*, 7(6): 776-782.

3. Erman, M., S. Demir, E. Ocak, S. Tufenkci, F. Oguz and A. Akkopru, (2011). Effects of Rhizobium, Arbuscular mycorrhiza and whey Applications on some properties in chickpea (*Cicer arietinum* L.) under Irrigated and Rainfed Conditions 1-Yield, Yield Components, Nodulation and AMF Colonization. *Field Crops Res.*, 122(1): 14-24.

4. Namvar, A., R.S. Sharifi, M. Sedghi, R.A. Zakaria, T. Khandan and B. Eskandarpour, (2011). Study on the Effects of Organic and Inorganic Nitrogen Fertilizer on Yield, Yield Components and Nodulation State of Chickpea (*Cicer arietinum* L.). Commun. *Soil Sci. Plant Anal.* 42(9): 1097-1109.

5. Salvagiotti, F., K.G. Cassman, J.E. Specht, D.T. Walters, A. Weiss and A. Dobermann, (2008). Nitrogen uptake, Fixation and Response to N in Soybeans: *A Review. Field Crops Res.*, 108: 1-13.

6. Caliskan, S., I. Ozkaya, M.E. Caliskan and M. Arslan, (2008). The Effect of Nitrogen and Iron Fertilization on Growth, Yield and Fertilizer use Efficiency of Soybean in Mediterranean *Type Soil. Field Crops Res.*, 108: 126-132.
7. McKenzie, B.A. and G.D. Hill, (1995). Growth and Yield of two chickpea (*Cicer arietinum* L.) Varieties in Canterbury, New Zealand. New Zealand *J. Crop Hortic. Sci.*, 23: 467-474.
8. Achakzai, A.K.K., (2012). Effect of Various Levels of Nitrogen Fertilizer on some Vegetative Growth Attributes of pea (*Pisum sativum* L.) cultivars. *Pak. J. Bot.*, 44(2): 655-659.
9. Miah, M.G., O. Hirota and J. Chikushi, (1991). Influence of Water Status, photosynthesis Rate and Plant Growth under different Temperatures and Water Regimes during Pod Formation Phase of Mungbean (*Vigna radiata*). *J. Fac. Agric. Kyushu Univ.*, 41(1-2): 17-28.
10. Ayallew, D. and R.A. Tabbada, (1987). Influence of Soil Moisture Levels on the Growth and Development of the Mungbean Plant (*Vigna radiate* L.). *Nat. Appl. Sci. Bull.*, 39(4): 273-280.
11. Kumar, S., B.R.T. Singh and R.C. Tyagi, (1995). Effect of Irrigation on Growth Parameters of Lentil (*Lens culinaris L.*) In: *Field Crop Abst.*, 48(5): 428-29.
12. Saraf, C.S., B. Baldev, M. Ali and S.N. Slim, (1990). Improved Cropping Systems and Alternative Cropping Practices, pp. 105-108. In: Chickpea in the Nineties: Proceedings of the Second International Workshop on Chickpea Improvement, ICRISAT Center, India Patencheru, A. pp. 502-524.
13. Bicer, B.T., A.N. Kalender and D. Sakar, (2004). The Effect of Irrigation on Spring-sown Chickpea. *J. Agron.*, 3(3): 154-158.
14. Patil, A.A., S.M. Maniur and U.G. Nalwadi, (1987). Effect GA_3 and NAA on Growth and Yield of Pulses. *South Indian Hortic.* 35(5): 393-394.
15. Dharmender, K., K.D. Hujar, R. Paliwal and D. Kumar, (1996). Yield and Yield Attributes of Chickpea as Influenced by GA_3 and NAA. Crop Res. Hisar, 12(1): 120-122.
16. Brar, Z.S., J.S. Deol and J.N. Kaul, (1992). Influence of Plant Growth Regulators on Grain Production and dry Matter Partitioning in Chickpea. *Int. Chickpea Newsl.*, 27: 25-27.
17. Gardner, F.P., R.B. Pearce and R.L. Mistechell, (1985). Physiology of Crop Plants. Iowa State Univ. Press. Iowa, 500010. pp. 66.
18. Russell, O.F. (1994). MSTAT-C v.2.1 (a computer based data analysis software). Crop and Soil Science Department, Michigan State University, USA.
19. Mirzakhani, S., M. Yarnia and F.R. Khoei, (2013). Effects of Water deficit Stress on Grain Related Traits in Cultivars of Chickpea (*Cicer arietinum* L.). *Res. Crops.*, 14(3): 769-776.
20. Sadeghipour, O. and P. Aghaei, (2012). Comparison of Autumn and Spring Sowing on Performance of Chickpea (*Cicer arietinum* L.) Varieties. *Int. J. Biosci.*, 2(6): 49-58.
21. Hafiz, S.I., (2000). Response of three Chickpea Cultivars to Late Foliar Spraying with urea as a Supplement for Early Soil Applied Nitrogen in Sandy Soils. *Ann. Agril. Sci.*, 38(1): 31-46.

22. Mukherjee, D. and R.K. Singh, (2005). Influence of Weed Flora Density on Yield of Chickpea Cultivars. *Indian J. Pulses Res.*, 18(2): 222-223.

23. Fallah, S., P. Ehsanzadeh and M. Daneshvar, (2005). Grain Yield and Yield Components in three Chickpea Genotypes under Dryland Conditions with and Without Supplementary Irrigation at different Plant Densities in Khorram-Abad, Lorestan. *Iranian J. Agril. Sci.*, 36(3): 719-731.

24. Palta, J.A., A.S. Nandwal, K. Sunita and N.C. Turner, (2005). Foliar Nitrogen Applications Increase the Seed Yield and Protein Content in Chickpea (*Cicer arietinum* L.) Subject to Terminal drought. Australian.

25. Mohammadi, G., K.G. Golezani, A. Javanshir and M. Moghaddam, (2006). The Influence of Water Limitation on the Yield of three chickpea Cultivars. *J. Sci. Tech. Agric. Nat. Resour.*, 10(2): 109-120.

26. Singh, Y.P. and C. Smita, (2006). Response of Varieties to Sources of Phosphorus and Irrigation Schedule on Growth, Quality, Yield, Sulphur Uptake and Water use by Chickpea (*Cicer arietinum* L.). *Res. Crops.*, 7(1): 84-87.

Pages 46-62

INTEGRATED NUTRIENT MANAGEMENT IN CHICKPEA
Edited by **: Dr. Virendra Kumar** and **Dr. Nirmal Kumar Katiyar**
Edition **: 2017**
ISBN : 978-93-5056-872-9
Published by **: Discovery Publishing House Pvt. Ltd., New Delhi (India)**

Growth and Reproductive Behaviour of Chickpea (*Cicer arietinum* L.) as Influenced by Supplemental Application of Nitrogen, Irrigation and Hormone

Indrajit Roy[1], Parimal Kanti Biswas[1]
Md. Hazrat Ali[1], Md. Nazmul Haque[1]*
Khursheda Parvin[2]

ABSTRACT

The experiment was conducted during the period from 11 December, 2012 to 30 March 2013 to study the effect of supplementary nitrogen, irrigation and hormones on flower droppings, growth and reproductive behaviour of chickpea. Statistically significant variation was recorded for different growth and reproductive parameters. Results showed that BARI chola 9 gave the highest plant height, number of branches plant^{-1}, dry matter content plant^{-1}, pod remaining, pod length, seed yield and the lowest flower dropping, pod dropping, total dropping. Among the supplemental treatments, the highest plant height, number of branches plant^{-1}, dry matter content plant^{-1}, pod remaining, pod length, seed yield and the lowest flower dropping, pod dropping, total dropping were found from supplemental irrigation + aqueous N before flowering. In case of treatment combination, the highest plant height (39.31 cm), number of branches plant^{-1} (6.53), dry matter content plant^{-1} (7.02 g), pod remaining (39.67 %), pod length (1.96 cm), seed yield (1.94 t ha^{-1}) and the lowest flower dropping (57.27 %), pod dropping (3.07 %), total dropping (60.33 %) was recorded from BARI chola 9 with supplemental irrigation + aqueous N before flowering.

Keywords: *Cicer arietinum* L., Hormone, Irrigation, Nitrogen, Seed Yield.

1. Department of Agronomy, Faculty of Agriculture, Sher-e-Bangla Agricultural University, Sher-e-Bangla Nagar, Dhaka - 1207, Bangladesh.
2. Department of Horticulture, Faculty of Agriculture, Sher-e-Bangla Agricultural University, Sher-e-Bangla Nagar, Dhaka - 1207, Bangladesh.

INTRODUCTION

Chickpea (*Cicer arietinum L.*), commonly known as gram, is one of the important pulse crops in Bangladesh. Today, chickpea is the 3rd most important pulse crop and about 15 per cent of the world's total pulse productions belong to this crop (FAO, 2010). Among the major pulses that grown in Bangladesh chickpea ranked 5th in area and production but 2nd in consumption priority (BBS, 2010).

Various environmental, physiological and pathological reasons are responsible for low yield of chickpea. Flower and pod droppings play an important role for the lower yield of chickpea.

Aziz *et al.* (1960) reported 20-50 per cent flower and pod dropping in chickpea. Being leguminous in nature, chickpea needs low but optimum nitrogen during onset of flowering and podding. Mansoor (2007) noted that lack of attention on fertilizer application in proper way with appropriate amount is identified for lowering chickpea yields. Experimental findings revealed that pulse crop stop to nourish Rhizobia rather translocally energy towards development of flowers and pods. Thus, nitrogen fixation is totally ceased during reproductive stage which eventually hampers the development of reproductive traits. In this situation nitrogen given as basal to the crop is not sufficiently available to the plant for nourishing its flowers and pods thus seed yield value is lower (Patel *et al.* 1984; BARC, 2005). Triggering nitrogen at the plant demand would be attempt towards yield improvements of pulse (Deolankar, 2005; Mukesh, 2006).

Water deficiency has adverse effects on growth, average yield and crude protein in legume crops. The flowering stage is the most vulnerable stage for water stress and chickpea is somewhat tolerant to deficit water but susceptible to excess water (Miah *et al.* 1991). Adequate supply of irrigation water along with chemical fertilizer is essential for normal growth and yield of a crop (Ayallew and Tabbada, 1987; Kumar *et al.* 1995). On the other hand, chickpea is grown in rabi season when lack of water becomes a serious restriction specially after flowerings. Saraf *et al.* (1990) stated that excess and deficient moisture conditions both are detrimental and reduce yield of chickpea. Nayyar *et al.* (2006) reported that the flowering and pod setting stages appear to be the most sensitive stages to water stress. Supplemental irrigation was applied to compare the treatment with control for identification of its role in flower droppings.

Plant growth regulators (PGR's) are organic compounds, which in small amounts, somehow modify a given physiological plant process. It plays an essential role in many aspects of plant growth and development (Patil *et al.* 1987; Dharmender *et al.* 1996). PRH is an organic product of Natural Bio

Agro Tech Co. (Pvt.) Ltd. (NBAT) - a Japan-Bangladesh Joint Venture agro based company. The product is a hormone made from fruits vinegar and other natural ingredients. The composition of the product is their patent. As per NBAI, the PRH is used in cereal crops, vegetables, fruit crops, cash crops, pulses and oil crops, fisheries, poultry and livestock (www.nbatbd.com). Studies showed that nitrogen and hormone have role to check droppings and hence application of nitrogen and PRH before flowering was included in the study. The main objective of the experiment was to check the reproductive behaviour specially flower droppings.

Materials and Methods

Experimental Site and Climate

A field experiment was conducted at Sher-e-Bangla Agricultural University, Dhaka, Bangladesh situated at 23°74°N latitude and 90°35°E longitude at an altitude of 8.6 meter above the sea level during the period from December 11, 2012 to March 30, 2013. The soil of the experimental site was sandy loam with pH and Cation Exchange capacity (CEC) 5.6 and 2.64 meq/100 g soil, respectively. The experimental site is under subtropical humid climatic conditions. The mean relative humidity, minimum temperature, maximum temperature and total rainfall during the crop growing period have been presented in Table 5.1.

Table 5.1: Records of meteorological observation (monthly) for the period of experiment (December 2012-March 2013)

Month	Mean Relative Humidity (%)	Mean Temperature (°C)		Total Rainfall (mm)
		Minimum	Maximum	
December 2012	78.58	14.54	23.93	5
January 2013	65.39	12.09	24.55	14
February 2013	47.16	16.5	27.86	34
March 2013	43.8	23.3	31.6	43.4

Experimental Treatments

The experiment was consists of two chickpea varieties *viz;* V_1-BARI chola 8, V_2-BARI chola 9 and five supplementary treatments *i.e.* T_1-(no spray at flowering and afterwards) (control), T_2-supplemental irrigation before flowering, T_3-supplemental irrigation + aqueous N before flowering, T_4-PRH (a phytohormone) spray before flowering and T_5-Kinetine spray before flowering.

Planting Materials, Design and Plot Size

The variety BARI chola 8 and BARI chola 9 were used as the test crops. The two factors experiment was laid out in split-plot design with three replications. The two varieties were assigned in the main plot and five supplementary treatments in sub-plot. The size of the each unit plot was 4.0 m × 3.2 m. The space between two blocks and two plots were 1.0 m and 0.5 m, respectively.

Fertilizer Application

Urea, Triple super phosphate (TSP), Muriate of potash (MoP), gypsum, zinc sulphate and boric acid were used as a source of N, P, K, Ca, S and B, respectively. Urea, Triple super phosphate (TSP), Muriate of potash (MoP), gypsum, zinc sulphate and boric acid were applied at the rate of 50, 90, 40, 110, 7 and 10 kg ha^{-1}, respectively. All of the fertilizers except urea were applied during final land preparation.

Supplemental Irrigation before Flowering (SIBF)

Supplementary irrigation was applied before flowering and it was done at 15 February at 65 Days after Sowing (DAS). Selected 6 plots were provided with flood irrigation.

SIBF + Aqueous N before Flowering

SIBF + Aqueous N before flowering was applied before flowering and done at 05 February at 55 DAS. Selected 6 plots were provided with flood irrigation and aqueous N. For aqueous nitrogen 153.6 g urea were mixed with 6 liter of water and sprayed in the plots.

PRH (a phytohormone) Spray before Flowering

PRH were sprayed before flowering and solution were made by adding 12 spoons of PRH with 6 liter of water and applied at 05 February at 55 DAS.

Kinetine Spray before Flowering

Kinetine (kinetine puriss CHR : 6-Furfurylaminopurine, $C_{10}H_5OH$) were sprayed before flowering and soluation were made by adding 150 mg kinetene and 10 ml ethanol (C_6H_5OH) with 6 liter of water and applied at 05 February at 55 DAS.

Dry Matter Content Plant[1]

After taking fresh weight at 60, 75, 90 and 105 DAS, the sample was sliced into very thin pieces and put into envelop then placed in oven maintained at 70°C for 72 hours. It was then transferred into desiccators and allowed to cool down at room temperature. The final dry matter content was taken by following formula:

$$\text{Dry matter content} = \frac{\text{Dry weight of plants (g)}}{\text{Fresh weight of plants (g)}} \times 100$$

Flower and Pod Dropping

Flower and pod dropping was counted for 5 selected plants and recorded in each plot. Dropping of flower and pod was counted in every morning by using clean paper during flowering time and pod development stage, respectively and recorded.

Statistical Analysis

Collected data were statistically analysed to find out the level of significance using MSTAT-C computer package programme developed by Freed (1986). The mean differences were assessed by least significant difference (LSD) at 5 per cent level of probability (Gomez and Gomez, 1984).

Results and Discussion

Plant Height

Varieties had significant effect on plant height of chickpea at different DAS (Fig. 5.1). Plant height increased with advancing growing period irrespective of varieties. Plant height increased rapidly at the early stages of growth; however, rate of progression in height was slow at the later stages. Different varieties produced different plant height on the basis of their varietal characters and improved varieties is the first and foremost requirement for initiation and accelerated production programme. Ozgun *et al.* (2004); Golldani and Moghaddam (2006) reported various plant heights for different chickpea varieties. Plant height significantly influenced by different supplementary treatments at different DAS (Fig. 5.2). Supplemental irrigation along with aqueous N before flowering produced the tallest plant height and control treatment produced the shortest plant. Supplementary spraying ensured favorable condition for chickpea plant with longest plant. Junttila (1992) reported that auxin type growth regulators had significant effect on the elongation of shoots of crop plants. Fallah *et al.* (2005) recorded longest plant growth applying supplementary irrigation.

The interaction effect of chickpea varieties and different supplementary treatments on plant height was significantly reflected at different stages of chickpea (Table 5.2). At 60, 75, 90 and 105 DAS the tallest plant (30.13, 32.66, 37.13 and 39.31 cm, respectively) was recorded from BARI chola 9 with supplemental irrigation along with aqueous N before flowering, while the shortest plant (21.13, 24.13, 25.00 and 25.94 cm, respectively) was obtained from BARI chola 8 with control treatment *i.e.*, no spray at flowering and afterwards. Kang *et al.* (2008) reported that to achieve yield potential, crops should be irrigated over the whole of crop growth.

Number of Branches Plant^{-1}

Chickpea varieties showed significant variation on number of branches plant^{-1} at different DAS (Fig. 5.3). Management practices influence the number of branches plant^{-1} but varieties itself also manipulated it. Ozgun *et al.* (2004);

Solaiman *et al.* (2007) reported that chickpea cultivars differed significantly with respect to number of branches plant^{-1}. Supplemental nitrogen, irrigation and hormone showed significant variation on number of branches plant^{-1} at 60, 75, 90 and 105 DAS (Fig. 5.4). Supplemental irrigation along with aqueous N before flowering ensured favourable growth condition which produced maximum branches plant^{-1} of chickpea plant. Hafiz (2000) reported that late supplementary foliar spraying with aqueous solution of 1 per cent urea significantly increased all the studied growth characters. Eid *et al.* (1991) and Iqbal *et al.* (2001) reported that branches of pea plants increased with foliar application of growth regulators.

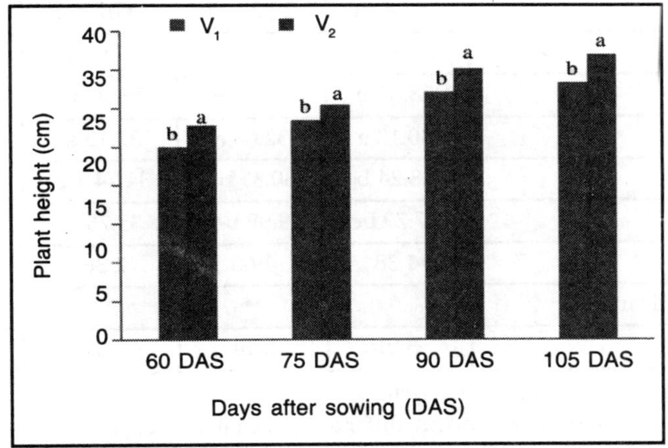

Fig. 5.1: Effect of variety on plant height of chickpea at different DAS (LSD value = 1.959, 1.630, 2.958 and 3.520 at 60,75,90 and 105 DAS, respectively

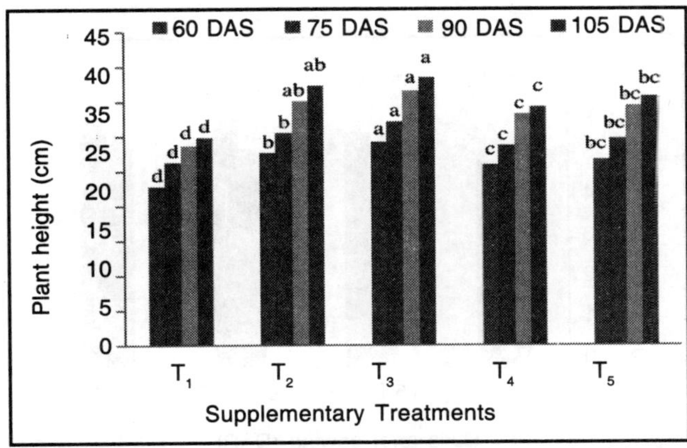

Fig. 5.2: Effect of supplementary treatments on plant height of chickpea at different DAS (LSD value = 0.975, 1.130, 1.665 and 1.600 at 60, 75, 90 and 105 DAS respectively)

V_1: BARI chola 8; V_2: BARI chola 9; T_1: Control *i.e.*, no spray at flowering and afterwards; T_2; Supplement ittigation before flowering T_3: Supplemental irrigation + Aqueous N before flowering T_4: PRH (a phyothormone) spray before flowering T_5: Kinetine spray before flowering

Table 5.2: Interaction effect of variety and supplementary nitrogen, irrigation and hormone spray on plant height of chickpea at different DAS

Treatment Combination	Plant Height (cm) at			
	60 DAS	75 DAS	90 DAS	105 DAS
V_1T_1	21.13 g	24.13 f	25.00 e	25.94 e
V_1T_2	26.62 cd	30.23 bc	34.74 a-c	36.65 b
V_1T_3	28.16 b	31.62 ab	36.00 a	37.47 ab
V_1T_4	23.43 f	26.94 e	31.56 d	32.45 d
V_1T_5	25.46 de	29.25 cd	33.07 b-d	33.99 cd
V_2T_1	24.44 ef	28.33 de	32.33 cd	33.74 cd
V_2T_2	28.51 b	30.74 bc	35.36 ab	37.89 ab
V_2T_3	30.13 a	32.66 a	37.13 a	39.31 a
V_2T_4	28.24 b	30.39 bc	34.74 a-c	36.08 bc
V_2T_5	27.79 bc	29.99 b-d	35.75 a	37.37 ab
$LSD_{(0.05)}$	1.38	1.60	2.36	2.26
Level of significance	*	**	**	**
CV (%)	3.01	3.14	4.05	3.72

**: significant at $p<0.01$, *: significant at $p<0.05$.

Values followed by the same letters do not differ at 5 per cent level of significance.

V_1: BARI chola 8; V_2: BARI chola 9; T1: Control *i.e.*, no spray at flowering and afterwards; T_2: Supplemental irrigation before flowering; T_3: Supplemental irrigation + Aqueous N before flowering; T_4: PRH (a phytohormone) spray before flowering; T_5: Kinetine spray before flowering.

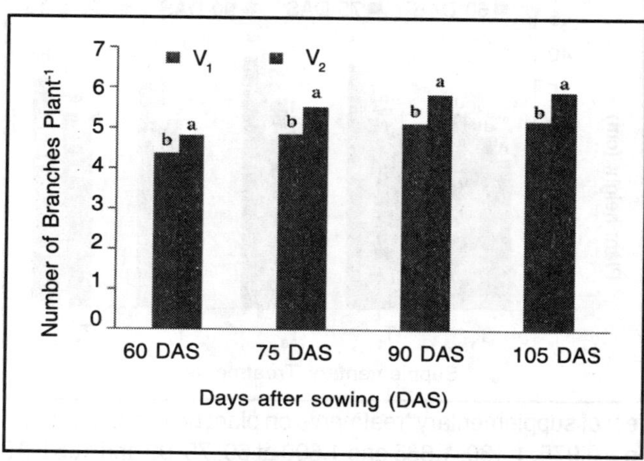

Fig. 5.3: Effect of varety on number of branches plant^{-1} of chickpea at different DAS (LAD value = 0.172, 0.455, 0.489 and 0.344 at 60,75, 90 and 105 DAS respectively)

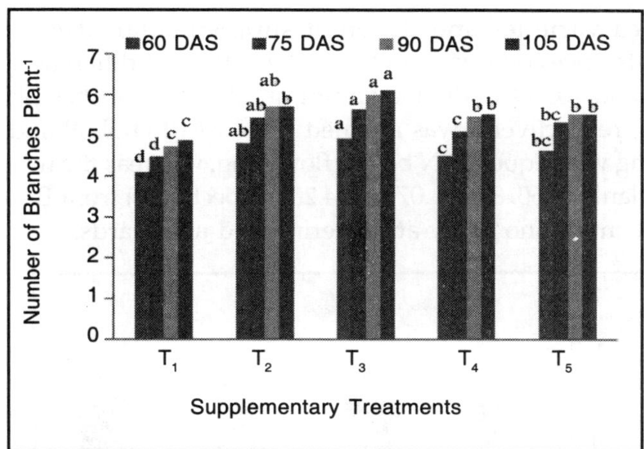

Fig. 5.4: Effect of supplementary treatment on number of branches plant[1] of chickpea at different DAS (LSD value = 0.242, 0.274, 0.391 and 0.373 at 60, 75, 90 and 105 DAS, respectively)

V_1: BARI chola 8; V_2: BARI chola 9; T_1: Control *i.e.*, no spray at flowering and afterwards; T_2; Supplement ittigation before flowering T_3: Supplemental irrigation + Aqueous N before flowering T_4: PRH (a phyothormone) spray before flowering T_5: Kinetine spray before flowering

Table 5.3: Interaction effect of variety and supplementary nitrogen, irrigation and hormone spray on number of branches plant^{-1} of chickpea at different DAS

Treatment Combination	Number of Branches Plant^{-1} at			
	60 DAS	75 DAS	90 DAS	105 DAS
V_1T_1	3.60 e	3.80 d	4.07 d	4.20 e
V_1T_2	4.67 a-c	5.07 bc	5.40 bc	5.40 cd
V_1T_3	4.87 a-c	5.33 b	5.53 bc	5.67 b-d
V_1T_4	4.20 d	4.80 c	5.13 c	5.13 d
V_1T_5	4.53 cd	5.27 b	5.53 bc	5.53 b-d
V_2T_1	4.60 bc	5.13 bc	5.40 bc	5.53 b-d
V_2T_2	4.93 ab	5.80 a	6.00 ab	6.00 b
V_2T_3	5.00 a	5.93 a	6.47 a	6.53 a
V_2T_4	4.80 a-c	5.40 b	5.80 b	5.93 bc
V_2T_5	4.73 a-c	5.40 b	5.53 bc	5.53 b-d
$LSD_{(0.05)}$	0.34	0.39	0.55	0.53
Level of significance	**	**	*	*
CV (%)	4.30	4.29	5.82	5.50

**: significant at $p<0.01$, *: significant at $p<0.05$.

Values followed by the same letters do not differ at 5 per cent level of significance.

V_1: BARI chola 8; V_2: BARI chola 9; T_1: Control *i.e.*, no spray at flowering and afterwards; T_2: Supplemental irrigation before flowering; T_3: Supplemental irrigation + Aqueous N before flowering; T_4: PRH (a phytohormone) spray before flowering; T_5: Kinetine spray before flowering.

Chickpea varieties and different supplementary treatments showed significant differences on number of branches plant^{-1} at different DAS (Table 5.3). At 60, 75, 90 and 105 DAS the maximum number of branches plant^{-1} (5.00, 5.93, 6.47 and 6.53, respectively) was attained from BARI chola 9 and supplemental irrigation along with aqueous N before flowering, whereas the minimum number of branches plant^{-1} (3.60, 3.80, 4.07 and 4.20, respectively) from BARI chola 8 with control treatment *i.e.*, no spray at flowering and afterwards.

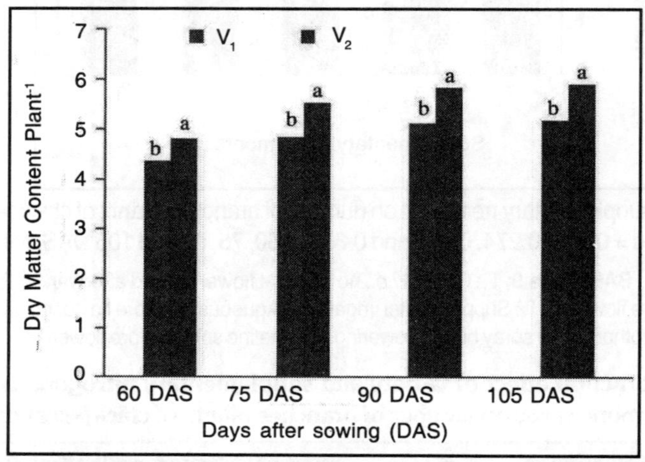

Fig. 5.5: Effect of variety on dry matter content plant^{-1} of chickpea at different DAS (LSD value = 0.436, 0.322, 0.497 and 0.272 at 60, 75, 90 and 105 DAS)

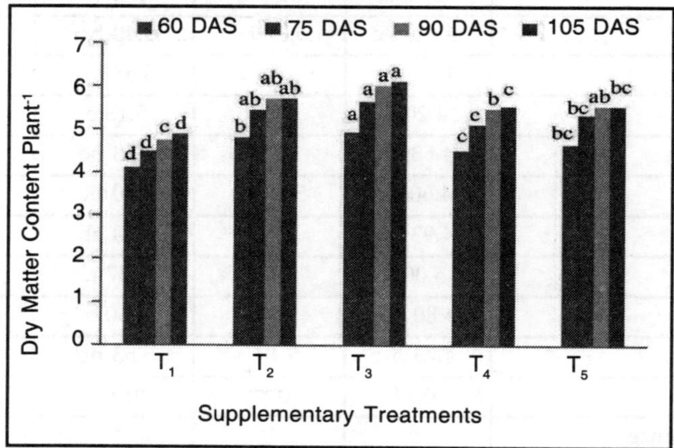

Fig. 5.6: Effect of supplementary treatment on dry matter content plant^{-1} of chickpea at different DAS (LSD value = 0.242, 0.274, 0.391 and 0.373 at 60, 75, 90 and 105 DAS)

V_1: BARI chola 8; V_2: BARI chola 9; T_1: Control *i.e.*, no spray at flowering and afterwards; T_2; Supplement ittigation before flowering T_3: Supplemental irrigation + Aqueous N before flowering T_4: PRH (a phyothormone) spray before flowering T_5: Kinetine spray before flowering

Table 5.4: Effect of variety and supplementary nitrogen, irrigation and hormone spray on dry matter content plant^{-1} of chickpea at different DAS

Treatment Combination	Dry Matter Content Plant^{-1} at			
	60 DAS	75 DAS	90 DAS	105 DAS
V_1T_1	3.14 d	3.83 f	4.10 e	4.25 e
V_1T_2	4.15 b	5.11 b-d	5.68 bc	6.08 b
V_1T_3	4.27 b	4.80 c-e	5.23 cd	5.47 cd
V_1T_4	3.65 c	4.57 de	5.33 bc	5.67 bc
V_1T_5	3.97 bc	4.73 de	5.35 bc	5.68 bc
V_2T_1	3.55 cd	4.40 e	4.66 de	5.05 d
V_2T_2	4.44 b	5.57 b	5.98 b	6.21 b
V_2T_3	5.23 a	6.25 a	6.75 a	7.02 a
V_2T4	4.24 b	5.07 b-d	5.68 bc	5.86 bc
V_2T_5	4.39 b	5.37 bc	5.82 bc	6.04 b
LSD (0.05)	0.47	0.55	0.62	0.49
Level of significance	*	*	*	**
CV (%)	6.63	6.40	6.60	4.94

**: significant at $p<0.01$, *: significant at $p<0.05$.
Values followed by the same letters do not differ at 5 per cent level of significance.
V_1: BARI chola 8; V_2: BARI chola 9; T_1: Control *i.e.*, no spray at flowering and afterwards; T_2: Supplemental irrigation before flowering; T_3: Supplemental irrigation + Aqueous N before flowering; T4: PRH (a phytohormone) spray before flowering; T_5: Kinetine spray before flowering

Dry Matter Content Plant^{1}

Dry matter content plant^{-1} varied significantly between varieties at different DAS (Fig. 5.5). Data revealed that at 60, 75, 90 and 105 DAS the maximum dry matter content plant^{-1} was found from BARI chola 9, while the minimum was recorded from BARI chola 8. Variability in chickpea varieties for dry matter content had been reported by Solaiman *et al.* (2007); Sadeghipour and Aghaei (2012). Statistically significant variation was recorded for dry matter content plant^{-1} at different DAS due to supplemental nitrogen, irrigation and hormones (Fig. 5.6). Supplemental irrigation along with aqueous N before flowering produced the highest dry matter content plant^{-1} at different DAS. Supplementary spraying ensured favourable condition for the growth of chickpea plant with optimum vegetative growth and the ultimate results was the highest dry matter content plant^{-1}.

Table 5.5: Effect of variety and/or supplemental nitrogen, irrigation and hormone spray on flower, pod, total dropping, pod remaining, pod length and seed yield of chickpea

Treatments	Flower Dropping (%)	Pod Dropping (%)	Total Dropping (%)	Pod Remaining (%)	Pod Length (cm)	Seed Yield ($t\ ha^{-1}$)
Variety						
V_1	64.98 a	3.79 a	68.77 a	31.23 b	1.75 b	1.43 b
V_2	60.27 b	3.62 b	63.89 a	36.11 a	1.85 a	1.69 a
LSD (0.05)	4.42	0.15	4.45	4.45	0.09	0.12
Level of significance	*	*	*	*	*	*
CV (%)	4.49	2.56	5.27	8.41	3.04	4.97
Supplemental treatments						
T_1	67.07 a	4.82 a	71.88 a	28.12 c	1.63 d	1.25 c
T_2	61.57 bc	3.27 c	64.83 bc	35.17 ab	1.89 b	1.71 a
T_3	59.17 c	3.10 d	62.27 c	37.73 a	1.95 a	1.84 a
T_4	62.70 b	3.62 b	66.32 b	33.68 b	1.74 c	1.49 b
T_5	62.63 b	3.72 b	66.35 b	33.65 b	1.79 c	1.51 b
LSD(0.05)	2.66	0.10	2.66	2.66	0.06	0.17
Level of significance	**	**	**	**	**	**
CV (%)	3.48	2.26	3.27	6.45	2.49	9.73
Treatment combination						
V_1T_1	71.20 a	4.97 a	76.17 a	23.83 e	1.45 e	1.19 e
V_1T_2	63.40 b-d	3.30 f	66.70 b-d	33.30 b-d	1.90 ab	1.55 cd
V_1T_3	61.07 b-e	3.13 gh	64.20 c-e	35.80 a-c	1.93 a	1.74 a-c
V_1T_4	64.33 bc	3.73 cd	68.07 bc	31.93 cd	1.70 d	1.32 de
V_1T_5	64.90 b	3.80 c	68.70 b	31.30 d	1.75 cd	1.33 de
V_2T_1	62.93 b-d	4.67 b	67.60 bc	32.40 cd	1.80 c	1.32 de
V_2T_2	59.73 de	3.23 fg	62.97 de	37.03 ab	1.88 ab	1.87 ab
V_2T_3	57.27 e	3.07 h	60.33 e	39.67 a	1.96 a	1.94 a
V_2T_4	61.07 b-e	3.50 e	64.57 b-d	35.43 b-d	1.79 c	1.65 bc
V_2T_5	60.37 c-e	3.63 de	64.00 c-e	36.00 a-c	1.83 bc	1.69 a-c
LSD(0.05)	3.767	0.149	3.76	3.758	0.077	0.263
Level of significance	*	*	*	*	**	*
CV (%)	3.48	2.26	3.27	6.45	2.49	9.73

**: significant at $p<0.01$, *: significant at $p<0.05$.

Values followed by the same letters do not differ at 5 per cent level of significance.

V_1: BARI chola 8; V_2: BARI chola 9; T_1: Control *i.e.*, no spray at flowering and afterwards; T_2: Supplemental irrigation before flowering; T_3: Supplemental irrigation + Aqueous N before flowering; T_4: PRH (a phytohormone) spray before flowering; T_5: Kinetine spray before flowering.

Dry matter content plant^{-1} at 60, 75, 90 and 105 DAS varied significantly due to the interaction effect of chickpea varieties and different supplementary treatments (Table 5.4). At 60, 75, 90 and 105 DAS the maximum dry matter content plant^{-1} (5.23 g, 6.25 g, 6.57 g and 7.02 g, respectively) was attained from BARI chola 9 and supplemental irrigation along with aqueous N before flowering and the minimum dry matter content plant^{-1} (3.14 g, 3.83 g, 4.10 g and 4.25 g, respectively) was recorded from BARI chola 8 with control treatment *i.e.*, no spray at flowering and afterwards.

Flower Dropping

The results regarding flower dropping of chickpea varieties are given in Table 5.4, which showed that flower dropping of chickpea varieties differed significantly (Table 5.5). The lower flower dropping (60.27%) was recorded from BARI chola 9, whereas the higher flower dropping (64.98%) was recorded from BARI chola 8. Flower dropping of chickpea showed statistically significant differences for different supplementary treatments that applied as supplementary nitrogen, irrigation and hormones (Table 5.5). The lowest flower dropping (59.17%) was found from supplemental irrigation along with aqueous N before flowering, which was statistically similar (61.17%) with supplemental irrigation before flowering and closely followed (62.63% and 62.70%, respectively) by kinetine spray before flowering and PRH spray before flowering, while the highest flower dropping (67.07%) was observed from control treatment. This might be due to suppression of apical dominance and increase in lateral branching that results in more number of branches plant-1 which ultimately produced more number of flowers plant^{-1}. Increased number of flower production may also be attributed to more flower retention (Singh *et al.* 2014). Interaction effect of chickpea varieties and different supplementary treatments varied significantly in terms of flower dropping (Table 5.5). The lowest flower dropping (57.27%) was recorded from BARI chola 9 and supplemental irrigation along with aqueous N before flowering and the highest flower dropping (71.20%) from BARI chola 8 with control treatment *i.e.*, no spray at flowering and afterwards. Singh (2002) reported that application of growth regulator had a significant effect on number of flowers plant^{-1} over water spray treatment.

Pod Dropping

The statistical analysis for pod dropping of chickpea varieties showed significant variation (Table 5.5). The lower pod dropping (3.62%) was observed from BARI chola 9, while the higher pod dropping (3.79%) was found from BARI chola 8. Statistically significant variation was recorded for pod dropping of chickpea due to the application of different supplementary treatments that applied as supplementary nitrogen, irrigation and hormones (Table 5.5). The lowest pod dropping (3.10%) was recorded from supplemental irrigation along with aqueous N before flowering, which was closely followed (3.27%) by supplemental irrigation before flowering, while the highest pod dropping (4.82%) was found from control *i.e.*, no spray at flowering and afterwards which was closely followed (3.72% and 3.62%, respectively) by kinetine spray before flowering and PRH spray before flowering. Singh *et al.* (2014) reported that different growth regulation practices were significantly better than control in producing more number of pods. Interaction effect of chickpea varieties and different supplementary treatments showed significant differences on pod dropping (Table 5.5). The minimum pod dropping (3.07%) was recorded from BARI chola 9 and supplemental irrigation along with aqueous N before flowering, whereas the maximum pod dropping (4.97%) from BARI chola 8 with control treatment *i.e.*, no spray at flowering and afterwards.

Total Dropping

Significant difference was found in terms of total dropping in chickpea varieties (Table 5.5). The lower total dropping (63.89%) was observed from BARI chola 9 and the higher (68.77%) was found from BARI chola 8. Total dropping of chickpea showed significant variation for different supplementary treatments (Table 5.5). The lowest total dropping (62.27%) was found from supplemental irrigation along with aqueous N before flowering, which was statistically similar (64.83%) with supplemental irrigation before flowering and closely followed (66.32% and 66.35%, respectively) by PRH spray before flowering and kinetine spray before flowering and they were statistically similar, whereas the highest total dropping (71.88%) was observed from control *i.e.*, no spray at flowering and afterwards. Interaction effect of chickpea varieties and different supplementary treatments showed significant differences on total dropping (Table 5.5). The lowest total dropping (60.33%) was observed from BARI chola 9 and supplemental irrigation along with aqueous N before flowering, while the highest total dropping (76.17%) was found from BARI chola 8 with control treatment *i.e.*, no spray at flowering and afterwards.

Pod Remaining

Significant difference was recorded among the varieties with respect to the pod remaining (Table 5.5). The higher pod remaining (36.11%) was found from BARI chola 9, while the lower pod remaining (31.23%) from BARI chola 8. Different supplementary treatments that applied as supplementary nitrogen, irrigation and hormones showed significant variation in terms of pod remaining of chickpea (Table 5.5). The highest pod remaining (37.73%) was found from supplemental irrigation along with aqueous N before flowering, which was statistically similar (35.17%) with supplemental irrigation before flowering and closely followed (33.68% and 33.65%, respectively) by PRH spray before flowering and kinetine spray before flowering. The lowest pod remaining (28.12%) was observed from control treatment *i.e.*, no spray at flowering and afterwards. The increase in number of pods might be due to increase in number of branches and increase in total number of flowers plant^{-1} (Singh *et al.* 2014). Chickpea varieties and different supplementary treatments varied significantly for pod remaining due to interaction effect (Table 5.5). The highest pod remaining (39.67%) was found from BARI chola 9 and supplemental irrigation along with aqueous N before flowering and the lowest (23.83%) from BARI chola 8 with control treatment *i.e.*, no spray at flowering and afterwards. Singh (2002) revealed that application of growth regulator had a significant bearing on number of pods plant^{-1} over water spray treatment.

Pod Length

Pod length of chickpea varieties varied significantly under the present trial (Table 5.5). The longer pod (1.85 cm) was recorded from BARI chola 9, whereas the shorter pod (1.75 cm) was found from BARI chola 8. Different varieties responded differently for pod length to input supply, method of cultivation and the prevailing environment during the growing season. Significant variation was recorded in terms of pod length of chickpea for different supplementary treatments (Table 5.5). The longest pod (1.95 cm) was found from supplemental irrigation along with aqueous N before flowering, which was followed (1.89 cm) by supplemental irrigation before flowering. On the other hand, the shortest pod (1.63 cm) was recorded from control treatment which was followed (1.74 cm and 1.79 cm) by PRH spray before flowering and kinetine spray before flowering. Bicer *et al.* (2004) reported that pod length were higher under irrigated than rainfed conditions. Interaction effect of chickpea varieties and different supplementary treatments exerted significant differences on pod length (Table 5.5). The longest pod (1.96 cm) was found from BARI chola 9 and supplemental irrigation along with aqueous N before flowering, while the shortest pod (1.45 cm) was observed from BARI chola 8 with control treatment *i.e.*, no spray at flowering and afterwards.

Seed Yield

A significant effect of varieties was found on the seed yield of chickpea (Table 5.5). The higher seed yield (1.69 t ha^{-1}) was observed from BARI chola 9, whereas the lower seed yield (1.43 t ha^{-1}) was found from BARI chola 8. Varieties plays an important role in producing high yield of chickpea and yield also varied for different varieties might be due to genetical and environmental influences as well as management practices. Mukherjee and Singh (2005); Solaiman *et al.* (2007) reported that chickpea genotypes differed significantly with respect to seed yield. The results of this experiment showed that different supplementary treatments had significant effect on seed yield of chickpea (Table 5.5). The highest seed yield (1.84 t ha^{-1}) was recorded from supplemental irrigation along with aqueous N before flowering, which was statistically similar (1.71 t ha^{-1}) with supplemental irrigation before flowering and closely followed (1.51 t ha^{-1} and 1.49 t ha^{-1}, respectively) by kinetine spray before flowering and PRH spray before flowering, while the lowest seed yield (1.25 t ha^{-1}) was attained from control treatment. It was revealed that supplementary spraying of nitrogen, irrigation and hormones ensured favorable condition for the growth of mungbean plant with optimum vegetative growth and the ultimate results was the highest yield. Fallah *et al.* (2005) reported that planting Greet palong with supplementary irrigation, may lead to a significant increase in grain yield under dryland conditions. Palta *et al.* (2005) reported that the potential to increase yields of chickpea by application of foliar nitrogen near flowering in environments in which terminal droughts reduce yield. Hafiz (2000) reported that late supplementary foliar spraying with aqueous solution of 1 per cent urea significantly increased yield and yield quality compared to the unsprayed control. Mohammadi *et al.* (2006) reported that among phenological stages of chickpea, pod formation was the most sensitive to water deficit and that under water limitation conditions chickpea yield could be improved by irrigation at this stage. Seed yield of chickpea significantly varied due to interaction between varieties and different supplementary treatments (Table 5.5). The highest seed yield (1.94 t ha^{-1}) was found from BARI chola 9 with supplemental irrigation along with aqueous N before flowering and the lowest seed yield (1.19 t ha^{-1}) from BARI chola 8 with control treatment *i.e.*, no spray at flowering and afterwards. Increased seed yield might be cumulative result of increased number of branches, flowers and pods plant^{-1}.

Conclusion

Different variety varied significantly for growth and reproductive behaviour of chickpea. Among the varieties, BARI chola 9 showed lower flower and pod droppings which resulted higher yield. Supplemental irrigation before flowering along with 5.5 g aqueous nitrogen m -2 showed significant role to reduce flower and pod droppings of chickpea. Considering the findings of the present study, it is concluded that BARI chola 9 cultivated with applying supplemental irrigation along with aqueous N before flowering gave better growth, lower droppings and higher yield of chickpea.

REFERENCES

Ayallew, D., and R.A. Tabbada. (1987). Influence of Soil Moisture Levels on the Growth and Development of the Mungbean Plant (*Vigna radiata L.*). *Nat Applied Sci Bulletin* 39(4): 273-280.

Aziz, M.A., M.A. Khan, and S. Shah. (1960). Causes of Low Setting of Seed in Gram (*Cicer arietinum*). Agric Pakistan 11(1): 37-48.

BARC. (2005). Fertilizer Recommendation Guide. Bangladesh Agriculture Research Council, Farmgate, Dhaka, p. 219.

BBS (Bangladesh Bureau of Statistics). (2010). Yearbook of Agricultural Statistics of Bangladesh. Planning Division. Ministry of Planning. Government of the People's Republic of Bangladesh. Dhaka, pp. 54-111.

Bicer, B. T., A. N. Kalender, and D. Sakar. (2004). The Effect of Irrigation on Spring-sown Chickpea. *J. Agron* 3(3): 154-158. doi:10.3923/ja.2004.154.158.

Deolankar, K.P. (2005). Effect of Fertigation on Growth and Yield of Chickpea. *J. Maharashtra Agril Uni* 30(2): 170-172.

Dharmender, K., K.D. Hujar, R. Paliwal, and D. Kumar. (1996). Yield and Yield Attributes of Chickpea as Influenced by GA3 and NAA. Crop Res Hisar 12(1): 120-122.

Eid, S. M.M., H.H. Abbas, and F. A. Abu-Sedra. (1991). Effect of GA Foliar Spray on Plant Growth, Chemical Composition, Flowering, Pod Yield and Chemical Composition of Green Seeds for Pea Plants Grown Under Salinity Stress. *Ann Agril Sci, Moshtohor* (Egypt) 30: 1443-1458.

Fallah, S., P. Ehsanzadeh, and M. Daneshvar. (2005). Grain Yield and Yield Components in three Chickpea Genotypes under Dryland Conditions with and Without Supplementary Irrigation at different Plant Densities in Khorram-Abad, Lorestan. *Iranian J. Agril Sci.* 36(3): 719-731.

FAO (Food and Agriculture Organization of the United Nations). (2010). Agricultural Production year book/ or http://faostat.fao.org.

Freed, D.R. (1986). MSTAT-C Programme. Crop and Soil Science Department. Michigan State University, USA.

Golldani, A., and P.R. Moghaddam. (2006). Effect of different Irrigation Levels on Phenology, Physiology Characteristics, and Yield Components of Three Chickpea (*Cicer arietinum L.*) Cultivars in *Mashhad. Agril Sci Tech* 20(3): 21-32.

Gomez, K.A., and A.A. Gomez. (1984). Statistical Procedures for Agricultural Research. Jhon Wiley and Sons, New York.

Hafiz, S.I. (2000). Response of Three Chickpea Cultivars to Late Foliar Spraying with urea as a Supplement for Early Soil Applied Nitrogen in Sandy Soils. *Ann Agril Sci* 38(1): 31-46.

Iqbal, H.F., A. Tahir, M.N. Khalid, I. Haq, and A.N. Ahmad. (2001). Response of Chickpea Growth towards Foliar Application of Gibberellic Acid at different Growth Stages. *Pakistan J Biol Sci.* 4(4): 433-434. doi:10.3923/pjbs.2001.433.434.

Junttila, O. (1992). Gibberellin and Elongation Growth. *Nordisk Jordbruksforskning,* 74: 74.

Kang, S., B.A. McKenzie and G.D. Hill. (2008). Effect of Irrigation on Growth and Yield of Kabuli Chickpea (*Cicer arietinum L.*) and Narrow-Leafed lupin (*Lupinus angustifolius L.*). Agron New Zealand 38: 11-32.

Kumar, S., B.R. T Singh, and R.C. Tyagi. (1995). Effect of Irrigation on Growth Parameters of Lentil (*Lens culinaris L.*). In: *Field Crop Abst.* 48(5): 428-29.

Mansoor, M. (2007). Evaluation of Various Agronomic Management Practices for Increased Productivity of Mungbean (*Vigna radiata L.*). Ph.D. Thesis, Department of Agron, Faculty of Agric, Gomal University, Dera Islam Khan.

Miah, M.G., O. Hirota, and J. Chikushi. (1991). Influence of Water Status, Photosynthesis Rate and Plant Growth under different Temperatures and Water Regimes during Pod Formation phase of Mungbean (*Vigna radiata*). *J.Faculty Agric Kyushu Uni* 41(1): 17-28.

Mohammadi, G., K.G. Golezani, A. Javanshir, and M. Moghaddam. (2006). The Influence of Water Limitation on the Yield of Three Chickpea Cultivars. JWSS-Isfahan Uni Technol 10(2): 109-120.

Mukesh, K. (2006). Impact of the Starter Doses of Nitrogen on Nodulation, Yield and Yield Attributes of Chickpea under Irrigated Conditions. *Int J. Agril Sci.* 2(1): 253-255.

Mukherjee, D., and R.K. Singh. (2005). Influence of Weed Flora Density on Yield of Chickpea Cultivars. *Indian J Pulses Res* 18(2): 222.

Nayyar, H., S. Singh, S. Kaur, S. Kumar, and H.D. Upadhyaya. (2006). Differential Sensitivity of Macrocarpa and Microcarpa Types of Chickpea (*Cicer arietinum L.*) to Water Stress: Association of Contrasting Stress Response with Oxidative Injury. *J. Integrative Plant Biol* 48(11): 1318-1329. doi:10.1111/j.1744-7909.2006.00350.x

Ozgun, O. S., B.T. Bicer, and D. Sakar. (2004). Agronomic and Morphological Characters of Chickpea under Irrigated Conditions in Turkey. *Int J. Agric Biol* 6(4): 606-610.

Palta, J. A., A.S. Nandwal, K. Sunita, and N.C. Turner. (2005). Foliar Nitrogen Applications Increase the Seed Yield and Protein Content in Chickpea (*Cicer arietinum L.*) Subject to Terminal Drought. *Australian J. Agril Res* 56(2): 105-112. doi:10.1071/AR04118.

Patel, R.G., M.P. Palel, H.C. Palel, and R.B. Palel. (1984). Effect of Graded Levels of Nitrogen and Phosphorus on Growth, Yield and Economics of Summer Mungbean. *Indian J. Agron* 29(3): 42-44.

Patil, A.A., S.M. Maniur, and U.G. Nalwadi. (1987). Effect GA3 and NAA on Growth and Yield of Pulses. *South Indian Hort* 35(5): 393-394.

Sadeghipour, O. and P. Aghaei. (2012). Comparison of Autumn and Spring Sowing on Performance of Chickpea (*Cicer arietinum L.*) Varieties. *Int J Biosci* 2(6): 49-58.

Saraf, C. S., B. Baldev, M. Ali, and S. N. Slim. (1990). Improved Cropping Systems and Alternative Cropping Practices, pp. 105-108. In: Chickpea in the Nineties: Proceedings of the Second International Workshop on Chickpea Improvement, ICRISAT Center, India Patencheru, A, pp. 502-524.

Singh, S. (2002). Studies on the Modification of Microclimate in Chickpea (*Cicer arietinum L.*) through the Ecological Manipulations. M. Sc. Thesis, P. A. U., Ludhiana, India.

Singh, S., J.S. Deol, and A.S. Brar. (2014). Growth and Yield of kabuli gram (*Cicer arietinum L.*) as Influenced by Plant Growth Regulation and Sowing Time. *Crop Res* 48(1, 2 and 3): 32-37.

Solaiman, A. R. M., D. Hossain, and M.G. Rabbani. (2007). Influence of Rhizobium Inoculant and Mineral Nitrogen on some Chickpea Varieties. *Bangladesh J. Microbiol* 24(2): 146-150.

Pages 63-71

INTEGRATED NUTRIENT MANAGEMENT IN CHICKPEA
***Edited by*: Dr. Virendra Kumar** and **Dr. Nirmal Kumar Katiyar**
***Edition*: 2017**
ISBN : 978-93-5056-872-9
***Published by*: Discovery Publishing House Pvt. Ltd., New Delhi (India)**

Effect of Iron on Yield Quality and Nutrient uptake of Chickpea (*Cicer arietinum* L.)

K.K. Pingoliya[1]
M.L. Dotaniya[2]
M. Lata[3]

ABSTRACT

The role of micronutrients in crops is well known in the present context. Research already proved the micronutrient deficiency in various crops as well as in the human beings and which results as drastic reduction in crop yield. Chickpea (Cicer arietinum L.) is an important grain legume crop in the World, and being a rich and cheap source of protein can help people to improve the nutritional quality of their diets. It is also the premier food legume crop in India, ranks first among all pulse crops. Iron (Fe) play vital role in several enzymatic reactions and metabolism in plants. A little amount of Fe enhanced the chickpea yield and quality. Application of Fe fertilizer for crop production also reduces the malnourishment in human and animals. At present, more emphasis is on biofortification aspect through agronomic as well as breeding techniques. Application of Fe fertilizers in chickpea crop production may be a better sustainable option to overcome these problems in the future. This review article described the Fe role in yield, quality and nutrient uptake by chickpea.

Keywords: Chickpea, Micronutrient, Nutrient Management.

1. Department of Agricultural Chemistry and Soil Science, Maharana Pratap University of Agriculture and Technology, Udaipur, India.
2. Indian Institute of Soil Science, Nabi Bagh, Berasia Road, Bhopal - 462 038, India.
3. Rajasthan University, Jaipur, India.

INTRODUCTION

The word' micronutrient' represent some essential nutrients that are required in very small quantities for the growth of plants and microorganisms. Essential micronutrients for plant growth are iron (Fe), manganese (Mn), zinc (Zn), copper (Cu), boron (B), molybdenum (Mo), nickel (Ni) and chlorine (Cl). Amongst these eight micronutrients, the content of Fe in soil as well as in plants is the highest than even P and S contents (Tisdale *et al.* 1985). It plays a crucial role in enzyme like: cytochrome oxidase, catalase and peroxidase. Although most of the Fe on the earth crust is in the form of Fe^{3+}, the Fe^{2+} form is physiologically more significant for plants. This form is relatively soluble, but is readily oxidized to Fe^{3+}, which then precipitates. The major natural source Fe are hematite (Fe_2O_3), goethite (FeOOH), magnetite (Fe_3O_4), pyrite (FeS_2) and olivine [$(Mg, Fe)_2 SiO_4$]. The total contents in the surface of soil is 4000 to 2,73,000 ppm whereas Fe available content in surface soil is 0.36 to 174 ppm DTPA-$CaCl_2$ extractable. Its deficiency is a limiting factor for plant growth and affected crop yield adversely (Kobayashi and Nishizawa, 2012). Symptoms include leaves turning yellow or brown in the margins between the veins which may remain green, while young leaves may appear to be bleached. It is present at high quantities in soils, but its availability to plants is usually very low, and therefore Fe deficiency is a common problem (Nozoye *et al.* 2011). The Fe deficiency in soil was reported in early sixties (Katyal and Rattan, 1995); and found in most of the state of India (Fig. 6.1 and Table 6.1). Excessive application of Zn, Mn and Cu induces Fe deficiency in crops. The rood exudates enhanced the mobilization of in situ Fe for plant uptake (Xiong *et al.* 2013; Ueno *et al.* 2007).

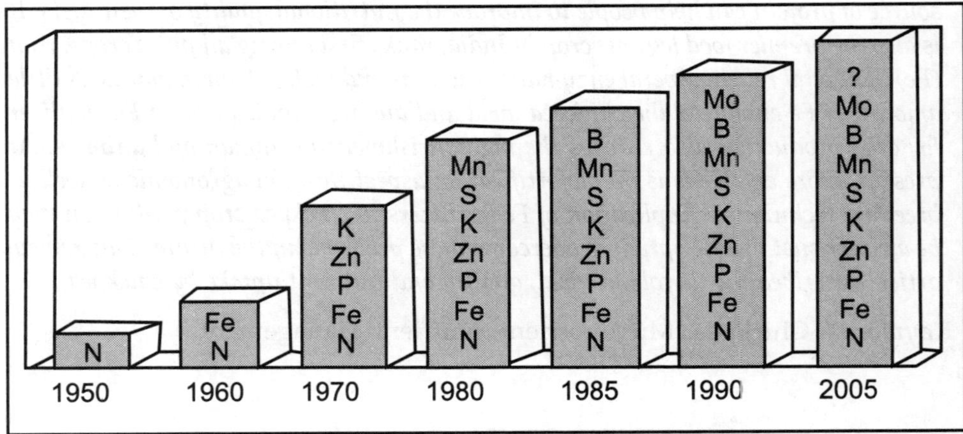

Fig. 6.1: Progressive expansion in occurrence of nutrient deficiencies (Katyal and Rattan, 1995)

Table 6.1: Extent of micronutrient deficiencies in soils of various states (Singh, 2009)

Name of State	Percent Sample Deficient (PSD)			
	Zn	Cu	Fe	Mn
Andhra Pradesh	49	< 1	3	1
Assam	34	< 1		-
Bihar	54	3	6	2
Gujarat	24	4	8	4
Haryana	61	2	20	4
Himachal Pradesh	42	0	27	5
Karnataka	73	5	35	17
Kerala	34	31 <	1	0
Madhya Pradesh	44	< 1	7	1
Maharashtra	86	1	24	0
Meghalaya	57	2	0	-3
Orissa	54	<1	0	0
Punjab	48	<1	14	2
Tamil Nadu	58	6	17	6
Uttar Pradesh	46	1	6	3
West Bengal	36	<1	0	3
All States	48	3	12	5

Chickpea (*Cicer arietinum* L.) is an important pulse crop in India. It significantly contributed in protein requirement of poor peoples. It is a highly nutritious pulse and places third in the importance list of the food legumes that are cultivated throughout the world. It contains 25 per cent proteins, which is the maximum provided by any pulse and 60 per cent carbohydrates (Singh *et al.* 1993). India is the largest producer of this pulse contributing to around 70 per cent of the world's total production. Fe plays the crucial role in enhancing crop yield. This review paper described the role of Fe in chickpea production.

Effect of Iron on Growth Attributes

Bhanavase *et al.* (1994) reported that the soil application of ferrous sulphate at 25 kg ha^{-1} to soybean crop increased nodulation, nodules dry weight per plant and dry matter accumulation as compared to control. Mundra and Bhati (1994) conducted a field experiment in loamy sand soil and they concluded that the application of Fe through ferrous sulphate at 10 kg ha^{-1} significantly increased the number of branches per plant, dry matter accumulation per plant and nodules per plant in cowpea over control. Shukla and Shukla (1994) at Allahabad, India applied 25 and 50 kg $FeSO_4$ ha^{-1} to chickpea crop which resulted in increased number of nodules per plant, dry weight of root nodules, leg haemoglobin content of root nodules and rate of N_2 fixation as compared to control treatment. Singh *et al.* (1998) working on mung bean under clay loam soil of Kanpur found that the plant height, branches per plant, dry matter partitioned by stem and leaves as well as the total dry weight. Mung bean did not differ with soil applied 15 kg $FeSO_4$ ha^{-1} and foliar applied $FeSO_4$ (0.5%) compared to control treatment at 40 day after sowing. Mahriya and Meena (1999) conducted a field trial at Jobner (Rajasthan), and they concluded that all the growth characters *viz;* plant height, number of branches per plant, dry matter production per meter row length were increased with the application of 4 kg Fe ha^{-1} in cowpea.

Balachander *et al.* (2003) reported that the application of Fe at 2 kg ha^{-1} through ferrous sulphate significantly increased the number and weight of nodules, biomass production, plant height and grain yield of black gram over control. Thapu *et al.* (2003) concluded that the application of micronutrients like: Fe (as ferrous sulphate at 0.4%), Mn, Cu, Zn significantly increased the growth characters in pea. Kumawat *et al.* (2006) conducted an experiment at Bikaner in mung bean and reported that the application of 25 kg $FeSO_4$ ha^{-1} gave the higher chlorophyll content in leaves, shoot weight and root nodules weight over control. Nenova (2006) revealed that pea plants were supplied with different amount of Fe, ranging from complete deficient to toxicity, higher plant growth, chlorophyll and carotenoid content and chlorophyll fluorescence parameters were recorded at 7 days intervals from day 20 to day 91. Sahu *et al.* (2008) reported that the application of $FeSO_4$ at 2 kg ha^{-1} significantly increased the growth characters over control in chickpea. Kumar *et al.* (2009) conducted an experiment at Kanpur and reported that the branches per plant, number of pods per plant, number of grains per pod and test weight significantly increased with levels of Fe up to 10 kg Fe ha^{-1} over control in chickpea.

Effect of Iron on Yield and Yield Attributes

Singh and Varun (1989) conducted a pot experiment on alluvial sandy loam soil with cowpea and concluded that the application of 0 to 20 mg kg^{-1} Fe increased the yield components. Gawad *et al.* (1991) reported that the application of 25 or 50 mg kg^{-1} Fe as ferrous sulphate along with 15.5, 31.0 or 46.5 kg P_2O_5 feddon^{-1} significantly increased the yield attributes in chickpea crop. Mundra and Bhati (1991) reported that the application of 20 kg $FeSO_4$ along with Rhizobium inoculation increased the seed yield in cowpea over control. Kumpawat and Manohar (1994) reported that the application of 20 kg $FeSO_4$ ha^{-1} significantly increased the dry weight of nodules, seed protein content and seed yield increased over control in gram. Kumpawat and Manohar (1994) reported that the seed yield of gram was increased by the application of 30 kg P_2O_5 ha^{-1} and 20 kg $FeSO_4$ ha^{-1} along with seed inoculation over control. Singh *et al.* (1995) observed that the application of Fe at 5 kg ha^{-1} increased seed yield of french bean by 26 per cent over control. Sakal *et al.* (1996) opined that the application of 1 per cent ferrous sulphate + 0.2 per cent citric acid solution as foliar spray increased grain yield of black gram and chickpea over control.

Singh *et al.* (1998) reported that the soil application of 15 kg $FeSO_4$ ha^{-1} significantly increased grain and straw yield of mung bean by 9.78 and 11.81 per cent over 0.1 per cent $FeSO_4$ foliar treated plots. Further yield attributes were also increased significantly with 15 kg $FeSO_4$ ha^{-1} over foliar applied $FeSO_4$ and control treatment. Sawires (2001) reported that the seed yield of gram was increased by the application of 20 kg $FeSO_4$ ha^{-1} along with seed inoculation over control. Gupta *et al.* (2002) conducted a field experiment at Kota (Rajasthan) and results revealed that the application of Fe either through soil (2.2 and 5.0 mg kg^{-1}) or foliar (0.5% $FeSO_4$ two spray) increased grain yield of mung bean over control. Yadav *et al.* (2002) reported that the seed and stover yield of mung bean significantly increased with the application of 4 kg Fe ha^{-1} over control. Balachander *et al.* (2003) reported that the application of Fe at 2 kg ha^{-1} through ferrous sulphate significantly increased the number and weight of nodules, biomass production, plant height and grain yield of black gram over control. Thapu *et al.* (2003) observed that the application of micronutrients like: Fe (as $FeSO_4$ at 0.4%), Mn, Cu, Zn significantly increased the grain yield in pea. Salam *et al.* (2004) conducted a field experiment at Raipur, Chhatisgarh and concluded that the seed yield of urdbean under application of $FeSO_4$ at 2-20 kg Fe ha^{-1} was maximum over control. Mevada *et al.* (2005) conducted a field experiment on sandy loam soil to study the effect the application of micronutrients (Zn, B, Mo, Fe) on the performance of urdbean and reported that the maximum grain yield (1180 kg ha^{-1}) was obtained under the application of chelated Fe (1 kg ha^{-1}) over control (924 kg ha^{-1}). Kumawat *et al.* (2006) observed that the soil application of Fe at 25 kg $FeSO_4$ ha^{-1} recorded significantly higher seed and straw yield of summer mung bean as compared to control. Sahu *et al.* (2008) reported that the application of $FeSO_4$ at 2 kg ha^{-1} along with biofertilizer inoculation gave the highest grain yield (1473 kg ha^{-1}) and straw yield (1423 kg ha^{-1}) as compared to control in chickpea.

Kumar *et al.* (2009) conducted an experiment at Kanpur and results revealed that the application of 10 kg Fe ha^{-1} enhanced the grain yield of chickpea by 17.3 per cent over control. Similar trend in straw yield response was also recorded. Sharma *et al.* (2010) reported that the application of chelated Fe (1 or 2 kg ha^{-1}), all the yield contributing characteristics *viz;* number of pods per plant, number of seeds per pod and 100 seeds weight were significantly increased in pigeon pea crop.

Effect of Iron on Nutrient Content, Uptake and Quality

Mundra and Bhati (1991) conducted a field experiment at Jobner (Rajasthan), revealed that the application of 10 and 20 kg $FeSO_4$ ha^{-1} significantly reduce P and Mn concentration in seed and its uptake but increased the uptake of N and Fe compared to control. Singh and Tiwari (1992) reported that the concentration and plant uptake of Zn were increased by Zn application while plant concentration of P, Fe and Cu were generally decreased due to Zn application in chickpea crop. Patel *et al.* (1993) conducted a field trial on calcareous soils of Gujarat revealed that foliar spray of one per cent $FeSO_4$ + 0.1 per cent citric acid and 2 per cent ferric citrate solution significantly increased concentration of Fe in groundnut leaves by 160.78 and 166.00 per cent at 60 days of crop over control. Both the treatments were at per in their effect and significantly reduces the concentrations of P at all stages of crop growth. Whereas, in another experiment results revealed the foliar spray of 3 per cent $FeSO_4$ to groundnut increased uptake of N, K, and Fe as compared to foliar spray of 0.5, 1.0 and 2.0 per cent $FeSO_4$ and soil applied $FeSO_4$ at 25 and 50 kg ha^{-1} (Pande *et al.* 1993). Kumpawat and Manohar (1994) reported that the seed protein content of gram was increased by the application of 30 kg P_2O_5 $ha^{-1}$and 20 kg $FeSO_4$ ha^{-1} along with seed inoculation over control. Shukla and Shukla (1994) observed that increase in Fe and P concentration in seeds of chickpea with increasing levels of $FeSO_4$ up to 50 kg ha^{-1} over control. Singh *et al.* (1995) reported that the uptake of N by French bean crop increased with increasing application of Fe up to 5 kg ha^{-1} but uptake of P remained unaffected.

Mahriya and Meena (1999) conducted a field trial at Jobner (Rajasthan), and they concluded that all the growth characters as well as protein content in seed were increased with the application of 4 kg Fe ha^{-1} in cowpea.

Yadav *et al.* (2002) reported that the protein content in seeds increased significantly with application of 30 kg P_2O5 ha^{-1} and 4 kg Fe ha^{-1} over their lower levels in mung bean. The Fe content and uptake in seed and stover increased significantly with the application of 6 kg Fe ha^{-1} but decreased the content and uptake of phosphorus. Kumawat *et al.* (2006) observed that the application of 25 kg $FeSO_4$ ha^{-1} to summer mung bean increased the activities of the catalase, guaiacol peroxidase synthesis of chlorophyll and active Fe content of green leaves over lower doses of $FeSO_4$ and controlled treatment.

While on calcareous soils of western Rajasthan, Kumawat *et al.* (2006) noted that soil application of 25 kg $FeSO_4$ ha^{-1} significantly increased Fe concentration in green leaves of mung bean as compared to control, further N, P, K and S uptake by grain and straw also increased due to 25 kg $FeSO_4$ ha^{-1} compared to control. Sahu *et al.* (2008) reported that the application of $FeSO_4$ at 2 kg ha^{-1} along with biofertilizer inoculation gave the highest grain yield (1473 kg ha-1) and nutrient uptake with Rhizobium + PSB inoculation compared to control in chickpea. Kumar *et al.* (2009) reported that the uptake of P and Fe by grain and straw increased significantly by application of varying levels of P and Fe up to 50 kg P_2O_5 and 10 kg Fe ha^{-1}over control in chickpea. Sharma *et al.* (2010) reported that the application of chelated Fe (1 or 2 kg ha^{-1}), all the yield contributing characteristics as well as protein content in seed were significantly increased in pigeon pea crop.

Conclusions

Chickpea is one of the leading pulse crop of India, contributing larger portion of dietary protein. But last few years, use of Fe fertilizers showed the higher yield. Application of Fe fertilizer enhanced the quality as well as chickpea yield. Spread the awareness of Fe fertilizer use in crop production by government and non-government organizations (NGOs), a potential strategy to enhance the crop yield. More initiative should be taken by research institute, so that Fe plays a vital role in sustainable chickpea production in future.

REFERENCES

Balachandar D., Nagarajan P., Gunasekaran S. (2003). Effect of Organic Amendments and Micronutrients on Nodulation and Yield of Black Gram in *Acid Soil. Legumes Res.* 26:192-195.

Bhanavase D.B., Jadhav B.R., Kshirsagar C.R., Patil P.L. (1994). Studies on chlorophyll, Nodulation, N - Fixation, Soybean Yield and their Correlation as Influenced by Micronutrients. *Madras Agric. J.* 81:325-328.

Dotaniya M.L., Kushwah S.K. (2013). Nutrients Uptake Ability of Various Rainy Season Crops Grown in a Vertisol of Central India. *Afr. J. Agric. Res.* 8(44):5592-5598. DOI: 10.5897/AJAR2013.7969.

Dotaniya M.L., Meena H.M., Lata M, Kumar K. (2013). Role of Phytosiderophores in Iron uptake by Plants. *Agric. Sci. Digest.* 33(1):73-76.

Gawad A.A., Hariri D.M., Shetaia AMA, Bahr AA (1991). Yield and Yield Components Responses of Chickpea (*Cicer arietinum* L.) to phosphorus fertilization and micronutrients. *Afr. J. Agric. Sci.* 18:61-71.

Gupta P.K., Sharma N.N., Acharaya H.K., Gupta S.K., Mali G.S. (2002). Response of mung bean to zinc and Iron on Vertisols of South-Western Plains of Rajasthan. National Symposium on Arid Legumes for Food Security and Promotion Trade, October, 2002. Sponsored by Indian Arid Legumes Society, CAZRI, Jodhpur.

Katyal J.C., Rattan R.K. (1995). Genetic Variations in Tolerance to Nutrient Deficiencies. In Genetic Research and Education: Current Trends and the Next Fifty Years (B. Sharma *et al.* Eds), Indian Society of Genetics and Plant Breeding, New Delhi, pp. 468-479.

Kobayashi T., Nishizawa N.K. (2012). Iron uptake, Translocation, and Regulation in Higher Plants. *Ann. Rev. Plant Biol.* 63:131-152. http://dx.doi.org/10.1146/annurev-arplant-042811-105522.

Kumar V., Dwivedi V.N., Tiwari D.D. (2009). Effect of phosphorus and iron on Yield and Mineral Nutrition in Chickpea. *Ann. Plant Soil Res.* 11:16-18.

Kumawat R.N., Rathore P.S., Pareek N. (2006). Response of mung Bean to Sulphur and Iron Nutrition Grown on Calcareous Soil of Western Rajasthan. *Indian J. Pulse Res.* 19:228-230.

Kumpawat B.S., Manohar S. (1994). Effect of Rhizobium Inoculation, phosphorus and Micronutrients on Nodulation and Protein Content of Gram. *Madras Agric. J.* 81: 630-631.

Mahriya A.K., Meena N.L. (1999). Response of phosphorus and Iron on Growth and Quality of Cowpea (*Vigna unguiculata* L.). *Ann. Agric. Biol. Res.* 4:203-205.

Mevada K.D., Patel J.J., Patel K.P. (2005). Effect of Micronutrients on Yield of Urdbean. *Indian J. Pulse Res.* 18:214-216.

Mundra S.L., Bhati D.S. (1991). Effect of Iron, Manganese and Rhizobium Inoculation on Nutrient Content and Uptake by Cowpea (Vigna unguiculata). *Indian J. Agron.* 36: 294-296.

Mundra S.L., Bhati D.S. (1994). Effect of Iron, Manganese and Rhizobium Inoculation on Growth, Nodulation, Iron: Manganese Ratio and Protein Content of Cowpea. *Farm. Syst.* 10:1-2.

Nenova V. (2006). Effect of Iron Supply on Growth and Photosystem II Efficiency of Pea Plants. *General Appl. Plant Physiol.* 32:81-90.

Nozoye T., Nagasaka S., Kobayashi T., Takahashi M., Sato Y., Uozumi N., Nakanishi H., Nishizawa N.K. (2011). Phytosiderophore efflux Transporters are Crucial for Iron Acquisition in Graminaceous Plants. *J. Biol. Chem.* 286:5446-5454. http://dx.doi.org/10.1074/jbc.M110.180026.

Pande P.K., Ravankar H.W., Laharia G.S., Ganwande R.P., Padole V.R. (1993). Effect of Iron on Yield and Uptake of Nutrients in Groundnut. *PKV Res. J.* 17:135-137.

Patel M.S., Suthar D.M., Kanzaria M.V. (1993). Effect of Foliar Application of Iron and Sulphur in Curing Chlorosis in Groundnut. *J. Indian Soc. Soil Sci.* 41:103-105.

Sahu S., Lidder R.S., Singh P.K. (2008). Effect of Micronutrients and Biofertilizers on Growth, Yield and Nutrient uptake by Chickpea (*Cicer aeritinum* L.) in Vertisols of Madhya Pradesh. *Adv. Plant Sci.* 21:501-503.

Sakal R., Singh A.P., Sinha R.B., Bhogal M.S. (1996). Twenty Five Years of Research on Micro and Secondary Nutrients in Soils and Crops of Bihar. *Res. Bull. Agric., Rajendra Agric. Uni. Pusa,* Samastipur, Bihar, pp. 1-207.

Salam P.K., Rajput R.S., Mishra P.K., Anita, Shrivastava G.K. (2004). Effect of Micronutrients Fertilization on Productivity Potential of Urdbean. *Ann. Agric. Res.* New Series 25: 329-332.

Sawires E.S. (2001). Effect of Phosphorus Fertilization and Micronutrients on Yield and Yield Components in Chickpea (*Cicer arietinum* L.). *Ann. Agric. Sci.* 46:155-164.

Sharma A., Nakul H.T., Jelgeri B.R., Surwenshi A. (2010). Effect of Micronutrients on Growth, Yield and Yield Components in Pigeon Pea (*Cajanus cajan* L.). *Res. J. Agric. Sci.* 1: 142-144.

Shukla V., Shukla I.C. (1994). Effect of Fe, Mo, Zn and P on Symbiotic Nitrogen Fixation of Chickpea. *Indian J. Agric. Chem.* 32:118-123.

Singh A.K., Singh K., Raju M.S., Singh J.P. (1995). Effect of Potassium, Zinc and Iron on Yield, Protein Content and Nutrient uptake in French bean (*Phaseolus vulgaris* L.). *J. Potassium Res.* 11:75-80.

Singh M.V. (2009). Micronutrient Nutritional Problems in Soils of India and Improvement for Human and Animal Health. *Indian J. Fert.* 5:11-16.

Singh S.K., Saxena H.K., Das T.K. (1998). The Effect of Kind of Micronutrients and their Method of Application of Mung bean under Zaid Conditions. *Ann. Agric. Res.* 19: 454-457.

Singh T., Tiwari K.N. (1992). Effect of Zinc Application on Yield and Nutrient Content in Chickpea,. *Maharashtra Agric. J.* 79: 87-91.

Singh V., Singh P.R., Khan N. (1993). Effect of P. and Fe Application on the Yield and Nutrient Content in Chickpea. *J. Indian Soc. Soil Sci.* 41:186-187.

Singh V., Varun G.S. (1989). Effect of Potassium and Iron Application on Yield and Nutrient uptake by Cowpea (*Vigna sinensis*). *J. Potassium Res.* 5:152-156.

Thapu U., Rai P., Suresh C.P., Pal P. (2003). Effect of Micronutrients on the Growth and Yield of Pea in Gangetic Alluvial of West Bengal. *Environ. Ecol.* 21:179-182.

Tisdale S.L., Nelson W.S., Beaton J.D. (1985). Soil Fertility and Fertilizers. Mcmillan Publishers Company, New York.

Ueno D., Rombola A.D., Iwashita T., Nomoto K., Ma JF (2007). Identification of two Novel Phytosiderophores Secreted by Perennial Grasses. *New Phytol.* 174:304-310. http://dx.doi.org/10.1111/j.1469-8137.2007.02056.x

Xiong H., Kakei Y., Kobayashi T., Guo X., Nakazono M., Takahashi H., Nakanishi H., Shen H., Zhang F., Nishizawa NK, Zuo Y (2013). Molecular Evidence for Phytosiderophore-induced Improvement of Iron Nutrition of Peanut Intercropped with Maize in Calcareous Soil.Plant Cell Environ. 36(10):1888-1902. http://dx.doi.org/10.1111/pce.12097.

Yadav P.S., Kameriya P.R., Rathore S. (2002). Effect of Phosphorus and Iron Fertilization on Yield, Protein Content and Nutrient Uptake in Mung Bean on Loamy Sand *Soil. J. Indian Soc. Soil Sci.* 50:225-226.

Pages 72-99

INTEGRATED NUTRIENT MANAGEMENT IN CHICKPEA
***Edited by* : Dr. Virendra Kumar** and **Dr. Nirmal Kumar Katiyar**
***Edition* : 2017**
ISBN : 978-93-5056-872-9
***Published by* : Discovery Publishing House Pvt. Ltd., New Delhi (India)**

The Effect of Molybdenum and Iron on Nodulation, Nitrogen Fixation and Yield of Chickpea Genotypes (*Cicer Arietinum* L.)

Nawaz Khan[1], Muhammad Tariq[1], Khitab Ullah[1]
Dost Muhammad[1], Imran Khan[1], Kamran Rahatullah[2]
Nazeer Ahmed[3], Saeed Ahmed[4]

ABSTRACT

The present study was based on the hypothesis that the applied molybdenum and iron influence the nodulation, nitrogen fixation and yield by chickpea genotypes. For this purpose a field experiment was conducted to study the influence of different levels of molybdenum and iron on the nodulation, nitrogen fixation and yield of chickpea genotypes (Cicer arietinum L.) growing two different genotypes such as: Desi (sheenghar) and Kabuli (Karak-II) during, 2011-12 at Malakandher Farm, The University of Agriculture, Peshawar. Different levels of molybdenum and iron were applied at the rate of 0, 0.25 and 0.50 and 0, 2 and 5.0 kg ha^{-1}, respectively along with a basal dose of 25 N, 60 P_2O_5 and 60 K_2O in randomized complete block design with split plot arrangement and replicated three times. Results revealed that maximum yield and yield parameters, numbers of root nodules and nitrogen concentration were observed in those treatment plots where Mo 0.5 and Fe 2.0 kg ha^{-1} were applied simultaneously for both genotypes. The grain yield, nodulation and nitrogen concentration were recorded significantly more in Kabuli (Karak-II) as compared to Desi (sheenghar) of chickpea genotypes, perhaps due to the formation

1. Department of Soil and Environmental Sciences, The university of Agriculture, Peshawar, Pakistan.
2. Department of Food Science and Technology, The University of Agriculture, Peshawar, Pakistan.
3. Department of Entomology, The University of Agriculture, Peshawar, Pakistan.
4. Department of Horticulture, The University of Agriculture, Peshawar, Pakistan.

of maximum nodulation and nitrogen concentration by plants. Results revealed that with increasing the levels of Mo and Fe in soil, the concentration of Fe and N in plant leaves were significantly increased in both genotypes at flowering stage. Moreover, in the present study the number of nodules were correlated with N concentration of plants for both genotypes and found as the nodules formation increases the plant N concentration linearly increased and showed close relationship with one another. Similarly, the Fe-concentration increases in plant leaves, N-concentration also increases in a similar fashion, indicated that Fe-played a vital role in N-fixation by chickpea genotypes. The present study suggests that the application of Mo 0.5 and Fe 2.0 kg ha^{-1} is important which play a significant role in getting the maximum yield, nodules and nitrogen concentration in chickpea genotypes.

INTRODUCTION

Chickpea (*Cicer arietinum* L.) is an annual legume belongs to family Leguminoseae and is grown throughout the world for grain pulse. There are two main kinds of chickpea *Desi* and *Kabuli*. *Desi*, has small, darker seeds and a rough coat, grown mostly in semi-arid regions, while *Kabuli* has lighter coloured, larger seeds with smoother coat, mainly grown in temperates regions of Pakistan. Chickpea is leguminous crop which fix nitrogen in the root nodules; and this process depend on various factors, like molybdenum and iron nutrition which play a key role in symbiotic nitrogen fixation by legumes. Chickpea is an important cool season legume of arid tropics due to its ability to fix atmosphere nitrogen, it is considered to sustain cropping system productivity. This crop having nodules on their roots where some bacteria, called rhizobia live with a specific function to fix atmosphere nitrogen into plant available form called biological nitrogen fixation. By this process a maximum amount of free lost nitrogen is deposited in to the soil which can be used by the same plant and the next can also. The maximum nitrogen fixation by the crop depend upon the cultivar, nodules numbers, nodule weight and the efficient strain of bacteria survive in their root nodules. Sufficient amount of nitrogen can be fix by the chickpea to replace the removed nitrogen in harvested grains (FAO, 1984; Schwenke *et al.* 1998). It contains sufficient amount of protein that meets protein requirement of the bulk of population of our country (Shah *et al.* 1998).

Molybdenum is required for growth of most biological organisms including plants (Graham and Stangoulis, 2005). Generally, molybdenum is an essential micronutrient for plants and bacteria (Williams and Fraustoda Silva 2002). Meagher *et al.* (1991) reported the role of molybdenum in normal assimilation of nitrogen by plants is well known, because molybdenum is an essential component of nitrate reductase and nitogenase, which control the reduction of inorganic nitrate and helps in fixing N_2 to NH_3. Thus, molybdenum is the key to nitrogen fixation by legumes. Brkics *et al.* (2004)

and Jongruaysup *et al.* (1993) also stated that the application of molybdenum stimulated nodulation and biological nitrogen fixation, thus increasing the legume yield. Moreover, Katyal and Randhawa (1983) stated that molybdenum is required in the synthesis of ascorbic acid is implicated in making iron physiologically available.

Similarly, iron plays a key role in several enzyme systems in which haem or haemin functions as the prothectic group. These haem enzyme systems comprise the catalases, peroxidases and several cytochromes. Cytochromes operate the respiratory metabolism of living cell. Among the haem Fe enzyme is ferredoxin which regulates oxidation reduction reaction its role in photosynthesis, NO^{-}_{2} and SO_4^{-2} reduction and nitrogen assimilation underlines the vital functions iron performs in over all plant metabolism. Iron deficiencies are mainly manifested by yellow leaves due to low levels of chlorophyll. Leaf yellowing first appears on the younger upper leaves in interveinal tissues. Severe iron deficiencies cause leaves to turn completely yellow or almost white, and then brown as leaves die. Hageman and Burris (1978) reported that the enzyme nitrogenase contained two proteins: Fe protein (component containing iron and protein) and Mo-Fe protein (component containing molybdenum, iron and protein). Therefore, iron and cobalt are essential for the nitrogen fixation process (Meagher *et al.* 1991).

Haque *et al.* (1979) reported that micronutrients molybdenum and iron are very important for chickpea and other legumes to fix atmospheric nitrogen because molybdenum and iron are essential constituents of nitrogenase enzyme which is responsible for biological nitrogen fixation and their deficiency in soil may affect nitrogen fixation and yield of chickpea.

In alkaline-calcareous soils, the yield of grain legumes specifically chickpea crop is often limited by lower availability of molybdenum and iron, especially when they depend upon symbiosis with root nodules bacteria for their nitrogen nutrition. However, the effect of molybdenum and iron limitation upon nitrogen fixation are not fully understood in the indigenous conditions for leguminous crop like chickpea, therefore keeping in view, the nutritional importance of molybdenum and iron on nitrogen fixation by chickpea crop, a field experiment was carried out in Malakandher Farm The university of Agriculture, Peshawar with the following main objectives:

Objectives

- To determine the effect of applied molybdenum and iron on the yield and yield parameters of chickpea genotypes.
- To study the effect of applied molybdenum and iron on root nodulation chickpea genotypes.
- To find out the effect of applied molybdenum and iron on the uptake of nitrogen by chickpea genotypes.

Materials and Methods

Experimental Description

A field experiment was conducted at Malakandher Farm, The University of Agriculture Peshawar, during 3rd November, 2011 to study the effect of molybdenum and iron on the nitrogen fixation by two chickpea genotypes, such as: *Desi* (Sheenghar) and *Kabuli* (Karak-II). The chickpea seeds were sown in randomized complete block design with split plot arrangement and replicated 3 times. A plot size was 6 m^2. Each plot was comprised of 3 rows containing row to row distance of 30 cm and plant to plant distance was of 20 cm. Different levels of molybdenum at the rate of 0, 0.25 and 0.5 and iron at the rate of 0, 2 and 5 kg ha^{-1} was applied in the form of ammonium molybdate and iron sulfate, respectively. A basal dose of 25 N, 60 P_2O_5 and 60 K_2O kg $ha^{-1}$was applied in the form of urea, di ammonium phosphate and potassium sulfate before sowing. Before fertilizer application a composite soil sample was collected for the determination of physico-chemical characteristics and desired nutrients status of the test soil.

Table 7.1: Physico-chemical characteristics of the experimental soil

Properties	Units	Values
Sand	%	21.98
Silt	%	54.42
Clay	%	23.60
Textural class	–	Silt Loam
pHs (1:5)	–	7.98
ECs (1:5)	dSm^{-1}	0.24
Lime	%	9.34
Organic matter	%	0.68
Total mineral nitrogen (NH_4-N + NO_3-N)	%	0.065
Fe (AB-DTPA)	mg kg^{-1}	4.33

The physico-chemical characteristics of the experimental soil (Table 7.1) shows that the soil was silt loam in texture, alkaline in reaction, non-saline in nature, low in organic matter content, moderately calcareous and slightly deficient in available-N, while soluble Fe was adequate (Katyal and Randhawa 1982).

All culture practices were performed when required. Data on the following parameters were recorded during field and laboratory investigations:

- Days to emergence.
- Days to flowering.
- Shoot biomass.
- Seed yield.
- Number of pods plant^{-1}.
- Number of seeds pod^{-1}.
- 100 seeds weight.
- Fresh mass of nodules plant^{-1}.
- Number of nodules plant^{-1}.
- N concentration in plant leaves.
- N uptake by plant.
- Fe concentration in plant leaves.
- Fe uptake by plant.

Soil Analysis

The physico-chemical properties of the experimental site such as: soil texture (Gee and Budr, 1982), soil pH (McLean, 1982), electrical conductivity (Rhoades, 1982), lime (Cottenie, 1980) and organic matter (Nelson and Sommers, 1996) contents were measured using the standard routine methods following in the laboratory of Soil and Environmental Sciences.

Plant Analysis

At flowering stage, fully developed leaves from each treatment plot were collected from randomly selected plants (5) for the determination of elemental N and Fe concentration. Fresh leaves were washed with distilled water, blotted with tissue paper and air dried in open air under shade. The samples were then oven dried at 70°C for 48h to a constant weight. The leaves were chopped with a mini grinder followed by wet acid digestion of leaves by procedure of Benton *et al.* (1991). The total N concentration in leaves was determined by micro Kjeldhal apparatus as described by Mulvaney (1996). While Fe concentration was estimated by atomic absorption spectrophotometer (Issac and Kerber, 1971).

Nitrogen Concentration

Total nitrogen in soil and plant simple was determined by the Kjeldahl method of Bremner and Mulvaney (1982). In this method, 0.2 g of soil or plant simple was digested with 3ml of concentrated H_2SO_4 in the presence of 1.1 g digestion mixture containing K_2SO_4, $CUSO_4$ and Se on block digestion for about 4-5 hours. After cooling, the digest was transferred quantitatively to a 100ml volumetric flask and made the volume using distilled water. 20ml of the digest was distilled in presence of 5ml of 40 per cent NaOH solution into a 5ml boric acid mixed indicator solution. The distillate was titrated against standard 0.005 M HCl. Blank was also run at the same time and subtracted its reading from the simple. The amount of nitrogren was calculated using the following expression:

$$\text{Total N (\%)} = \frac{(\text{Sample - Blank}) \times 0.005 \times 0.014 \times 100 \times 100}{\text{Weight of plant sample} \times 20}$$

S = volume of acid (0.1 N) used for sample.

B = volume of acid (0.1 N) used for blank.

Iron Concentration

Iron concentration in chickpea leaves was determined in digested sample using atomic absorption spectrophotometer (Perkin Elmer 2380) a 0.25 g sample was digested with nitric acid and perchloric acid as suggested by Walsh and Beaton (1977).

Statistical Analysis

The statistical analysis of data was carried out by conducting ANOVA and the treatment differences were estimated by LSD-test of significance. In addition, multiple regression models were used to find out the relationship between fixed N in plants and applied Mo-Fe to soil (Steel *et al.* 1997).

Results and Discussion

The effect of different levels of molybdenum (Mo) and iron (Fe) was evaluated on the yield, nodulation and nitrogen concentration of chickpea crop under agro-climatic conditions of Malakandher Farm, The University of Agriculture, Peshawar, during Rabbi 2011-12. The test verities were *Sheenghar* and *Karak-II*. The field and laboratory findings are presented in Tables 7.1 to 7.13 along with Figs. 7.1 to 7.6 and complete analysis of variance along with replication wise-data for each parameter is given in Appendices 1 to 13. The results obtained are presented and discussed in the following sections.

Days to Emergence

Nutrients uptake and yield of plants were directly affected by seed emergence. Non-significant differences were observed among the different combination of molybdenum and iron. The data regarding to days to germination from the date of sowing are given in (Table 7.1a). The emergence data were recorded after 7 days of sowing. Maximum days (11 days) were taken by *Sheenghar* as compared to *Karak-II* and this difference was probably due to climatic effect *i.e.,* continuous rainfall on crop genotypes or genetic factor not due to nutritional problem of the seed. However, in the treatment plots where no molybdenum was applied took more days to emergence for both chickpea genotypes. Due to the different levels of iron ranging from complete deficiency to toxicity, increased or decreased the growth rate and physiological components were reported by Nenova, (2006). The emergence was delay due to environmental factors *i.e.,* absence of sun light and continues rainfall during the experimental time. Results also showed that the emergence rate in molybdenum and iron plots were comparatively better than those plots, which received no molybdenum and iron fertilizer as shown in Fig. 7.1.

Table 7.1a: Effect of molybdenum and iron application on the days to emergence of chickpea genotypes

Genotypes	Mo (kg ha^{-1})	Fe (kg ha^{-1}) 0	2	5	Mean (V × Mo)
		(V × Mo × Fe)			
Sheenghar	0	10.5	10	11	10.5
	0.25	9.3	9	10.3	9.5
	0.5	9.3	10	10.4	9.9
Karak-II	0	10.3	10.2	10.7	10.4
	0.25	10.3	10	10.6	10.3
	0.5	9.5	9	10.6	9.7
		(Mo × Fe)			(Mo)
	0	10.4	10.1	10.9	10.5
	0.25	9.8	9.5	10.5	9.9
	0.5	9.4	9.5	10.5	9.8
		(V × Fe)			(V)
Sheenghar		9.7	9.7	10.6	10.0
Karak-II		10.0	9.7	10.6	10.1
Mean		9.9	9.7	10.6	

LSD value of P< 0.05 for genotypes = 0.28.

Days to Flowering

The data pertaining to number of days to flowering are given in Table 7.2a. Non significant differences were observed between chickpea genotypes in terms of days to flowering. After 130 days of sowing the flowering data were recorded. The maximum numbers of days (138 days) for flowering were recorded in control, while the minimum numbers of days to flowering (133 days) were observed where Mo 0.5 and Fe 2 kg ha^{-1} were applied in both genotypes of chickpea. Furthermore, statistically no differences in days to flowering were recorded between chickpea genotypes. These results are supported by the previous work of Tahir *et al.* (2011).

Table 7.1b: Effect of molybdenum and iron application on the per cent emergence of chickpea genotypes

Verities	Treatments		D7	D8	D9	D10	D11
	Mo (kgha^{-1})	Fe					
Sheenghar	0	0	24.0	43.0	64.7	76.0	83.3
		2	24.3	40.0	67.0	79.0	84.0
		5	23.3	40.3	63.0	79.0	81.3
	0.25	0	24.3	41.3	66.0	80.0	86.3
		2	25.0	43.0	67.0	79.7	87.3
		5	23.7	42.0	67.7	79.0	86.3
	0.5	0	24.3	43.7	68.7	80.7	86.0
		2	26.0	45.3	69.7	81.3	89.3
		5	24.0	43.7	68.3	80.0	86.0
Karak-II	0	0	28.0	42.3	66.3	72.7	82.0
		2	26.3	43.3	67.0	75.3	83.3
		5	27.0	44.3	70.0	74.3	81.3
	0.25	0	25.7	47.0	70.7	74.3	86.7
		2	29.3	49.0	71.0	80.7	88.3
		5	28.3	48.3	69.0	78.0	86.7
	0.5	0	26.7	50.3	70.0	79.0	85.7
		2	30.7	51.0	72.7	81.3	90.3
		5	25.0	47.3	70.0	80.3	88.7
LSD (P<0.05)			NS	NS	2.25	NS	NS
% CV			13.71	10.92	8.19	7.27	5.23

NS=Non-significant.

Moreover, the treatment plots where no molybdenum was applied took more days to flowering. It showed that the unavailability of molybdenum reduced the days to flowering of chickpea crop. Same observations were reported by Nautiyal *et al.* (2005). They observed that the low availability of molybdenum is known to disrupt formation development and viability of pollen grains. Therefore the number and size of flowers were reduced and consequently the seed yield was also decreased significantly. Generally, genotypes *Sheenghar* took more days to flowering than *Karak-II,* which may be due to genetic difference not due to nutritional on chickpea genotypes. Yield and uptake of nutrients by plants were directly affected by flowering. Flowering data also shows that the emergence rates in molybdenum and iron plots were comparatively better than those plots, which received no molybdenum and iron fertilizer as shown in Fig. 7.2. Similar observations were reported by Truong and Duthion (1993).

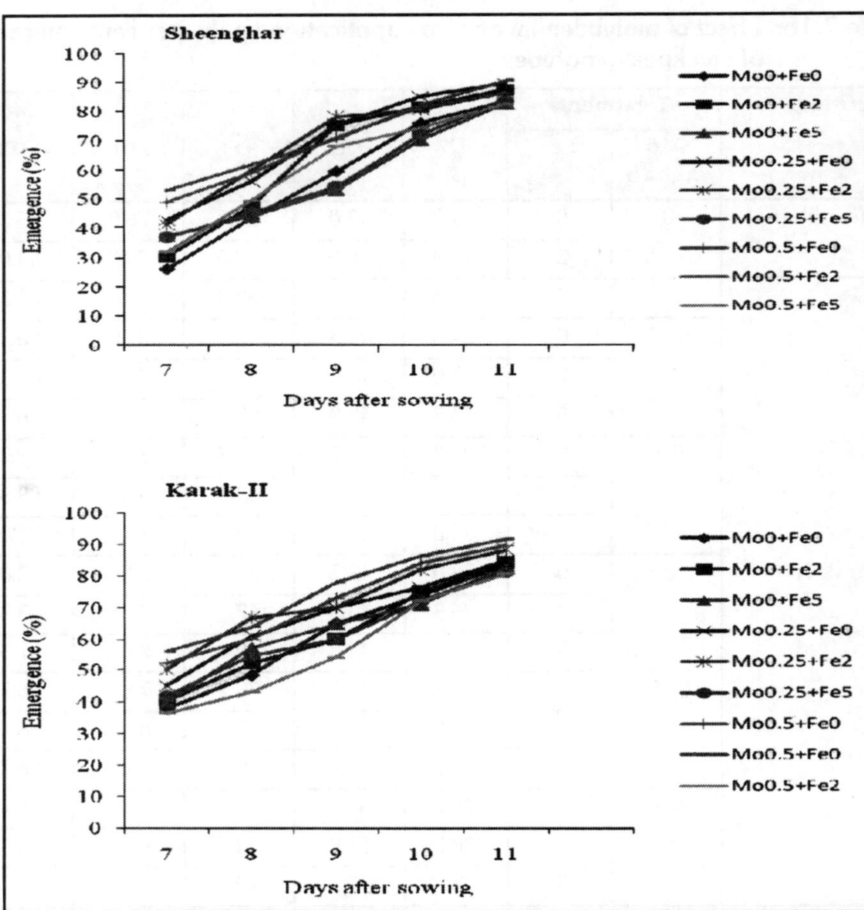

Fig. 7.1: Effect of applied molybdenum and iron on the % emergence of chickpea genotypes

Table 7.2a: Effect of molybdenum and iron application on days to flowering of chickpea genotypes

Genotypes	Mo (kg ha^{-1})	Fe (kg ha^{-1}) 0	2	5	Mean (V × Mo)
		(V × Mo × Fe)			
Sheeenghar	0	138	135.5	135.7	136.4
	0.25	136	136	136	136.0
	0.5	136	135	137.5	136.2
Karak-II	0	138	136	137	137.0
	0.25	137	135	137.2	136.4
	0.5	137	134	137.3	136.1

Contd...

		(Mo × Fe)			(Mo)
	0	138.0	135.8	136.4	136.7
	0.25	136.5	135.5	136.6	136.2
	0.5	136.5	134.5	137.4	136.1
		(V × Fe)			(V × Fe)
Sheenghar		136.7	135.5	136.4	136.2
Karak-II		136.7	135.7	136.8	136.4
Mean		136.7	135.6	136.6	

LSD value of P< 0.05 for Mo = 9.56.

LSD value of P< 0.05 for Fe = 1.54.

Table 7.2b: Effect of molybdenum and iron application on the days to flowering of chickpea genotypes

Verities	Treatments		D130	D131	D132	D133	D134	D135
	Mo (kgha^{-1})	Fe						
Sheenghar	0	0	13.7	27.0	37.3	54.0	64.0	81.0
		2	15.3	26.7	37.0	55.0	65.0	80.0
		5	14.3	25.3	38.3	52.7	62.7	81.0
	0.25	0	14.3	26.7	39.7	55.7	67.7	82.0
		2	16.0	26.0	41.0	56.0	68.7	86.3
		5	15.3	26.7	37.7	53.0	66.0	81.7
	0.5	0	14.7	27.3	36.7	54.7	66.3	81.7
		2	16.0	28.7	43.3	57.7	69.0	89.0
		5	14.7	26.3	38.0	55.7	66.0	80.0
Karak-II	0	0	15.3	26.3	37.5	54.3	68.7	76.7
		2	15.7	26.3	36.9	56.3	69.3	79.7
		5	16.0	25.7	39.6	53.0	68.7	80.3
	0.25	0	16.0	27.7	36.2	56.3	68.0	82.7
		2	15.7	27.3	47.5	57.7	70.0	85.0
		5	15.3	26.3	45.5	53.0	68.0	83.0
	0.5	0	16.0	27.0	39.0	53.0	67.0	84.3
		2	17.0	28.7	55.8	59.0	71.3	87.7
		5	16.3	27.0	43.5	56.3	68.0	80.3
LSD (P<0.05)			NS	NS	NS	2.04	3.21	NS
% CV			15.83	8.67	744	5.26	3.81	4.12

NS=Non-significant.

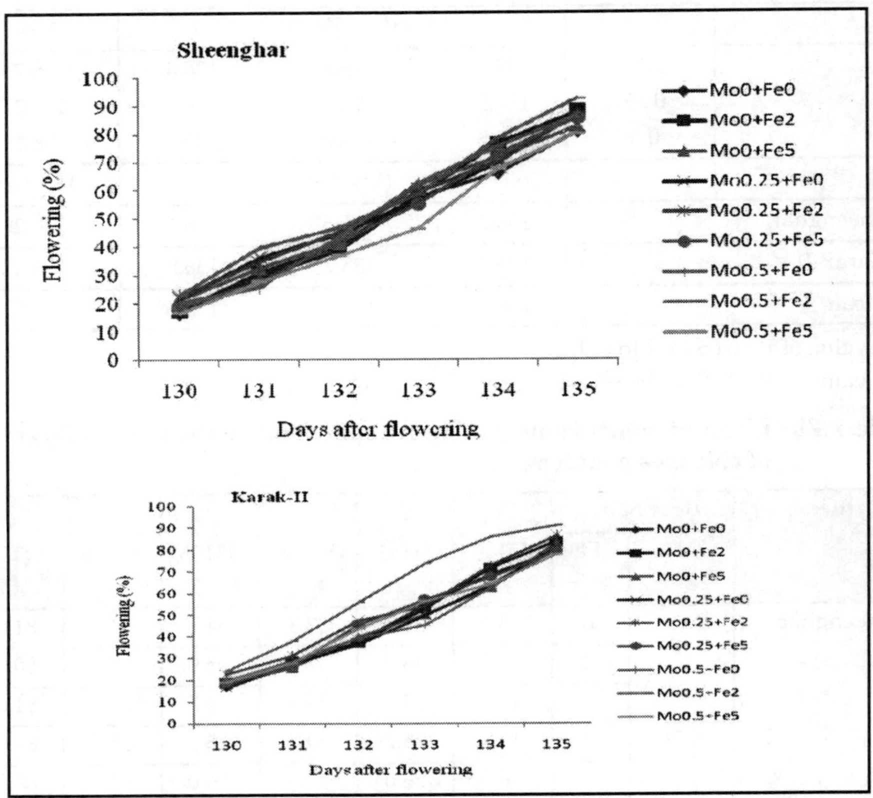

Fig. 7.2: Effect of applied molybdenum and iron on the % flowering of chickpea genotypes

Shoot Biomass

The data regarding shoot biomass is presented in Table 7.3. Results showed that significant differences were found among various molybdenum and iron treatments for shoot biomass of chickpea genotypes. However, maximum shoot biomass 6210 and 6434 kg ha^{-1} were found in treatment plot, where Mo 0.5 and Fe 2 kg ha^{-1} were applied for both genotypes, while the minimum shoot biomass 4125 and 4375 were recorded in control, (where no molybdenum and iron were applied) in both chickpea genotypes. It showed that both the micronutrients application had positive effect on the production of shoot biomass. The finding results suggested that a normal level molybdenum and iron produced maximum shoot biomass above and below this level the shoot biomass significantly reduced in both chickpea genotypes. Same results were obtained by Sarivestava and Ahlavat (1995). It is observed that the *Karak-II* genotype yielded more than the *Sheenghar* genotype of chickpea. Furthermore, beside the poor growth performance of *Sheenghar* genotype this may also evident from the lower nodules formation and non-significant nitrogen uptake, which directly affected the shoot biomass of chickpea genotype. Sawires (2001) supported our results, who stated that molybdenum, iron and zinc application at 15-30 mg kg^{-1} increased the straw yield of chickpea.

Table 7.3: Effect of molybdenum and iron application on biomass of chickpea genotypes

Genotypes	Mo (kg ha^{-1})	Fe (kg ha^{-1}) 0	2	5	Mean (V × Mo)
		(V × Mo × Fe)			
Sheenghar	0	4125	5215	5467	4936
	0.25	5735	5780	5813	5776
	0.5	5725	6210	5825	5920
Karak-II	0	4375	5355	5800	5177
	0.25	5876	5890	6100	5955
	0.5	6125	6434	6040	6200
		(Mo x Fe)			(Mo)
	0	4250	5285	5634	5056
	0.25	5806	5835	5957	5866
	0.5	5925	6322	5933	6060
		(V × Fe)			(V × Fe)
Sheenghar		5195	5735	5702	5544
Karak-II		5459	5893	5980	5777
Mean		5327	5814	5841	

LSD value of $P < 0.05$ for Mo × Fe = 80.6.6
LSD value of $P < 0.05$ for Mo = 32.93.

Grain Yield

The result showed that the different level of the micronutrients (Molybdenum and Iron) significantly increases the yield of chickpea over control Table 7.4. The maximum grain yield of 433 kg ha^{-1} and 465 kg ha^{-1} were obtained for treatment receiving Mo at 0.5 and Fe at 2 kg ha^{-1}, while minimum grain yield of 280 kg ha^{-1} and 307 kg ha^{-1} were obtained in control for both chickpea genotypes. These result suggested that the normal level of micronutrients enhance the grain yield of chickpea above and below this level the grain yield significantly reduced in both chickpea genotypes. Similar observations were found by Sarivestava and Ahlavat (1995) and Sarie *et al.* (1983). Results showed that genotype *Karak-II* yielded more than the *Sheenghar*, this is not only due to the genetic development but it may be due to the environmental conditions, perhaps the environmental conditions were not favorable for *Sheenghar* genotype, which indicate poor growth performance. Furthermore, beside the poor growth performance of *Sheenghar* genotype this may be due to the lower nodulation and non-significant nitrogen uptake, which directly affected the total grain yield of chickpea genotype. Results are in line with the previous work of Kothari (2002) and Johansen *et al.* (2007) who stated that lower nodules formation and nitrogen uptake by legumes consequently reduced grain yield of crops. The application of molybdenum progressively increases the yield of chickpea reported by (Shil *et al.* 2007). Abd-el-Gawad *et al.* (1993) reported positive response of chickpea to phosphorus, molybdenum, iron and zinc. Similarly, Abo-shetaia and Soheir (2001) also observed that the application of phosphorus at 95.2 kg ha^{-1} 47.6-95.2 mg kg^{-1} ha $^{-1}$ of micronutrient (molybdenum) significantly increased the number of pods plant^{-1}, seed yield and grain yield kg ha^{-1} in chickpea (*cv.Giza195*). The combined application of molybdenum and iron with inoculation gave significantly higher grain yield over control reported by (Singh 2004). Boto *et al.* (2010) reported that the applications of molybdenum, zinc and boron enhance seed yield mainly due to the number of pods plant^{-1}.

Table 7.4: Effect of molybdenum and iron application on the grain yield (kg ha^{-1}) of chickpea genotypes

Genotypes	Mo (kg ha^{-1})	Fe (kg ha^{-1}) 0	2	5	Mean (V × Mo)
		(V × Mo × Fe)			
Sheenghar	0	280	350	300	310
	0.25	380	366	316	354
	0.5	416	433	310	386
Karak-II	0	307	344	315	322
	0.25	400	365	330	365
	0.5	438	465	345	416
			(Mo x Fe)		(Mo)
	0	294	347	308	316
	0.25	390	366	323	360
	0.5	427	449	328	401
			(V×Fe)		(V×Fe)
Sheenghar		359	383	309	350
Karak-II		382	391	330	368
Mean		370	387	319	

LSD value of $P< 0.05$ for Mo = 29.61.

LSD value of $P< 0.05$ for Mo × Fe = 51.29.

Pods Plant^{-1}

The data regarding number of pods plant^{-1} is presented in Table 7.5. Results showed that significant differences were found among various molybdenum and iron treatments for number of pods plant^{-1}. However, more pods (32) and (33) were found in the treatment plot, where Mo 0.5 and Fe 2 kg ha^{-1} were applied for both genotypes and less pods plant^{-1} were recorded in control. Srivastava and Ahlawat (1995) and Rabbani *et al.* (2005) also observed positive effect of molybdenum and reported that applied molybdenum gave statistically significance effect on the average number of pods plant^{-1}. Similarly, Boto *et al.* (2010) reported that the application of molybdenum, zinc and boron enhance the number of pods plant^{-1}. Results further showed that the performance of genotype *Karak-II* was found better than the *Sheenghar* in terms of pods plant^{-1}, suggested *Karak-II* is more productive which gave higher yield than *Sheenghar* under the conditions of the experiment.

Table 7.5: Effect of molybdenum and iron application on pods plant^{-1}of chickpea genotypes

Genotypes	Mo (kg ha^{-1})	Fe (kg ha^{-1}) 0	2	5	Mean (V × Mo)
			(V × Mo × Fe)		
Sheenghar	0	27	23	16	22
	0.25	28	29	33	30
	0.5	28	32	25	28
Karak-II	0	20	23	18	20
	0.25	21	23	31	25
	0.5	28	33	22	28
			(Mo x Fe)		(Mo)
	0	24	23	17	21
	0.25	25	26	32	28
	0.5	28	33	24	26
			(V x Fe)		(V x Fe)
Sheenghar		28	25	25	26
Karak-II		23	26	24	24
Mean		25	26	25	

LSD value of $P < 0.05$ for Mo = 1.66.

LSD value of $P < 0.05$ for Mo × Fe = 2.88.

Seeds Pod^{-1}

The data observed on number of seeds pod^{-1} are given in Table 7.6. Non-significant differences were observed among various molybdenum and iron treatments for number of seeds pod^{-1}. However, maximum seeds pod^{-1} (1.6) and (1.7) were found in treatment plot where Mo 0.5 and Fe 2 kg ha^{-1} were applied for both chickpea genotypes and minimum seed pod^{-1} (1.3) and (1.0) were recorded in control, (where no molybdenum and no iron were applied). The increase in number of seeds pod^{-1} by the application of molybdenum along with iron may be due to the fact that molybdenum and iron may fixed that much amount of nitrogen which was required by the plant to show better performance as molybdenum is related directly to nitrogen fixation by legumes. Result also showed that the molybdenum and iron nutrition had similar effect on both chickpea genotypes. Similar observations were found by Landge *et al.* (2002) and Tahir *et al.* (2011).

Table 7.6: Effect of molybdenum and iron application on seeds pod^{-1} of chickpea genotypes

Genotypes	Mo (kg ha^{-1})	Fe (kg ha^{-1}) 0	2	5	Mean (V × Mo)
		(V × Mo × Fe)			
Sheenghar	0	1.3	1.4	1.6	1.4
	0.25	1.5	1.4	1.4	1.4
	0.5	1.5	1.6	1.3	1.5
Karak-II	0	1.0	1.4	1.2	1.2
	0.25	1.5	1.3	1.3	1.4
	0.5	1.4	1.7	1.4	1.5
			(Mo x Fe)		(Mo)
	0	1.2	1.4	1.4	1.3
	0.25	1.5	1.4	1.4	1.4
	0.5	1.5	1.7	1.4	1.5
			(V × Fe)		(V × Fe)
Sheenghar		1.4	1.5	1.4	1.4
Karak-II		1.3	1.5	1.3	1.4
Mean		1.4	1.5	1.4	

LSD value of $P < 0.05$ for Mo = 0.42.

100 Seeds Weight

Data regarding that 100-seed weight was significantly affected by the application of molybdenum and iron presented in Table 7.7. The maximum

100-seed weight 17.30 g was obtained in treatment plot, where Mo 0.5 and Fe 2 kg ha^{-1} were applied in genotype *Sheenghar* and 22.2 g was obtained in *Karak-II* where Mo 0.5 and Fe 2 kg ha^{-1} were used as treatment. While, the minimum 100-seed weight 16.75 and 22.03 g were observed in control treatment for both chickpea genotypes. Rabbani *et al.* (2005) found that the application of *Rhizobium* inoculant in combination with phosphorus and molybdenum gave statistically significant 100-seed weight. These results indicated that nil or excess molybdenum and iron reduced the 100-seed weight as compared to those plots which received normal levels of molybdenum and iron. These results are supported by previous work of Kevresan *et al.* (2001). Moreover, Nautiyal *et al.* (2005) stated that leguminous plants are very sensitive to molybdenum effects, but excess molybdenum may impair growth and decrease the seed yield of the crops. In the present experiment excess molybdenum reduced the seed yield of both chickpea genotypes. Results also showed that the seeds of Kabuli genotype (*Karak-II)* were heavier than the Desi genotype (*Sheenghar)*, perhaps this may be due to genetic difference not due to nutritional effect.

Table 7.7: Effect of molybdenum and iron application on 100 seeds weight (g) of chickpea genotypes

Genotypes	Mo (kg ha^{-1})	Fe (kg ha^{-1}) 0	2	5	Mean (V × Mo)
		(V × Mo × Fe)			
Sheenghar	0	16.8	17.2	17.2	17.1
	0.25	17.3	17.3	17.3	17.3
	0.5	17.3	17.3	17.3	17.3
Karak-II	0	22.0	22.2	22.2	22.1
	0.25	22.2	22.1	22.1	22.1
	0.5	22.0	22.2	22.1	22.1
			(Mo × Fe)		(Mo)
	0	19.4	19.7	19.7	19.6
	0.25	19.7	19.7	19.7	19.7
	0.5	19.7	19.7	19.7	19.7
			(V × Fe)		(V × Fe)
Sheenghar		17.0	17.1	17.3	17.3
Karak-II		22.0	22.1	22.1	22.1
Mean		19.3	19.6	19.7	19.7

LSD value of $P < 0.05$ for Mo = 8.783.

Fresh Weight of Nodules

The data obtained on fresh weight of nodules plant^{-1} are presented in Table 7.8. Highly significant differences were observed among the different molybdenum and iron treatments. The maximum fresh weight of nodules 3.13 g and 2.84 g were obtained in the treatment plots, where Mo 0.5 and Fe 2 kg ha^{-1} were applied for both chickpea genotypes, while minimum fresh weight of nodules 1.45 g and 1.59 g were recorded in the treatment plots, where Mo 0 and Fe 5 kg ha^{-1} were applied respectively. These results indicated that fresh weight of nodules was affected by the nutrition of molybdenum and iron application. Bhanavase and Patil (1994) reported that molybdenum enhance nodule numbers, nodule weight plant^{-1} and nitrogen concentration of nodules.

Table 7.8: Effect of molybdenum and iron application on nodules fresh weight (g) of chickpea genotypes

Genotypes	Mo (kg ha^{-1})	Fe (kg ha^{-1}) 0	2	5	Mean (V × Mo)
		(V × Mo × Fe)			
Sheenghar	0	2.0	1.7	1.6	1.8
	0.25	2.3	2.5	2.4	2.4
	0.5	2.6	2.8	2.6	2.7
Karak-II	0	1.7	1.8	1.5	1.6
	0.25	2.2	2.7	2.6	2.5
	0.5	2.9	3.1	2.7	2.9
			(Mo × Fe)		(Mo)
	0	1.8	1.7	1.5	1.7
	0.25	2.2	2.6	2.5	2.4
	0.5	2.8	3.0	2.6	2.8
			(V × Fe)		(V × Fe)
Sheenghar		2.3	2.3	2.2	2.3
Karak-II		2.3	2.5	2.2	2.3
Mean		2.3	2.4	2.2	

LSD value of $P< 0.05$ for Mo = 0.06.

Effect on Nodulation

The results obtained on number of nodules in chickpea genotypes are presented and discussed below:

Number of Nodules

The data obtained on numbers of nodules plant^{-1} at flowering stage are presented in Table 7.9. It has a direct effect on the grain yield of chickpea genotypes. The data showed that molybdenum highly significantly and iron significantly affected the number of nodules plant^{-1} in chickpea compared with control. The maximum nodules of 49 and 54 were obtained for treatment receiving Mo at 0.5 and Fe at 2 kg ha^{-1}, in both chickpea genotypes, while the minimum nodules of 28 and 25 were obtained for treatment receiving Mo at 0 and Fe at 5 kg ha^{-1} in both chickpea genotypes. The result suggested that molybdenum generally enhanced the number of nodules in chickpea genotypes. Bhanavase and Patil (1994) reported that molybdenum increased nodule numbers, nodule weight plant^{-1} and nitrogen concentration of nodules. Verma *et al.* (1988) observed in their pot experiment that molybdenum at 0.5-2 mg kg^{-1} increases the number of nodules in chickpea *(cv. Radhey)*. Moreover, in the present study the number of nodules were regressed with nitrogen content of plants for both genotypes (Fig. 7.3) and observed as the formation of nodules increases the nitrogen content of plant linearly increased. Generally *Karak-II* genotype showed maximum nodulation and maximum nitrogen uptake compared to *Sheenghar* genotype, but the r^2 value (r^2=0.224) was slightly lower than *Karak-II* genotype (r^2=0.366). These results suggest that the *Sheenghar* genotype utilized more nitrogen than *Karak-II* genotype. Cutcliffe (1986) and Brkics *et al.* (2004) observed same correlation between nodules and plant nitrogen in legumes, who reported that as the nodulation increases the nitrogen content in plants increased and consequently the grain yield increased.

Table 7.9: Effect of molybdenum and iron application on nodules plant^{-1} of chickpea genotypes

Genotypes	Mo (kg ha^{-1})	Fe (kg ha^{-1}) 0	2	5	Mean (V × Mo)
		(V × Mo × Fe)			
Sheenghar	0	35	30	28	31
	0.25	40	43	41	41
	0.5	46	49	44	46
Karak-II	0	30	31	25	29
	0.25	38	47	45	43
	0.5	50	54	48	51
			(Mo × Fe)		(Mo)
	0	33	31	27	30
	0.25	39	45	43	42
	0.5	48	52	46	49
			(V × Fe)		(V × Fe)
Sheenghar		40	40	41	38
Karak-II		39	39	44	39
Mean		40	40	42	39

LSD value of P< 0.05 for Mo = 3.21.
LSD value of P< 0.05 for Fe = 3.21.

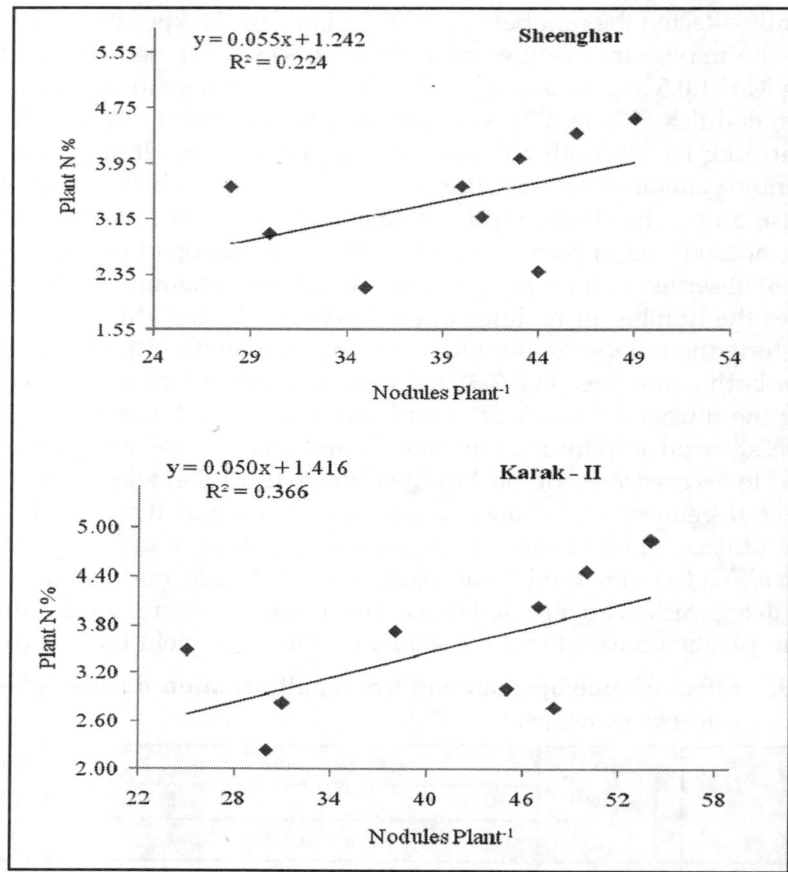

Fig. 7.3: Relationship between nodulation and plant N % in chickpea genotypes

Nutrient Contents in Plant Leaves

N Concentration

At flowering stage plant leaves were analyzed for nitrogen concentration, to obtain that how much nitrogen concentration fixed by plant, which can be used for sowing in the subsequent season. The data obtained on the nitrogen concentration in shoot at maximum biomass stage of chickpea is presented in Table 7.10. Significant differences were found among the different treatments of molybdenum and iron for nitrogen concentration. The maximum nitrogen concentration of 4.60 per cent and 4.84 per cent in shoot biomass of chickpea genotypes were obtained for treatment receiving Mo at 0.5 and Fe at 2 kg ha^{-1} respectively. While, the minimum nitrogen concentration 2.18 per cent and 2.24 per cent were obtained for control, (where no molybdenum and iron were applied) in both genotypes of chickpea. The data showed that no treatment plot was found N-deficient for both chickpea genotypes as the threshold values reported by Westermann (2005) and Kaiser *et al.* (2005). This is good evidence that the leaves of chickpea plant still contain sufficient nitrogen because an adequate amount of nutrient is required for seed germination. Bhanavase and Patil (1994) reported that molybdenum enhance nodule numbers, nodule weight plant^{-1} and nitrogen concentration of nodules. Results further showed that significant differences were found in nitrogen contents for both genotypes and both genotypes increases nitrogen concentration in a similar fashion as the iron concentration increases in plant leaves, suggested iron played a key role in nitrogen fixation by chickpea genotypes. The previous work of Marschner (1995) and Vieira *et al.* (1998) support our result. Furthermore, in the present study plant iron were regressed with nitrogen for both chickpea genotypes (Fig. 7.5) and observed as the plant-Fe increases the N-concentration in plants linearly increased. However, the correlation of the *Karak-II* genotype as compared to *Sheenghar* genotype could not attain statistical significance because of little variation in Fe-content of chickpea leaves. Westermann (2005) and Kaiser *et al.* (2005) observed same relationship between plant iron and nitrogen, who stated that iron played a vital role in the nitrogen fixation by legumes.

Table 7.10: Effect of molybdenum and iron application on N concentration (%) of chickpea genotypes

Genotypes	Mo (kg ha^{-1})	Fe (kg ha^{-1})			Mean (V × Mo)
		0	2	5	
		(V × Mo × Fe)			
Sheenghar	0	2.18	2.95	3.61	2.91
	0.25	3.63	4.04	3.19	3.62
	0.5	4.40	4.61	2.41	3.81
Karak-II	0	2.24	2.83	3.49	2.85
	0.25	3.72	4.04	3.00	3.59
	0.5	4.46	4.84	2.78	4.03
			(Mo × Fe)		(Mo)
	0	2.21	2.89	3.55	2.88
	0.25	3.68	4.04	3.10	3.60
	0.5	4.43	4.73	2.60	3.92
			(V × Fe)		(V × Fe)
Sheenghar		3.40	3.87	3.07	3.07
Karak-II		3.47	3.90	3.09	3.09
Mean		3.44	3.89	3.08	3.08

LSD value of $P < 0.05$ for Fe = 0.48.
LSD value of $P < 0.05$ for Mo = 2.77.
LSD value of $P < 0.05$ for Fe × Genotypes = 0.83.

Iron Concentration

The data obtained on iron concentration in shoot at maximum biomass of chickpea is presented in Table 7.12. Significant differences were observed among the different treatments of molybdenum and iron. In both genotypes the maximum iron concentration was obtained for the treatment which receiving Mo at 0.5 and Fe at 2 kg ha^{-1} which is 248 µg g^{-1} in *Sheenghar* and 276 µg g^{-1} in *Karak-II* genotype respectively. While, the minimum iron concentration was 110 µg g^{-1} and 156 µg g^{-1} were observed in control, (where no molybdenum and iron were applied) in both chickpea genotypes. The iron concentration in plant leaves significantly increased with increasing levels of applied iron and molybdenum in both chickpea genotypes. Results showed that with increasing the levels of molybdenum and iron fertilizers the concentration of iron in plant leaves were also increased may be due to positive interaction between iron and molybdenum within legume plants. Moreover, these results showed that no treatment plot was found Fe-deficient for both chickpea genotypes, as the threshold values suggested by Katyal and Randhawa (1982).

Table 7.12: Effect of molybdenum and iron application on Fe (µg g^{-1}) concentration by chickpea genotypes

Genotypes	Mo (kg ha^{-1})	Fe (kg ha^{-1}) 0	2	5	Mean (V × Mo)
		(V × Mo × Fe)			
Sheenghar	0	110	148	158	139
	0.25	114	180	184	159
	0.5	124	248	212	195
Karak-II	0	156	178	186	173
	0.25	152	220	235	202
	0.5	162	276	272	237
			(Mo × Fe)		(Mo)
	0	133	163	172	156
	0.25	133	200	210	181
	0.5	143	262	242	216
			(V × Fe)		(V × Fe)
Sheenghar		116	180	197	164
Karak-II		157	223	232	204
Mean		136	202	215	

LSD value of $P< 0.05$ for Mo 20.57.

LSD value of $P< 0.05$ for Fe = 20.57.

LSD value of $P< 0.05$ for Mo × Fe = 35.63.

Summary

A field experiment was conducted at Malakandher Farm, The University of Agriculture Peshawar, during November, 2011 to study the effect of molybdenum and iron on the nodulation, nitrogen fixation and yield of two chickpea genotypes, such as: Desi (genotype *Sheenghar*) and Kabuli (genotype *Karak-II*). The chickpea seeds were sown in randomized complete block design with split plot arrangement and replicated 3 times. A plot size was kept 6 m^2. Each plot was comprised of 3 rows containing row to row distance of 30 cm apart and plant to plant distance was of 20 cm. Different levels of molybdenum at the rate of 0, 0.25 and 0.5 and iron at the rate of 0, 2 and 5 kg ha^{-1} was applied in the form of ammonium molybdate and iron sulfate, respectively. A basal dose of 25 N, 60 P_2O_5 and 60 K_2O kg ha^{-1} was applied in the form of urea, di ammonium phosphate and potassium sulfate, respectively before sowing. Before fertilizer application a composite soil sample was collected for the determination of physico-chemical characteristics and desired nutrients status of the test soil. All culture practices were performed when required.

Results showed that the maximum emergence and flowering were recorded in treatment plots where Mo 0.5 and Fe 2 kg ha^{-1} were applied for both chickpea genotypes. While, the minimum emergence and flowering was observed in those plots which received Mo 0 and Fe 0 kg ha^{-1}. Days to emergence and days to flowering data also showed that the emergence rate and number of flowering in molybdenum and iron plots were comparatively better than control plots. Moreover, results revealed that the different treatments of molybdenum and iron varied significantly regarded to days to emergence and number of days to flowering. Results also showed that significant differences were found among various molybdenum and iron treatments for number of pods $plant^{-1}$ and seed pod^{-1}. However, more pods and seeds were found in treatment plot, where Mo 0.5 and Fe 2 kg ha^{-1} were applied for both genotypes and less pods $plant^{-1}$ and seed pod^{-1} were recorded in treatment plot, where Mo 0 and Fe 2 kg ha^{-1} were applied. Results further showed that the performance of *Karak-II* genotype was found better than the *Sheenghar* genotype in terms of pods $plant^{-1}$ and seed pod^{-1} and suggested *Karak-II* genotype is more productive which gave higher yield than *Sheenghar* genotype under the conditions of the experiment. Results also showed that in general, the seeds of *Karak-II* genotype were heavier than the *Sheenghar* genotype of chickpea. Number of nodules has a direct effect on the grain yield of chickpea genotypes. The data showed that molybdenum and iron significantly affected the number of nodules $plant^{-1}$ and seed yield of chickpea compared to control. The maximum number of nodules $plant^{-1}$ and seed yield was obtained for treatment receiving Mo at 0.5 and Fe at 2 kg ha^{-1} in both chickpea genotypes. These results suggested that both micronutrients enhanced the grain yield of chickpea genotypes. The present results suggested that molybdenum has a positive effect on nodules formation in legume genotypes, because Mo-deficient plants result decreased number of nodules and seed yield compared to plots of molybdenum applied to chickpea genotypes. Generally Kabuli genotype (*Karak-II*) showed maximum nodulation and maximum nitrogen uptake compared to *Sheenghar* genotype, but the r^2 value (r^2=0.22) was slightly lower than Kabuli genotype (*Karak-II*) (r^2=0.37). These results suggest that Desi genotype (*Sheenghar*) utilized more nitrogen than (*Karak-II*) genotype. Results showed that significant differences were found among various molybdenum and iron treatments for shoot biomass of chickpea genotypes. However, maximum shoot biomass were found in treatment plot, where Mo 0.5 and Fe 2 kg ha^{-1} were applied for both genotypes, while the minimum shoot biomass were recorded in control (where no molybdenum and iron) were applied for both chickpea genotypes. It showed that both the micronutrients applications have positive effect on the production of shoot biomass.

The maximum nitrogen content and uptake was obtained for treatment receiving Mo at 0.5 and Fe at 2 kg ha^{-1} for both chickpea genotypes. The results suggested that both Mo and Fe increased the nitrogen concentration in shoot of chickpea genotypes. Results further showed that the differences found in nitrogen contents for both genotypes were not very large and both genotypes increases nitrogen concentration. Iron played a key role in nitrogen fixation by chickpea genotypes. In both genotypes the maximum iron concentration and uptake were obtained for the same treatment which receiving Mo at 0.5 and Fe at 2 kg ha^{-1}. Generally Kabuli genotype (*Karak-II*) showed maximum iron and nitrogen uptake compared to Desi genotype (*Sheenghar*), the r^2 value (r^2=0.10) was slightly lower than Kabuli genotype (*Karak-II*) (r^2=0.22). These results suggest that the Kabuli genotype (*Karak-II*) utilized more iron than Desi genotype (*Sheenghar*).

Based on the present findings it is recommend that the application of molybdenum at 0.5 kg ha^{-1} and iron at 2 kg ha^{-1} to chickpea genotypes for better growth performance, more nodulations and adequate nitrogen uptake by legume genotypes.

Conclusion

The following conclusions could be drawn from this study.

- Days to emergence and days to flowering were not significantly affected by the application of molybdenum and iron for both genotypes of chickpea. However, maximum emergence and flowering were recorded in treatment plots where Mo 0.5 and Fe 2 kg ha^{-1} were applied for both chickpea genotypes.

- The grain yield was significantly increased with application of Mo at 0.5 and Fe at 2 kg ha^{-1} for both chickpea genotypes Desi (*Sheenghar)* and Kabuli (*Karak-II)*. It was also noted that Kabuli genotype (*Karak-II)* yielded greater than Desi genotype (*Sheenghar)*.
- Maximum numbers of nodules were obtained in the treatment plots, where Mo 0.5 and Fe 2 kg ha^{-1} were applied for both chickpea genotypes. Generally Kabuli genotype (*Karak-II)* showed more nodulation and more N-uptake compared to Desi genotype (*Sheenghar)*. These results suggest that the *Karak-II* genotype utilized more nitrogen than *Sheenghar* genotype.
- At flowering stage, nitrogen concentration in leaves increased with increasing levels of Mo and Fe in soil in both genotypes, and the differences found in nitrogen contents for both genotypes were not very large and both genotypes increases nitrogen concentration in a similar fashion, suggested iron played a vital role in nitrogen fixation by chickpea genotypes.
- Similarly, the concentration of iron in leaves significantly increased with increasing levels of applied molybdenum and iron in both genotypes of chickpea. Generally, the concentration of iron was found more in chickpea genotype *Karak-II* than *Sheenghar*, indicating *Karak-II* genotype was more efficient than *Sheenghar* in absorbing the iron nutrition.
- The number of nodules were correlated with nitrogen content of plants for both genotypes and found as the nodules formation increases the plant nitrogen concentration linearly increased and showed close relationship with one another. Similarly, the iron uptake increases in plant leaves, nitrogen uptake also increases, indicated that iron played a vital role in nitrogen fixation by chickpea genotypes.
- The overall results suggested that Kabuli genotype (*Karak-II)* had the maximum grain yield, number of nodules and nitrogen uptake as compared to Desi genotype (*Sheenghar)* with the application of Mo 0.5 and Fe 2 kg ha^{-1} under the prevailing conditions of the experiment.

Recommendation

The following recommendations were formulated from the present study.

- Presently 0.5 kg ha^{-1} Mo and 2 kg ha^{-1} Fe is suggested for getting maximum yield, nodulation and nitrogen fixation by chickpea genotypes under the prevailing conditions.
- The suggested levels of molybdenum and iron for maximum yield, nodulation and nitrogen fixation need to be studied on different chickpea genotypes under different ecological conditions of the Khyber Pakhtoon Khwa Province.

REFERENCES

1. Abd. El. Gawad, A.A., D.M. El. Hariri, A.M.A. Abo-Shetaia, and A.A. Bahr. (1993). Yield and Yield Components Responses of Chickpea (*Cicer arietinum* L.) to phosphorus Fertilization and Micronutrients. *Afri. J. Agri. Sci.* 18: 61-71.
2. Abo-Shetaia,. A.M., and A.M. Soheir. (2001). Yield and Yield Components Responses of Chickpea (*Cicer arietinum* L.) to phosphorus Fertilization and Micronutrients. *Arab Univ. J. Agric. Sci.* 9: 235-243.
3. Ali, M., J.P. Mishera, and M. Ali. (2000). Nutrients Management in Pulses and Pulse-based Cropping System. *Fert.* News. 45: 57-69.
4. Anderson, A.J. and D. Spencer. (1999). Molybdenum and Sulphur in Symbiotic Nitrogen Fixation. Bioch.and Biophy. *Res. Commun.* 164:273-274.
5. Bambara, S. and P.A. Ndakidemi. (2010). The Potential Roles of Lime and Molybdenum on the Growth, Nitrogen Fixation and Assimilation of Metabolites in Nodulated Legume: A Special Reference to *Phaseolus vulgaris L. African. J. Biotech.* 8(17): 2482-2489.
6. Benton, J.J. R., B. wolf and H.A. Mills. (1991). Plant Analysis Hand Book. A Practical Sampling, Analysis and Interpretation Guide. Micro publ. Inc. USA.
7. Bhanavase, D.B., and P.L. Patil. (1994). Effect of Molybdenum on Nodulation in Gram. *J. Maharashtra. Agric. Univ.* 19: 127-129.
8. Boto, J. Valenciano and V. Marcelo (2010). Response of Chickpea (*Cicer arietinum* L.) Yield to Zinc, Boron and Molybdenum Application Under pot Conditions *Spanish J. Agric. Res.* 8(3), 797-807.
9. Brikics, S., Z. Milakovic, A. Kristek, M. Antunovic. (2004). Pea Yield and its Quality Depending on Inoculation, Nitrogen and Molybdenum Fertilization. *Plant, Soil and Environ.* 50(1): 39-45.
10. Cottenie, A. (1980). Soil and Plant Testing as a Basis of Fertilizer Recommendations. Food and Agriculture Organization. FAO. *Soil Bull.* 38(2): 64-67.
11. Cutcliffe, J.A. (1986). Effects of Boron, Molybdenum and Lime on Yield and Leaf Tissue Nutrient Concentration of Green Peas. *Can. J. Plant Sci.* 66: 971-976.
12. F.A.O. (1984). Legume Inoculants and their use. FAO., U.N. Rome, Italy, p. 1-63.
13. Gee, G.W. and J.W. Budr. (1982). Particle size Analysis. pp. 383-411. *In:* Methods of Soil Analysis. Physical and Mineralogical Properties. Part 1. Klute, A. (ed) 2nd. Ed. Agron. 9. Am. Soc. Agron. Inc. Wisconsin, USA.
14. Graham RD, Stangoulis JRS (2005). Molybdenum and Disease. In:Mineral Nutrition and Plant Diseases (Dantoff L., Elmer W, Huber D. Eds) St. Paul, MN: APS Press.
15. Hageman R.V., Burris R.H. (1978). Nitrogenase and Nitrogenase Reductase Associate and Dissociate with Each Catalytic Cycle. *Proc. Nat. Acad. Sci.* U.S.A., 75: 2699-2702.
16. Haque, I., R.T. odell, W.M. Walker, and C.S. Kamara. (1979). Micronutrients Cation Survey of Lowland Rice in Syria Leone. *Commun. Soil Sci. Plant Anal.* 10: 981-992.
17. Isaac R. and J.D. Kerber. (1971). Atomic Absorption and Flame Photometry: Techniques and uses in Soil, Plant and Water Analysis. In: Instrumental Methods for Analysis of Soil and Plant Tissue. M. L. Walsh. (ed). Soil Sci. Soc. Am. Madison, WI, USA.

18. Islam, M.A., U.K. Saha, M.S. Islam, and R.R. Saha. (1995). Fertilizing Chickpea for High Yield with Special Emphasis on Boron and Molybdenum in Grey Flood Plain Soils of Bangladesh. *Ann. Bangladesh Agric.* 5: 43-49.
19. Johansen L.M.A. Rondon. J. Ramírez and M. Hurtado. (2007). Biological Nitrogen Fixation by Common Beans (*Phaseolus vulgaris* L.) increases with bio-char additions. *Biol. Fert. Soil.* 43: 699-708.
20. Jongruaysup S., Ohara G.W., Dell B. and Bell R.W. (1993). Effects of Low Molybdenum Seed on Nodule Initiation, Development and N_2 Fixation in Black Gram (*Vigna mungo* L). *Plant-Soil,* 156: 345-348.
21. Kaiser, B.N., K. Gridley, J.N. Brady, T. Phillips and S.D. Tyerman. (2005). The Role of Molybdenum in Agricultural Plant Production. *J. Sci. Annals of Botany* 96(5): 745-754.
22. Katyal, J. and N. S. Randhawa. (1983). Micronutrients. FAO. Fertilizer and Plant Nutrition, Bulletin No. 7. United Nation.
23. Kevresan, S.M. Popovic and J. Kandrac. (2001). Nitrogen and Protein Metabolism in Young pea Plants as Affected by different Concentrations of Nickel, Cadmium, Lead and Molybdenum. *J. Plant Nutr.* 24: 1633-1644.
24. Kim, J. and D.C. Rees. (1992). Structural Models for the Metal Centers in the Nitrogenase Molybdenum-Iron Protein. Chemistry and Chemical Engineering, California Institute of Technology, Pasadena. 257 (5077):1677-1682.
25. Kothari M.L. (2002). Effect of Modes and Levels of Molybdenum Application on Grain Yield Protein Content and Nodulation of Chickpea Grown on loamy Sand Soil. *Commu. Soil Sci. Plant Anal.* 33(15): 18-23.
26. Kumpawat, B.S., and S. Manohar. (1994). Effect of *Rhizobium* Inoculation, Phosphorus and Micronutrients on Nodulation and Protein Content of Gram. *Madras Agric. J.* 81: 630-631.
27. Landge, S.K., S.U. Kakade, P.D. Thakare., A.P. Karunakar and D.J. Jiotode. (2002). Response of Soybean to Nitrogen and Phosphorus. *Pak. J. Genotypes Sci.* 3(3): 653-655.
28. Mahavir Singh, S.K. Chaudhary, S.R. Sharma and M.S. Rathore (2004). Effect of some Micronutrients on Content and uptake by Chickpea *(Cicer arletinum) Agric. Sci. Digest,* 24 (4): 268-270.
29. Marschner, H., M. Haussling and E. George. (1995). Ammonium and Nitrate Uptake Rates and Rhizosphere pH in Non-mycorrhizal Roots of Norway Spruce (*Picea abies* L.) *Karst.* Trees. 5:14-21.
30. McLean, E.O. (1982). Soil pH and Lime Requirement. pp. 199-224. *In:* Methods of Soil Analysis. Physical and Mineralogical Properties. Part 2. Page, A. L., M. H. Miller and D. R. Keeny. (eds.) 2nd. Ed. Am. Soc. Agron. Inc. Madison, WI, USA.
31. Meagher,W.R., M. Johnson and P.R. Stout. (1991). Molybdenum Requirement of Leguminous Plants Supplied with Fixed Nitrogen. *Plant Physiol.* 27(2): 623-629.
32. Mulvaney, R.L. and H.M. Brown. (1996). A Soil Organic Nitrogen Fraction that Reduces the need for Nitrogen Fertilization. *Soil Sci. Soc. Am. J.* 65: 1164-1172.
33. Nautiyal N., S. Singh and C. Chatterjee. (2005). Seed Reserves of Chickpea in Relation to Molybdenum Supply. *J. Sci. Food Agric.* 85:860-864.

34. Nelson, D.W. and L.E. Sommers. (1996). Total Carbon, Organic Carbon and Organic Matter. pp. 961-1010. *In:* Methods of Soil Analysis Part 3. Sparks, D. L. (ed) Soil Sci. Soc. Am. Inc. Book Series No. 5. Madison, Wisconsin, USA.

35. Nenova, V. (2006). Effect of Iron Supply on Growth and Photosystem and Efficiency of Pea Plants. *Gen. Appl. Plant Physiol.* Special Issue. 81-90.

36. Rabbani M.G., A.R. Solaiman, K.M. Hossain and T. Hossain. (2005). Effects of *Rhizobium* Inoculant, Nitrogen, Phosphorus and Molybdenum on Nodulation, Yield and Seed Protein in pea. Kor. *J. Genotypes Sci.* 50(2): 112-119.

37. Rhoades, J.D. (1982). Cation Exchange Capacity. pp. 149-157. In: Methods of Soil Analysis. Physical and Mineralogical Properties. Part 2. Page, A. L. M. H.Miller and D. R. Keeny. (eds.) 2nd. Ed. Am. Soc. Agron. Inc. Madison, WI, USA.

38. Rondon, M. A., J. Lehmann, J. Ramírez and M. Hurtado. (2007). Biological Nitrogen Fixation by Common Beans (*Phaseolus vulgaris* L.) increases with biochar additions Biol. Fert. Soils 43:699-708.

39. Saraie, J.M. Kitagawa, A. Shinohara and T. Tanaka. (1983). Heteroepitaxial Growth of $ZnSO_4$ by a Close-spaced Technique: Incorporation and Morphology. *J. Crystal Growth.* 63(2): 321-336.

40. Sarawgi, S. K. P.K . Tiwari and R.S Tripathi. (2000). Growth, Nodulation and Yield of Chickpea as Influenced Phosphorus. Bacterial Culture and Micronutrients under Rainfed Condition. *Madras Agric. J.* 86: 181-185.

41. Srivastava, S.N.L. and S.C. Varma. (1985). Effect of Nitrogen, Phosphorus and Molybdenum Fertilization on Growth, Nodulation and Residual Fertility in Field pea. *Ind. J. Agric. Res.* 19(3): 131-137.

42. Sawires, E.S. (2001). Effect of Phosphorus Fertilization and Micronutrients on Yield and Yield Components of Chickpea (*Cicer arietinum.*) *Ann. Agric. Sci. Cairo.* 46: 155-164.

43. Schwenke, G.D., M.B. Peoples, G.L. Turner, and D.F Her Ridge. (1998). Doses Nitrogen Fixation of Commercial, Dryland Chickpea and Faba Bean Genotypess in North West New South Wales Maintain or Enhance Soil Nitrogen. *Aust. J .Exp. Agric.* 38: 61-70.

44. Shah, Z., S.H . Shah, M. Aslam, S. Ali, D.F. Herridge, M.B. Peoples, and M. T. Jan. (1998). Pakistan's Agriculture Cereal and Legume Production. *J. Univ. Wales* 75: 89-97.

45. Shil, S. Noor And M.A. Hossain (2007). Effects of Boron and Molybdenum on the Yield of Chickpea, *J. Agric Rural Dev* 5(1&2*)*, 17-24.

46. Singh,V., G.P. Singh, and V. Singh. (1994). Effect of Applied Potassium and Molybdenum on Yield and Composition of Chickpea. *J. Potassium. Res.* 10: 411-414.

47. Srivastava, S.N.L. and S.C. Varma. (1995). Effect of Nitrogen, Phosphorus and Molybdenum Fertilization on Growth, Nodulation and Residual Fertility in Field pea. *Ind. J. Agric. Res.* 19(3): 131-137.

48. Steel, R.G.D., Torrie J.H. and Dickey, D.A. (1997). Principle and Procedure of Statistics. A Biometrical Approach. 3rd. (ed). McGraw Hill Companies, Inc. New York, USA.

49. Tahir, M., A. Ali, N. Aabidin, M. Yaseen and H. Rehman. (2011). Effect of Molybdenum and Seed Inoculation on Growth, Yield and Quality of Mungbean. *Genotypes and Environment*. 2(2): 37-40.

50. Truong, H.H. and C. Duthion. (1993). Time of Flowering of Pea (*PisumSatirum* L.) as a Function of Leaf Appearance Rate and Node of Flower. *Ann. Botany*. 72: 133-142.

51. Valenciano, J.A. Boto and V. Marcelo (2010). Response of Chickpea (*Cicer arietinum* L.) Yield to Zinc, Boron and Molybdenum Application under Pot Conditions Spanish *J. Agric. Res.* 8(3), 797-807.

52. Verma, L.P., P.C. Ram, and B.R. Maurya. (1988). Response of Chickpea to Phosphorus and Molybdenum of Eastern Uttar Pradesh, India. *Int. Chickpea Newsletter*. 18, 31-33. www.iosrjournals.org

53. Vieira, R.F., E.J. Cardoso, and C. Cassini. (1998). Foliar Application of Molybdenum in Common Beans. I. Nitrogenase and Reductase Activities in a Soil of High Fertility. *J. Plant Nutr.* 21:169-180.

54. Walsh, L.M and J.D. Beaton. (1977). Soil Testing and Plant Analysis. Soil Sci. Soc. Am. Inc. Madison, USA.

55. Wankhade, .S.G., R.C. Dakhore, S.S. Wanjari, D.B. Patil, N.R. Potdukhe, and R.W. Ingle. (1996). Response of Genotypess to Micronutrients. *Ind. J. Agric. Res.* 3: 164-168.

56. Westermann. D.T. (2005). Nutritional Requirements of Potatoes. *Am. J. Potato Res.* 82: 301-307.

57. Williams R.J.P., Frausto da Silva J.J.R. (2002). The Involvement of Molybdenum in Life. Bioch and Biophy. Res. Commun.292: 293-299.

58. Wolfe, M. (1994). The Effect of Molybdenum upon the Nitrogen Metabolism of *Anabaena cylindrica.* Ann. Bot. 18 (3): 309-325.

59. Zahid, M.A., A. Rashid, and J. Din. (2000). Balanced Nutrient Management in Chickpea. *Int. Chickpea and Pigeon Pea Newsletter*. 7: 24-26.

60. Zaman, M. Abdul Mazid and Golam Kabir (2011). Effect of Rhizobium Inoculant on Nodulation, Yield and Yield Traits of Chickpea (*Cicer arietinum* L.) in Four Different Soils of Greater Rajshahi *J. Life Earth Sci.,* Vol. 6: 45-50.

61. Zaroug, and N. Munns. (1997). Nodulation, Nitrogen Fixation, Leaf Area, and Sugar Content in *Lablab Purpureus* as Affected by Sulfur Nutrition by Plant and Soil. *Ann. Botany*. 53: 319-32.

Pages 100-103

INTEGRATED NUTRIENT MANAGEMENT IN CHICKPEA
Edited by **: Dr. Virendra Kumar** and **Dr. Nirmal Kumar Katiyar**
Edition **: 2017**
ISBN : 978-93-5056-872-9
Published by **: Discovery Publishing House Pvt. Ltd., New Delhi (India)**

Response of Chickpea to Levels of Zinc and Phosphorus

Anil Kumar Sharma
B.P.S. Raghubanshi
Pawan Sirothia

Chickpea (*Cicer arietinum* L.) is the major pulse crop of India. At global level, it ranks fifth in terms of area and production under legumes. It is grown with less care and less manurial requirement. Application of phosphorus and zinc are increased the pulse production. The response of phosphorus and zinc depends upon many factors like: climate, variety and soil type, pH, nutrient availability etc., during the growth. The requirement of phosphorus in leguminous crop like: chickpea is higher than other crops for their root development and metabolic activities. In recent years, zinc deficiency has been aggravated in Indian soils due to tremendous increase in cropping intensity and adoption of cultivation of high yielding varieties. Zinc is essential for promoting certain metabolic reactions. It is necessary for the production of chlorophyll and carbohydrates. Zinc is directly or indirectly required by several enzyme systems, auxin and protein synthesis. Zinc is believed to promote RNA sysnthesis, which in turn is needed for protein production. At several places normal yield of crops could not be achieved despite judicious use of NPK fertilizers due to deficiency of micronutrients in soil, in general, that of Zn in particular. A favourable balance between phosphorus and zinc should be maintained for optimum growth of plant. The information on Zn and P relationship in an important crop like: chickpea is not adequate; especially in situations where both the interacting nutrients

Deparment of Soil Science, M.G.C.G.V.V., Chirakoot (Satna) M.P. 485 331.

(P and Zn) are deficient is soil. Hence, the present investigation was conducted to study the effect of zinc and phosphorus on growth, yield, uptake and quality of chickpea crop.

A field experiment was conducted during *rabi* 2010-11 at M.G.C.G.V.V. farm, Chirakoot (M.P.). The experimental soil was sandy clay-loam in texture and laid out in factorial randomized design replicated three times. The treatment comprises 4 levels of zinc [0, 10, 20 and 30 kg Zn So_4 ha^{-1}] and five levels of phosphorus [0, 25, 40, 55 and 70 kg P ha^{-1}]. The experimental soil was sandy clay loam in texture, slightly alkaline in reaction, having electrical conductivity 0.3 dS/m at 25°C. Soils were poor in available nitrogen (168 kg ha^{-1}), phosphorus (20 kg ha^{-1}), rich in available potash (370 kg ha^{-1}), DTPA Zn (0.45 mg ha^{-1}) and organic carbon (0.45%). Before and after experiment, the soils samples were collected and analyzed for pH, electrical conductivity, and organic carbon, available N, P_2O_5, K_2O and DTPA-Zn were analyzed. After harvest of crop yield were recorded and uptake of zinc and phosphorus were determined. Protein content in seed was also determined as per standard procedure.

Table 8.1: Growth, yield, and quality of chickpea as affected by levels of zinc and phoaphorus

Treaments	Growth Characters			Yield Attributes		Yield (q ha^{-1})		Protein Content (%)
	Plant Height (cm)	Primary Branches/ Plant	Secondary Branches/ Plant	Pods/ Plant	Test Weight (g)	Seed	Straw	
Zinc sulphate (kg ha^{-1})								
0	44.9	7.5	25.7	62.9	15.0	18.0	33.2	20.7
10	46.4	7.7	26.5	65.0	15.5	18.6	34.3	21.3
20	47.9	8.0	27.4	67.0	16.0	19.2	35.4	22.0
30	48.7	8.1	27.8	68.2	16.2	19.5	36.0	22.4
CD (P=0.05)	1.22	0.21	0.68	1.71	0.41	0.49	0.89	0.57
Phosphorus (kg ha^{-1})								
0	44.3	7.4	25.3	62.1	14.8	17.7	32.8	20.4
25	45.9	7.6	26.2	64.2	15.3	18.3	33.9	21.1
40	47.2	7.9	26.9	66.0	15.7	18.9	34.9	21.7
55	48.4	8.1	27.6	67.7	16.1	19.4	35.8	22.3
70	49.2	8.2	28.1	68.8	16.4	19.7	36.4	22.6
CD (P=0.05)	1.17	0.58	0.67	1.64	0.39	0.47	0.87	0.53

Yield and growth characters like: plant height, primary and secondary branches/plant, pods/plant, test weight and seed and straw yield of chickpea were significantly influenced by the dose of zinc and phosphorus. Increasing dose of zinc increases the growth and yield characters up to 30 kg Zn So_4 ha^{-1}. However, significant response was noted up to 20 kg Zn So_4 ha^{-1}. Similarly, application of phosphorus increases the characters up to 70 kg P_20_5 ha^{-1} but the significant response was noted up to 55 kg ha^{-1}. There was no significant difference between 20 and 30 kg zinc sulphate ha^{-1} and 70 and 55 kg P_20_5 ha^{-1} (Table 8.1). It might be the due to supply of both nutrient in soil and their synegestic effect on other nutrients increases the yield and growth character. The results confirm the findings of Pathak *et al.* (2003) and Karwasra and Kumar (2007).

Quality

Protein content was significantly influenced by different doses of zinc and phosphorus (Table 8.1). Highest protein content was recorded at with 30 kg Zn ha^{-1} but it was at par with 20 kg Zn ha^{-1}. Similarly, highest protein content was recorded under 70 kg P ha^{-1} and it was at par with 55 kg P ha^{-1}. The beneficial effect of zinc and phosphorus levels on protein content may be due to the increase in cation exchange capacity of the roots which would enable to plant extracts more nutrients from soil. Pathak *et al.* (2003) reported similar findings.

Table 8.2: Nutrient uptake by crop and status of plants Zn in soil as affected by different levels of zinc and phosphorus

Treaments	Zinc Uptake (g ha^{-1})	Phosphorus Uptake (kg ha^{-1})	Available Zinc (mg kg-1)	Available P_2O_5 (mg kg^{-1})	B:C ratio
Zinc Sulphate (kg ha^{-1})					
0	52.7	23.8	0.38	21.4	5.3
10	56.3	25.4	0.40	20.4	5.5
20	59.9	27.1	0.43	19.4	6.5
30	61.9	28.0	0.45	18.9	6.6I
CD (P=0.05)	2.98	1.35	0.024	0.85	–
Phosphorus (kg ha^{-1})					
0	57.1	23.2	0.47	18.1	5.5
25	58.1	24.8	0.44	19.1	5.7
40	58.2	26.2	0.41	20.1	6.4
55	58.1	27.6	0:39	21.1	6.5
70	57.1	28.5	0.37	21.6	6.6
CD (P=0.05)	NS	1.29	0.025	0.81	-

Uptake of zinc and phosphorus significantly influenced by different zinc and phosphorus (Table 8.2). Increasing dose of zinc significantly increases the uptake of zinc by chickpea crop. It is well establish fact that the application of zinc in soil increases the uptake of zinc by plants. It is well established fact that the Zn present in water soluble, exchangeable and complexed fractions contributed maximum to the plant uptake. Results confirm the finding of Akay (2011). Uptake of zinc is not influenced by the increasing dose of phosphorus. It may be due to the fact that zinc had antagonistic effect with phoaphorus. Increasing dose of zinc increases the uptake of phosphorus. It may be due to inspite of antagonistic efeect higher yield iof chickpea increases the uptake of phosphorus. Phosphorus uptake increases with increasing level of phosporus. It is well establish fact that the application of P_2O_5 in soil increases the uptake of P by plants. Tomar and Tiwari (2005) also reported that application of P_2O_5 significantly increased uptake of phosphorus. Increasing dose of nitrogen increases the DTPA – Zn of Soil. However, it was decreases with increase in available phosphorus conent. On the other hand, available phosphorus has antagonistic effect with zinc. Highest build-up of Zinc was observed under 30 kg Zn So4 ha^{-1} and 0 kg P_2O_5 ha^{-1}. Phosphorus build-up was recorded contrary to the zinc. Increasing dose of either zinc or phosphorus increases the benefic coat ration of chickpea. Zinc beyond 20 kg ha^{-1} and phosphorus beyond 40 kg ha^{-1} given high B:C ratio. The result confirms the finding of Singh *et al.* (2005) and Deshmukh *et al.* (2005). The highiest seed, straw yield and protein content of chickpea was recorded due to application of Zn So_4 @ 30 kg ha^{-1} and P_2O_5 @ 70 kg ha^{-1} but the significient response was up to Zn So_4 @20 kg ha^{-1} and P_2O_5 55 kg ha^{-1}. The maximum gross return, net return and B:C Ratio were highest under 30 kg ha^{-1} and 70 kh ha^{-1}.

REFERENCES

Akay, A. (2011). 'Effect of Zinc Fertilizer Applications on Yield and Element Contents of some Registered Chickpeas Varieties' *African Journal of Biotechnology* 10 (61): 13090-13096.

Karwasra, R.S. and Kumar, Anil (2007). Effect of Phosphorus and Zinc Application on Growth, Biomass and Nutrient Uptake by Chickpea in Calcareous Soils, *Haryana Journal of Agronomy* 23: 111-112.

Pathak, Satyajit, Namdeo, K.N., Chakrawarti, V.K. and Tiwari, R.K. (2003). 'Effect of Biofertilizers, Diammonium Phosphate and Zinc Sulphate on Growth and Yield of Chickpea (*Cicer arietinum* L.)' Crop Research 26 (1): 42-46.

Tomar, S.S. and Tiwari, R.J. (2005). 'Response of Mustard Varieties to Fertility Levels under Normal Sown Condition' *Research on Crop Journal* 6: 214-216.

Singh, A.K., Bhagwan Singh and Singh, H.C. (2005). Response of Chickpea (*Cicer arietinum* L.) to Fertilizer Phosphorus and Zinc Application under Rainfed Condition of Eastern Uttar Pradesh, *Indian Journal of Dryland Agricultural Research and Development* 20: 114-117.

Pages 104-111

INTEGRATED NUTRIENT MANAGEMENT IN CHICKPEA
***Edited by* : Dr. Virendra Kumar** and **Dr. Nirmal Kumar Katiyar**
***Edition* : 2017**
ISBN : 978-93-5056-872-9
***Published by* : Discovery Publishing House Pvt. Ltd., New Delhi (India)**

Effect of Dual Bio-inoculants on Growth, Yield, Economics and Uptake of Nutrients in Chickpea Genotypes

Pavan Kumar Raj, S.B. Singh
K.N. Namdeo*, Yogendra Singh, S.S. Parihar
Manoj Kumar Ahirwar

ABSTRACT

A field experiment was conducted during winter seasons of 2009-10 and 2010-11 Rewa (M.P.) to study the effect of dual bio-inoculants on growth, yield, economics and uptake of nutrients in chickpea genotypes. Amongst the chickpea genotypes, JG-130 gave maximum grain (27.04 q ha^{-1}) and straw yield (31.89 q ha^{-1}) with the net income of '. 92756 ha^{-1} followed by JG-11 and Vijay. However, the grain protein was highest (24.3%) in Vijay genotype. Amongst the bio-inoculants, Rhizobium + phosphorus-solubilizing bacteria (PSB) recorded the highest grain (30.44 q ha^{-1}), straw (34.99 q ha^{-1}) yield and grain protein (24.4%) with the highest net income of '.108079 ha^{-1}. The second best treatment was Rhizobium + Azotobacter. The yield and net income were further augmented when JG-130 was grown with Rhizobium + PSB. The uptake of N, P, K and S was significantly higher in grain and straw of JG-130 over JG-11 and Vijay. The nutrients uptake by grain and straw was significantly higher due to Rhizobium + PSB over the single bio-inoculants. The highest total nutrients uptake by chickpea, due to Rhizobium + PSB, was 151.4 kg N, 18.0 kg P, 71.9 kg K and 18.1 kg S ha^{-1}.

Keywords: Chickpea Genotypes, Dual Bio-inoculants, Growth, Yield, Economics Nutrients Uptake.

Department of Botany, Government P.G. Science College, Rewa - 486 001 (M.P.) India.

INTRODUCTION

Chickpea is one of the important pulse crop of Madhya Pradesh where serious efforts are being made to economize the productivity by growing recently developed well-promising varieties. Dual inoculation of bio-inoculants in legumes not only reduces the input of chemical fertilizers but also reduces the cost of the system itself in terms of photosynthetic drain. Positive effect of phosphorus-solubilizing bacteria (PSB) and plant growth promoting rhizobacteria (PGPR) on legume *Rhizobium* symbiosis is well documented for effective nodulation (Sarna *et al.* 2008). Phosphorus is released in soil from inorganic compound due to local accumulation of lactic acid and action of H_2S developed by microbial metabolism. These organisms are known to produce amino acid, vitamins, growth promoting substances like: IAA and gibberelic acid which helps better growth and yield. The combined inoculation increases the yield which may be due to the antagonistic interaction of PGPR with various soil borne pathogens or due to production of metabolites for plant growth by increasing nutrient ability which is reflected in grain yield. The non-symbiotic *Azotobacter sp.*, provides positive influence on nodulation and N_2 fixing efficiency of *Rhizobium* in legumes (Sarna *et al.* 2008). The beneficial effects of *A. chroococcum* are attributed to production of plant growth hormones, improved nutrient uptake and antagonistic effect on plant pathogens (Parmar and Dadarwal, 1997). Due to fertility variations in different soil types, the response of a certain chickpea genotype to different microbial sources of nutrients is highly inconsistent, location and even site specific. Since very little information is available on these aspects, the present research work was carried out using chickpea genotypes.

Materials and Methods

A field experiment was conducted during *rabi* seasons of 2009-10 and 2010-11 at the Agriculture-cum-Research Farm, Beenda-Semariya Road, Rewa (M.P.). The soil of the experimental field was clay-loam having pH 7.1, electrical conductivity 0.23 dS m^{-1}, organic carbon 5.8 g kg^{-1}, available N 248 kg ha^{-1}, available P_2O_5 14.1 kg ha^{-1}, available K_2O and 404 kg ha^{-1} and available S 13.0 kg ha^{-1}. The rainfall received during the winter months was 78.8 and 101.8 mm in 2009-10 and 1010-11. The treatments comprised three chickpea genotypes (JG-11, JG-130 and Vijay) in main plots and six bioinoculant treatments (control, *Rhizobium, Azotobacter,* phosphate-solubilizng bacteria (PSB), Rhiz. + Azoto. and Rhiz. + PSB) in the sub-plots. The experiment was laid out in split-plot design with three replications. Chickpea genotypes were sown on 16 October, 2009 and 24 October, 2010 @ 80 kg seed/ha at 30 cm row spacing. A uniform dose of 20 kg N and 50 kg P_2O_5 ha^{-1} was applied through diammonium phosphate and 20 kg S ha^{-1} through elemental sulphur as basal dose in all the treatments. Before sowing, the seed were inoculated with Rhizobium or Azotobacter biofertilizer using 20 g/kg seed, and during sowing PSB (phosphate-solubilizing bacteria) was applied in the same furrows @ 20 g/kg seed mixed with FYM as per treatments. The crop was grown as per recommended package of practices. The crop was harvested on 20 March, 2010 and 28 March, 2011. The chlorophyll content in leaves was estimated at 60 days stage by acetone extraction method (Witham *et al.* 1971). The nitrogen content in grain was determined by Kjeldahl method (Jackson, 1973). The protein content in grain was obtained by multiplying the per cent N content in grain with 6.25. Grain and straw were digested in diacid (HNO_3 and $HClO_4$) mixture for estimation of P, K and S. Phosphorus was determined by molybdovanadate yellow colour method, K by flame photometer and S by turbidimetric method. The nutrients uptake was calculated by multiplying the grain or straw yield with the per cent nutrient content in grain or straw.

Results and Discussion

Nodulation and Physiological Parameters

Amongst the chickpea genotypes, JG-130 recorded significantly higher root nodulation, dry matter production and chlorophyll content in leaves. This may be due to rapid plant growth and development of new leaves which proved photosynthetically more active. Thus, the increased photosynthetic surface (leaf area) induced competition for light and shadding of leaves. The significant differences in physiological parameters in different genotypes might be owing to their genetic variability (Rajput *et al.* 2004). It is a natural phenomenon that the chlorophyll content in leaf tissue varies with species, age of plants and growth seasons. Increase in chlorophyll content with age of plants may be due to high magnesium and protein contents of leaves (Srivastava *et al.* 2012).

The dual inoculation of Rhizobia plus P-solubilizing bacteria resulted in significantly higher root-nodulation (25.6 nodules/plant) and chlorophyll content (0.277 mg g^{-1} leaf weight) in leaves. The second best mixed inoculation was *Rhizobium* plus *Azotobacter* which appeared to have supplemented the growing plants with fixed N only as well as growth promoting substances. Positive effect of PSB and PGRP on legume *Rhizobium* symbiosis is well documented in early events of nodulation (Sarna *et al.* 2008). The maximum chlorophyll content after multiple inoculation with R+Az+PGPR, was recorded followed by dual inoculation with R+Az Srinivasan *et al.* (1985) has reported a positive and significant correlation between photosynthesis and nitrogen fixation.

Table 9.1: Root nodulation, chlorophyll content and yield parameters of chickpea as influenced by genotypes and bio-inoculants (Pooled for 2 years)

Treatments	Root Nodules/ Plant at 50 DAS	Dry Weight of Root Nodules /Plant (g)	Dry Matter/ Plant at 50 DAS (g)	Chlorophyll Content (mg/g Leaf Weight) (95 DAS)	Pods/ Plant	Seeds/ Pod	1000-seed weight (g)
Genotypes							
JG-11	23.7	0.47	1.59	0.15	60.6	1.1	260.5
JG-130	24.0	0.50	1.71	0.29	64.8	1.2	277.5
Vijay	17.0	0.48	1.62	0.228\	56.9	1.1	238.6
CD (P=0.05)	2.00	NS	0.11	0.04	2.34	0.019	1.64
Bio-inoculants							
Control	17.9	0.39	1.47	0.18	35.1	1.0	236.8
Rhizobium	20.4	0.51	1.63	0.21	56.9	1.2	262.5
Azotobacter	23.0	0.43	1055	0.20	60.6	1.1	252.6
PSB	20.9	0.45	1.62	0.22	62.9	1.1	259.1
Rhiz. + Azoto.	21.5	0.52	1.70	0.24	68.4	1.2	267.4
Rhiz. + PSB	25.6	0.59	1.84	0.27	80.7	1.3	274.7
CD (P=0.05)	1.07	0.02	0.11	0.03	1.34	0.015	1.08

Yield-Attributes and Yield

The number of pods/plant, seeds/pod, 1000-seed weight and seed weight/plant were augmented significantly in JG-130 over other genotypes. The higher yield attributes of JG-130 may be owing to maximum increase in dry matter production as well as chlorophyll contents in leaves. The variation in these parameters among the genotypes is mainly due to the fact that such parameters are genetically governed (Shrivastava *et al.* 2000; and Singh *et al.* 2004). The grain yield was significantly higher (27.04 q ha^{-1}) in JG-130 over the remaining genotypes which may be due to higher yield attributes of this genotype. The productivity parameters are based on the cumulative effect of the genetic ability and production efficiency of the genotypes, their fertility management and the agro-climatic conditions. The best performance of JG-130 over others might be ascribed to its physiological role in synthesis and partitioning of the biomass (Patel *et al.* 2012). The mixed inoculation of *Rhizobium* + PSB resulted in significant rise in all the yield-attributes over the other treatments. However, the second best treatment was *Rhizobium* + *Azotobacter*. The higher yield attributes under these treatments might be due to increased growth and chlorophyll content in leaves as a result of increased microbial population and their biochemical activities as well as improved biological properties of the soil. All these favourable situations eventually brought about greater accumulation of carbohydrates, proteins and their translocation to the reproductive organs which in turn increased the yield components. Consequently the yield parameters were also found in the higher range in the above mentioned mixed bioinoculant treatments. These results are in close agreement with those of Verma *et al.* (2000), Tomar *et al.* (2001) and Zaidi *et al.* (2003).

Table 9.2: Yield and quality parameters and economical gain from chickpea as influenced by genotypes and bio-inoculants (Pooled for 2 years)

Treatments	Grain Yield (q ha^{-1})	Straw Yield (q ha^{-1})	Harvest Index (%)	Net Income ('. ha^{-1})	B:C ratio	Grain Protein Content (%) (kg ha^{-1})	Protein Yield
Genotypes							
JG-11	24.06	30.02	44.59	79249	3.56	23.66	570.5
JG-130	27.04	31.89	45.85	92756	4.01	23.60	'640.0
Vijay	23.26	28.83	44.73	75574	3.44	24.36	567.3
CD (P=0.05)	0.28	0.30	NS	–	–	0.15	7.2
Bio-inoculants							
Control	19.73	23.54	45.67	60175	3.00	23.41	461.2
Rhizobium	24.81	29.74	45.54	82429	3.66	23.79	590.0
Azotobacter	23.37	29.66	44.05	75967	3.45	23.84	557.5
PSB	22.95	30.43	43.13	74108	3.39	23.57	540.4
Rhiz. + Azoto.	27.42	33.12	45.39	94400	4.05	24.16	662.1
Rhiz. + PSB	30.44	34.99	46.57	108079	4.48	24.47	744.5
CD (P=0.05)	0.23	0.24	1.21	–	–	0.14	6.2

Grain Quality and Net Income

Amongst the genotypes, Vijay recorded significantly higher grain protein (24.36%), however the protein yield and net income were found highest from JG-130 (640 kg ha^{-1} and Rs. 92756 ha^{-1}, respectively). The higher grain protein in Vijay may be owing to the increased synthesis of protein through amino acids as a result of N-metabolism (Dwivedi and Bapat, 1998). The higher protein yield from JG-130 was due to its increased productivity. Similarly the highest net income was owing to the highest grain yield. Amongst the bio-inoculant treatments, *Rhizobium* + PSB recorded significantly higher grain protein (24.47%), protein yield (774.5 kg ha^{-1}) as well as net income (Rs. 108079 ha^{-1}, followed by *Rhizobium* + *Azotobacter*. The response of dual biofertilizers in improving seed quality may be attributed to their significant role in regulating the photosynthesis, root enlargement and better microbial activities.

Uptake of Nutrients

The uptake of N, P, K and S was, in general, higher in chickpea grain than in straw (Table 9.3). The nutrients uptake was significantly higher in

JG-130, whereas lower uptake in case of JG-11 and Vijay genotypes. The significant variation in nutrients uptake by genotypes was in accordance with the similar variations in their nutrient content and grain yield. The leading role of JG-130 may be due to the fact that the larger part of these nutrients absorbed by the plant would have migrated into the seeds (Tiwari *et al.* 2006). The impact of *Rhizobium* + PSB increased the nutrients uptake by chickpea biomass significantly over the remaining treatments. However, the second best treatment was *Rhizobium* + *Azotobacter*. *Rhizobium* + PSB producing a total removed of 151.43 kg N, 17.96 kg P, 71.91 kg K and 18.14 kg S ha^{-1}. The higher uptake of nutrients under different treatments might be owing to increased total biomass in these treatments. These results corroborate with those of Pathak *et al.* (2003), Singh *et al.* (2004), Sharma *et al.* (2006) and Singh *et al.* (2008). Under the present day of heavy crises of costly chemical fertilizers and deteriorating soil health, the addition of eco-friendly, renewable and cheaper biofertilizers would go a long way in bringing out efficient and economical utilization of chemical fertilizers. Chickpea var. JG-130 grown with *Rhizobium* + PSB recorded maximum grain yield and net income.

Table 9.3: Nutrient uptake of chickpea as influenced by genotypes and bio-inoculants (Pooled for 2 years)

Treatments	Nitrogen (kg ha^{-1})		Phosphorus (kg ha^{-1})		Potassium (kg ha^{-1})		Sulphur (kg ha^{-1})	
	Grain	Straw	Grain	Straw	Grain	Straw	Grain	Straw
Genotypes								
JG-11	91.9	25.9	9.9	3.6	29.2	27.9	7.6	6.0
JG-130	102.4	28.3	11.5	4.1	33.3	30.1	9.0	6.8
Vijay	90.7	25.3	9.6	3.6	28.2	26.6	7.6	5.9
CD (P=0.05)	1.07	0.80	0.61	0.14	0.47	0.32	0.16	0.11
Bio-inoculants								
Control	73.8	19.9	7.7	2.5	22.5	21.4	6.0	4.2
Rhizobium	94.4	25.6	9.8	3.6	29.6	27.4	7.8	6.1
Azotobacter	90.4	25.6	9.7	3.7	28.5	27.5	7.6	5.7
PSB	86.5	26.5	9.8	3.9	28.0	28.3	7.5	6.4
Rhiz. + Azoto.	105.9	29.3	11.5	4.2	34.1	31.2	9.1	7.2
Rhiz. + PSB	119.1	32.3	13.3	4.7	38.6	33.3	10.3	7.8
CD (P=0.05)	1.01	0.64	0.48	0.12	0.37	0.28	0.14	0.12

REFERENCES

Jackson, M.L. (1973). *Soil Chemical Analysis*, Prentica Hall of India Pvt. Ltd., New Delhi.

Khurana, A.S. and Sharma, Poonam (2000). Effect of Dual Inoculation of Phosphate-solubilizing Bacteria, *Bradyrhizobium sp.* (*Cicer*) and Phosphorus on Nitrogen Fixation and Yield of Chickpea. *Indian Journal of Pulses Research*, 13: 66-67.

Patel, M.P., Richhariya, G.P., Sharma, R.D. and Namdeo, K.N. (2012). Effect of Fertility Levels on Nutrient Contents and Uptake of Soybean Genotypes. *Crop Research*, 44: 71-74.

Parmar, N. and Dadarwal, K.R. (1997). Rhizobacteria from the Rhizosphere and Rhizoplane of Chickpea (*Cicer arietinum* L.). *Indian Journal of Microbiology*, 37: 205-10.

Pathak, Satyajit, Namdeo, K.N., Chakravarti, V.K. and Tiwari, R.K. (2003). Effect of Biofertilizers, Diammonium Phosphate and Zinc Sulphate on Growth and Yield of Chickpea. *Crop Research*, 26: 42-46.

Rajput, B.S., Mathur, C.M. and Sonakiya, V.K. (2004). Physiological Studies on Advanced Generation Short Duration Deshi Chickpea (*Cicer arietinum* L.) genotypes. *Advances of Plant Science*, 17: 513-517.

Sarna, S., Sharma, Poonam and Khurana, A.S. (2008). Combined Inoculation of *Azotobacter* and Plant Growth Promoting *Rhizobacteria* on the Efficiency of *Rhizobium* in chickpea. *Annals of Plant and Soil Research*, 10:39-43.

Sharma, J., Namdeo, K.N., Shrivastava, K.B.L., Patel, A.K. and Tiwari, O.P. (2006). Effect of Fertility Levels, Growth Regulators and Biofertilizers on Nutrient Contents and Uptake of Field Pea (*Pisum sativum* L.). *Crop Research*, 32: 192-95.

Shrivastava, G.K., Choubey, N.K., Pandey, R.L. and Tripathi, R.S. (2000). Chickpea (*Cicer arietinum* L.) Varieties Suitable for Rainfed and Irrigated Conditions of Chhattisgarh Plains. *Journal of Interacademicia*, 4: 516-19.

Singh, H., Chaudhary, B.S. and Ahmad, B. (2008). Effect of Phosphorus, Sulphur and phosphate-solubilizing Bacteria on Growth, Yield and Uptake of Nutrients by Cowpea. *Annals of Plant and Soil Research*, 10: 56-58.

Singh, Mukul, Namdeo, K.N. and Saraiya, A.B. (2004 b). Effect of Phosphorus, Sulphur, Growth Regulators and Biofertilizers on Yield and Nutrient Uptake of Blackgram. *Annals of Plant and Soil Research*, 6: 152-155.

Singh, Narpinder, Sandhu, K.S. and Maninder, Kaur (2004). Characterization of Starches Separated from Indian Chickpea (*Cicer arietinum* L.) Cultivars. *Journal of Food Engineering*, 63 441-449.

Srivastava, Manisha, Gupta, U.P. and Sinha, Asha (2012). Influence of Bean Common Mosaic Virus Infection on Chlorophyll Content and Primary Productivity in Hyacinth Bean (*Dolichos lablab* L.). *Crop Research*, 44:174-81.

Tiwari, M.K.; Patel, A.K. and Namdeo, K.N. (2006). Effect of Fertility Levels and Triacontanol on Yield, Quality and Nutrient Uptake of Soybean. *Annals of Plant and Soil Research*, 8:152-54.

Tomar, A., Kumar, N., Pareek, R.P. and Chaube, A.K. (2001). Synergism among VA mycorrhiza, Phosphate-solubilizing Bacteria and *Rhizobium* for blackgram (*Vigna mung* (L.) under Field Conditions. *Pedosphere*, 11: 327-32.

Verma, O.P., Paul, Sangeeta and Rathi, M.S. (2000). Synergistic Effect of Co-inoculation of *Azotobacter chroococcum* and *Rhizobium* on pea (*Pisum sativum*). *Annals of Agricultural Research*, 21: 418-20.

Witham, P.H.; Baiydes, D.F. and Devlin, R.M. (1971). Chlorophyll Absorption of Spectrum and Quantitative Determination. *Experimental Plant Physiology*. Von Nastrand Reinhold Co., New York, p. 245.

Zaidi, Almas, Khan, M.S. and Amil, M. (2003). Interactive Effect of Rhizotrophic Microorganisms on Yield and Nutrient Uptake of Chickpea (*Cicer arietinum* L.). *European Journal of Agronomy*, 19: 15-21.

Pages 112-117

INTEGRATED NUTRIENT MANAGEMENT IN CHICKPEA
Edited by **: Dr. Virendra Kumar** and **Dr. Nirmal Kumar Katiyar**
Edition **: 2017**
ISBN : 978-93-5056-872-9
Published by **: Discovery Publishing House Pvt. Ltd., New Delhi (India)**

10

Effect of Phosphorus on Growth, Productivity and Economics of Chickpea Varieties

V.K. Gulpadiya
D.S. Chhonkar

ABSTRACT

The effect of phosphorus on growth and productivity of chickpea varieties was studied during rabi Season of 2011-12 at Research farm, Raja Balwant Singh College, Bichpuri, Agra (U.P.). The experiment comprised of four levels of phosphorus (0, 30, 60 and 90 kg P_2O_5 ha^{-1}) and three chickpea varieties viz; Haryana-1, BG-7 and PBG-7. Results showed that the taller plants root growth and yield and yield attributes were obtained with higher Haryana-1 variety. Most of the growth parameters and yield attributes were increased significantly with every increase in levels of phosphorus up to 60 kg P_2O_5 ha^{-1} which were statistically at par with 90 kg P_2O_5 ha^{-1} but significantly higher than other levels of phosphorus. The increase in grain yield with 30, 60 and 90 kg P_2O_5 ha^{-1} were 42.6, 55.3 and 68.5 per cent, respectively over control. Haryana-1 recorded the highest grain yield (10.18 q ha^{-1}) excelling BG-7, by 15.2 per cent and PBG-7 by 21.2 per cent. Maximum net returns (32875 ha^{-1}) along with a B:C ratio of 2.41 was obtained in Haryana-1. Phosphorus use efficiency decreased with the increase in P level. Net returns (30334.8 ha^{-1}) and benefit cost (2.40) ratio were the highest with 60 kg P_2O_5 ha^{-1}.

Keywords: Chickpea, Varieties, Phosphorus, Growth yield, Economics.

Department of Agronomy, Raja Balwant Singh College (Dr. B.R.A. University) Bichpuri, Agra (U.P.) - 283105.

INTRODUCTION

Chickpea (*Cicer aritinum* L.) is the major pulse crop of India. At global level, it ranks fifth in terms of area and production under legumes. It is grown with less care and low manurial requirement. The productivity of chickpea is low because of its cultivation generally in poor soils. Pulses have inherent capacity to fix atmospheric nitrogen in symbiotic association with Rhizobium. This characteristic of pulses has helped in maintaining the sustainable fertility levels of soils. Under the pulses the soil does not allow water to run very fast which enhance the soil productivity, especially in case of the dry farming zones. Because of their better ground coverage, the pulses reduce water losses through evaporation from the soil surface. Application of phosphorus increased the production of pulse crops (Sharma *et al.* 2014). The response of phosphorus depends upon many factors like: climate, variety and soil type and availability of nutrients during the period of growth. The requirement of phosphorus in legumes like chickpea is higher than other crops for their root development and metabolic activities. Phosphorus is the vital component of DNA, RNA, ATP and photosynthetic system and catalyses a number of bio chemical reactions from the beginning of seedling growth through to the formation of grain at maturity. Selection of suitable variety plays a vital role in crop production. The choice of right variety of chickpea helps in augmenting crop productivity. Thus, the value of stable and high yield varieties has been universally recognized as an important non case input for boosting the production any crop. There is a possibility of ranging the productivity per unit area by essential use of phosphorus. Limited information is available on the aspect under agro climatic conditions of Agra reason of Uttar Pradesh. The present investigation was therefore carried out to the study the effect of phosphorus levels on yield and economics of chickpea varieties.

Methods and Material

A field experiment was carried out during *Rabi* season of 2011-12 at the Research farm of Raja Balwant Singh College, Bichpuri Agra (Uttar Pradesh), situated at latitude of 27°2′ N and longitude of 77°9′ E with an elevation of 163.4 m above the mean sea level having semi arid, sub tropical climate with extremes of temperature both in summers and winters. The soil was sandy loam with alkaline pH (7.9) low in organic carbon (3 g kg^{-1}), available nitrogen (170 kg ha^{-1}) phosphorus (18 kg ha^{-1}) and K (110 kg ha^{-1}) Treatments comprised of three chickpea varieties *i.e.* Haryana-1, BG-7 and PBG-7 and four phosphorus levels, *viz*; 0, 30, 60 and 90 kg. P_2O_5 ha^{-1} was tested in factorial randomized design with three replications. Entire quantities of K_2O (40 kg ha^{-1}), Nitrogen and quantity of P_2O_5 as per treatment were applied at the time of as basal dressing through and diammonium phosphate and muriate of potash respectively. The rest amount of N was applied as urea. The crop was sown on in second weak of November 2011. All agronomic practices like weeding intercultural practices and irrigation were done according to need of the crop. Growth and yield attributeds were recorded at maturity. The crop was harvested in the first week of April 2012. Data on grain and straw yields were recorded. Economics of various treatments was calculated on the basis of prevailing market prices of different input and final produce.

Results and Discussion

The results indicated that Variety Haryana-1 produced significantly taller plants, higher length and dry weight of root plant^{-1}, number and dry weight of nodules plant^{-1} than those of BG-7 and PBG-7. Sound root system with the variety Həryana-1 might be due its genetic characters. Variety Haryana-1 also produced significantly more number and weight of pods plant^{-1} than those of BG-7 and PBG-7 (Table 10.2). The number and weight of grains plant^{-1} were appreciably higher by 14.7 per cent and 15 per cent and 14.5 per cent and 16.7 per cent with the variety Haryana-1 over the BG-7 and PBG-7 varieties, respectively while number and weight of grains pod^{-1} and test weight did not modify due to varieties. Appreciably higher biological, grain and straw yield were recorded with the variety Haryana-1 as compared to BG-7 and PBG-7. The increase in grain yield with Variety Haryana-1 was to the tune of 15.2 per cent and 21.2 per cent over BG-7 and PBG-7. Markedly highest net return of 29397.5 ha^{-1} along with B: C ratio of 2.41 was obtained in variety Haryana-1. The lowest net return of 25071.5 ha^{-1} was observed in variety PBG-7. The plant growth attributes such as: plant height and number of secondary branches plant^{-1} appreciably improved with the application of phosphorus upto 60 kg P_2O_5 ha^{-1} Bahadur *et al.* 2002, Sahu *et al.* 2003, Length and weight of root plant^{-1} and number and weight of nodules plant^{-1} was increased appreciably with every increase in the rate of phosphorus application upto 60 kg P_2O_5 ha^{-1}, beyond that no significant advantage was noticed. It appears that with the increased supply of phosphorus, soil physical condition gets improved which, in turn, might have helped improving the root size and uptake of nutrients. With such improvements in root size, the noted enhanced rate of nodulation was possible. It may also be argued that in presence of adequate phosphorus, bacterial cells become motive and flagellate which, in turn, results in more N_2 fixation and finally better plant growth. It is also a well established fact that the application of phosphorus encourages the formation of new cells and thus promotes the root and shoot growth, whereas in the absences of phosphorus or with inadequate supply the infection remains latent leading to the poor development of roots and nodules, leaves and stem and finally reduce the amount of nitrogen fixed by restricting host plant growth. Some recent evidences (Vishwakarma *et al.* (2012) suggest that phosphorus requirements for nodulation and maximum nodules activities are much greater than poor host plant growth. Infection of Rhizobium bacteria depends on their interception with root hair, under adequate phosphorus application. Nodulation increased due to high bacterial interception on account of properly developed roots and increased density of nodule bacteria.

Table 10.1: Growth and root characters of chickpea varieties as affected by phosphorus at harvest

Treatment	Plant Height (cm)	Branches Plant^{-1}	Secondary Branches Plant^{-1}	Dry Matter Accumulation Plant^{-1} (g)	Root Length (cm)	Root Weight (cm)	Nodules Plant^{-1}	Dry Weight of Nodules Plant^{-1} (g)
Varieties								
Haryana-1	44.12	4.3	9.1	14.22	12.3	173.2	8.5	12.26
BG-7	41.15	3.7	8.1	12.88	11	165.6	7.7	10.96
PBG-7	40.13	3.6	8.1	12.44	10.9	163.5	7.6	10.92
SEm±	0.94	0.08	0.21	0.34	0.32	1.95	0.19	0.32
CD (P=0.05)	2.70	0.22	0.25	0.99	0.92	5.61	0.54	1.06
Phosphorus (kg ha^{-1})								
0	36.27	2.9	7.1	9.56	10	156.1	6.3	9.84
30	40.78	3.7	8.2	12.68	11.2	168.9	7.8	11.14
60	44.30	4.4	9.2	15.20	12.3	173.5	8.8	12.26
90	45.85	4.4	9.2	15.28	12.3	174.1	8.8	12.28
SEm±	1.08	0.09	0.61	0.40	0.37	2.26	0.21	0.37
CD (P=0.05)	3.10	0.25	0.71	1.14	1.07	6.48	0.62	1.06

Application of phosphorus significantly increased the dry matter accumulation in the plant and the differences were well marked upto 60 kg P_2O_5 ha^{-1} (Table 10.1). When the rate of phosphorus increased from 60 to 90 kg P_2O_5 ha^{-1}, the dry matter accumulation in plant increased marginally. At harvest, the increases in dry matter accumulation with30, 60 and 90 kg P_2O_5 ha^{-1} were 32.6, 59 and 59.8, respectively over the control. The favourable effect of phosphorus on plant growth might be due to the fact that phosphorus is the chief constituent of the lipids and nucleo-proteins, an abundance of phosphorus in the meristematic region might have helped in cell division and multiplication, it is also concerned with carbohydrate transformation, respiration and nitrogen fixation and hence it boosted plant growth. The response of phosphorus in terms of dry matter accumulation upto 60 kg P_2O_5 ha^{-1} have also been reported Singh *et al.* (2005) in chickpea.

Table 10.2: Effect of phosphorus on yield attributes of chickpea varieties

Treatments	Pods Plant^{-1}	Weight of Pods Plant^{-1} (g)	Grains Pods^{-1}	Weight of Grains Pods^{-1} (g)	1000 Grain Weight (g)
Varieties					
Haryana-1	30.1	60.66	1.7	3.30	302.48
BG-7	26	48.42	1.7	3.00	300.24
PBG-7	25	46.32	1.7	2.94	298.30
SEm±	1.13	1.25	0.50	0.87	1.24
CD (P=0.05)	3.25	3.58	NS	NS	NS
Phosphorus (kg ha^{-1})					
0	21	38.78	1.7	2.28	290.90
30	26.1	50.36	1.7	2.96	301.18
60	30.3	58.72	1.7	3.50	304.20
90	30.7	59.34	1.7	3.58	305.08
SEm±	1.31	1.42	0	1.04	1.48
CD (P=0.05)	3.75	3.92	NS	NS	4.24

The grain yield plant^{-1} is the combined effect of number and weight of pods plant^{-1}, number and weight of grains plant^{-1} and 1000 grain weight. Almost all yield contributing characters namely number and weight of grains plant^{-1} and 1000 grain weight were also improved appreciably with increasing levels of phosphorus upto 60 kg P_2O_5 ha^{-1}, except 1000 grain weight, where the differences among 30, 60 and 90 kg P_2O_5 ha^{-1}, were not significant.

Biological, grain and straw yields were significantly increased with increasing rates of phosphorus application up to 60 kg P_2O_5 ha^{-1}. The increases in grain yield with 30, 60 and 90 kg P_2O_5 ha^{-1} were to the tune of 42.6, 55.3 and 68.5 per cent, respectively over the control. Response of chickpea to phosphorus upto 60 kg P_2O_5 ha^{-1} was reported by Islam *et al.* (2011). Application of phosphorus also had significant effect on harvest index as compared with control. It may be recall that the application of 90 kg P_2O_5 ha^{-1} failed to bring any additional significant improvement over its lower dose (60 kg P_2O_5 ha^{-1}). It may be pointed out that initial status of the available phosphorus of the soil was in the low range and, therefore, addition of 60 kg P_2O_5 ha^{-1} could have become adequate for normal growth and development of the pulse crop Sahu *et al.* (2002) and Sharma *et al.* (2014).

It is evident from the Table 10.2 that the highest net returns of 32875 ha^{-1} and B:C ratio (2.52) were obtained with the 60 kg P_2O_5 ha^{-1} followed by application of 30 kg P_2O_5 ha^{-1}. This could be attributed to higher yields of chickpea varieties with 60 kg P_20_5 ha^{-1}. Similar results were reported by Sahu *et al.* (2005).

Table 10.3: Effect of phosphorus on yield and economics of chickpea varieties

Treatments	Biological Yield (q ha^{-1})	Grain Yield (q ha^{-1})	Straw Yield (q ha^{-1})	Harvest index (%)	Net Income ('/ha-^{1})	B/C ratio
Varieties						
Haryana-1	33.42	10.18	23.24	30.5	29397.5	2.41
BG-7	30.23	8.84	21.39	29.2	26104.5	2.25
PBG-7	29.50	8.40	21.10	28.5	25071.5	2.20
SEm±	0.93	0.33	0.60	0.73		
CD (P=0.05)	2.67	0.94	1.72	NS		
Phosphorus (kg ha^{-1})						
0	24.36	6.45	17.91	26.5	22419.8	2.20
30	30.38	9.22	21.16	30.4	27661.9	2.37
60	34.03	10.02	24.01	29.4	30334.8	2.40
90	35.43	10.87	24.56	30.7	27014.7	2.17
SEm±	1.07	0.38	0.69	0.85		
CD (P=0.05)	3.08	1.08	1.99	2.43		

On the basis results obtained in present study, it can be concluded that out of three varieties Haryana-1 was identified as best variety for cultivation in Agra region with 60 kg P_2O_5 ha^{-1}.

REFERENCES

Akinrinde, E.A. and Okeleye, K.O. (2005). 'Chickpea Performance and Phosphorus use Efficiency in Response to Sole and Combined Applications of Superphosphate and Market Waste-based Organic Fertilizers on a Loamy Sand Arenic Hapludalf. *Crop Research* (Hisar) 30(3):372-379.

Bahadur, M.M.; Ashrafuzzaman, M; Kabir. M.K.; Chowdhury. M.F. and Majumdar, D.A.N. (2002). Response of Chickpea (*Cicer arietinum* L.) Varieties to Different Levels of Phosphorus *Crop Research* (Hisar) 23(2): 293-299.

Islam, M.; Mohsan, S.; Ali, A.; Khalid, R.; Fayyaz-ul-Hassan Abid Mahmood, A. and Subhani, A. (2011) Growth, Nitrogen Fixation and Nutrient Uptake by Chickpea (*Cicer arietinum*) in Response to Phosphorus and Sulfur Application Under Rainfed Conditions in Pakistan. *International Journal of Agriculture and Biology*. 13: 5, 725-730.

Sahu, J.P. Singh, N.P. Kaushik, M.K.; Sharma, B.B. and Singh, V.K. (2002). Effect of Rhizobium, Phosphorus and Potash Application on the Productivity of Chickpea. *Indian Journal of Pulse Research*. 15 (1): 39-42.

Singh, Sher; Punia, S.S. and Sheoran, P. (2005). Effect of Irrigation, Phosphorus and Seed Inoculation on Chickpea (Cicer arietinum L.). *Haryana Journal of Agronomy*. 21(1):21-23. Sharma, A.K., Raghubanshi, B.P.S. and Sirothia, P. (2014) Response of Chickpea to Levels of Zink and Phosphorus. *Annals of Plant and Soil Research* 16(2):172-173.

Vishwakarma, S.K., Singh P. Singh, R.P. and Kawat, R.N. (2012). Yield and Quality of Chickpea as Affected by Rhizobuim Inoculation. *Annals of Plant and Soil Research* 14: 79-80.

Pages 118-129

INTEGRATED NUTRIENT MANAGEMENT IN CHICKPEA
***Edited by* : Dr. Virendra Kumar** and **Dr. Nirmal Kumar Katiyar**
***Edition* : 2017**
ISBN : 978-93-5056-872-9
***Published by* : Discovery Publishing House Pvt. Ltd., New Delhi (India)**

11

Effect of *Rhizobium* and Phosphate Solubilizing Bacterial Inoculants on Symbiotic Traits, Nodule Leghemoglobin, and Yield of Chickpea Genotypes

G.S. Tagore[1], S.L. Namdeo[2]
S.K. Sharma[2], Narendra Kumar[3]

A field experiment was carried out during the *rabi* season of 2004-05 to find out the effect of *Rhizobium* and phosphate solubilizing bacterial (PSB) inoculants on symbiotic traits, nodule leghemoglobin, and yield of five elite genotypes of chickpea. Among the chickpea genotypes, IG-593 performed better in respect of symbiotic parameters including: nodule number, nodule fresh weight, nodule dry weight, shoot dry weight, yield attributes and yield. Leghemoglobin content (2.55 mg g^{-1} of fresh nodule) was also higher under IG-593. Among microbial inoculants, the *Rhizobium* + PSB was found most effective in terms of nodule number (27.66 nodules $plant^{-1}$), nodule fresh weight (144.90 mg $plant^{-1}$), nodule dry weight (74.30 mg $plant^{-1}$), shoot dry weight (11.76 g $plant^{-1}$), and leghemoglobin content (2.29 mg g^{-1} of fresh nodule) and also showed its positive effect in enhancing all the yield attributing parameters, grain and straw yields.

INTRODUCTION

Pulses are the second most important group of crops after cereals. Developing countries contribute about 74 per cent to the global pulses

1. Department of Soil Science and Agricultural Chemistry, JNKVV, Jabalpur, M.P. 482 004, India.
2. College of Agriculture, Indore, Madhya Pradesh 452 001, India.
3. IIPR, Kanpur, Uttar Pradesh 208 024, India.

production and the remaining comes from developed countries. India, China, Brazil, Canada, Myanmar, and Australia are the major pulse producing countries with relative share of 25 per cent, 10 per cent, 5 per cent, 5 per cent, and 4 per cent, respectively. In 2009, the global pulses production was 61.5 million tonnes from an area of 70.6 million hectares with an average yield of 871 kg/ha. Dry beans contributed about 32 per cent to global pulses production followed by dry peas (17%), chickpea (15.9%), broad bean (7.5%), lentil (5.7%), cowpea (6%), and pigeonpea (4.0%). India is the largest producer and consumer of pulses in the world contributing around 25-28 per cent of the total global production. About 75 per cent of the global chickpea (*Cicer arietinum* L.) area falls in India [1]. Chickpea is one of the major post rainy seasonpulse crops in Madhya Pradesh, which occupies 3.09 m ha with production of 3.30 mt and productivity of 1071 kg ha^{-1} [2]. The poor productivity of chickpea in this region is mainly due to imbalance application of nutrients and use of traditional varieties. Under such situations, use of *Rhizobium* and phosphate solubilizing bacteria (PSB) had shown advantage in enhancing chickpea productivity [3, 4]. Microbial inoculants are cost effective, ecofriendly, and renewable sources of plant nutrients [5]. *Rhizobium* and PSB assume a great importance on account of their vital role in N-fixation and P-solubilisation. The 2 introduction of efficient strains of P-solubilizing species of Bacillus *megaterium* biovar *phosphaticum, Bacillus polymyxa, Pseudomonas striata, Aspergillus awamori,* and *Penicillium digitatum* in the rhizosphere of crops and soils has been reported to help in increasing phosphorus availability in the soil [6]. Since the information on response of elite genotypes 2 of chickpea to inoculation with *Rhizobium* and phosphate solubilizing bacterial inoculants is meager under such situ-ation, therefore, an experiment was designed to assess the productivity of chickpea genotypes in combinations with microbial inoculants in *Malwa* Region of Madhya Pradesh.

Material and Methods

Experimental Site

The field experiment was conducted at the Experimental Farm of College of Agriculture, Indore, Madhya Pradesh (22°43 N, 75°56 E and 555.7 m above mean sea level). The soil of the experimental site belongs to sarol series, which is a member of a fine montmorillonitic family of Vertic Ustochrept and Vertic Chromusters. The soil characteristics of the experimental site before start of the study were analysed and presented in Table 11.1.

Treatments Details and Crop Culture

The experiment was conducted during the winter (*rabi*) season of 2004-05. The experiment was laid out in split-plot design with three replications. The experiment was conducted with twenty treatment combinations comprising five genotypes, namely: IG-226, IG-370, IG-379, JG-412, and IG-593, in main plots and four microbial inoculants (no inoculum, *Rhizobium*, PSB, and *Rhizobium* + PSB) in sub-plots. The chickpea genotypes were collected from college of Agriculture, Indore and microbial inoculants from JNKVV, Jabalpur. The gross plot size was 5 m × 2.40 m^2. Chickpea crop was sown on a fine seed bed prepared after presown irrigation with a seed rate of 100 kg ha^{-1}. *Rhizobium* inoculant at 5 g kg^{-1} seed was applied as seed treatment, whereas, phosphate solubilizing bacterial inoculants were applied in soil at 3 kg ha^{-1} prior to sowing. The chickpea crop was given irrigation at 40 days after sowing.

Table 11.1: Soil properties before the start of the study

Soil Parameter	Value
pH	7.8
Electrical conductivity, dS m^{-1}	0.23
Soil organic carbon, %	0.45
Available nitrogen, kg ha^{-1}	204
Available phosphorous (Olsen' P), kg ha^{-1}	9.58
Available potassium, kg ha^{-1}	576
Available sulphur, kg ha^{-1}	12.88

Soil Analysis

Soil samples from surface soil (0-15 cm) were taken for chemical analysis after harvesting of rice crop. Random cores were taken from each plot with a 5 cm diameter tube auger and bulked. The moist soil samples were sieved (2 mm) after removing plant material and roots. Similarly, initial soil samples were collected from 10 random places of experimental site before start of study. All chemical results are means of triplicate analyses and are expressed on oven-dry basis. Soil was analyzed for pH in 1 : 2.5 soil : water suspension [7], SOC by the method of Walkley and Black [8], Kjeldahl N by FOSS Tecator (Model 2200), available P following the method of Bray and Kurtz [9], available K by 1 N NH OAc using a flame photometer [7], and available 4 S by using 0.15 per cent CaCl [10]. *Rhizobium* population in the 2 soil samples was enumerated by plant infection technique of Toomsan *et al.* [11] and phosphate solubilizing bacteria (PSB) by dilution plate count method as described by Sundara Rao and Sinha [12].

Nodulation, Growth, and Yield of Crops

Five plants were randomly selected and removed from each plot and recorded the nodule fresh weight at 35, 55, and 75 days after sowing (DAS). After removal of nodules, the plants were first sun International Journal of Agronomy dried for 3 days and then oven dried at 65°C for 48 hours to obtain dry weight. Leghemoglobin content in nodular tissues collected at

35, 55, and 75 DAS was determined by the procedure outlined by Beau [13]. The nodules were dried in oven at 65°C for 78 hours for dry weight of nodules. Plants were harvested at physiological maturity and plant height, and number of branches per plant, number of pods per plant, and number of seeds per pod and test weight (1000 seed weight) were recorded from 10 randomly selected plants at the time of harvest. Total dry matter and grain yield were also recorded for each plot.

Statistical Analysis

Effect of treatments were evaluated by split-plot analysis of variance (ANOVA) with chickpea genotypes as main and microbial inoculants as subfactors. Analysis of variance was performed using the programme SPSS 11.0 for windows. The significance of the treatment effect was determined using *F*-test. When ANOVA indicated that there was a significant value, multiple comparisons of mean value were performed using the least significant difference method (LSD).

Results and Discussion

Symbiotic Traits

The data on mean nodule number, nodule fresh weight, nodule dry weight, and shoot dry weight at 35, 55 and 75 days after sowing (DAS) are presented in Figs. 11.1(a), 1(b), 1(c), 1(d) and Table 11.2. The analysis of data revealed that among the genotypes, IG-593 exhibited the highest nodule number, namely: 19.91, 27.04, and 25.29 plant^{-1}, nodule fresh weight, namely: 86.79, 127.48, and 100.16 mg plant^{-1} and dry weight of nodules, namely: 46.16, 67.29, and 65.68 mg plant^{-1}at 35, 55, and 75 DAS, respectively.

Genotype IG-593 recorded maximum shoot dry weight, namely: 2.56, 12.55, and 25.53 g plant^{-1} and the minimum in IG-370, namely: 1.67, 8.03, and 14.98 g plant^{-1} at 35, 55, and 75 DAS, respectively. The data on symbiotic traits of chickpea genotypes indicated that shoot dry weight increased progressively and nodule number, nodule fresh weight, nodule dry weight also followed the similar trend at 35 and 55 DAS, but the decline was noted in nodule number, fresh weight, and dry weight of nodules at 75 DAS. This was mainly due to decay of nodular tissues at pod formation, which start from 60 to 65 DAS.

Coinoculation of *Rhizobium* and PSB recorded significantly higher nodule number and its fresh as well as dry weight than *Rhizobium* and PSB alone. The increase in nodulation might be due to synergistic effect of the two types of microorganisms for biological nitrogen fixation as against their individual application. Results of the similar kind have also been reported by Rudresh *et al.* [4]. It is also due to the fact that phosphate solubilizing bacteria by virtue of their property of producing organic acids solubilize insoluble or fixed form of phosphorus in the rhizosphere and make it available to the growing plants, which promotes root development in plants [14]. In the present study, a significant response of dual inoculation with *Rhizobium* and PSB was observed with respect to shoot dry weight per plant. Observations of the similar kind have been recorded by Gupta and Namdeo [15] and Barea *et al.* [16].

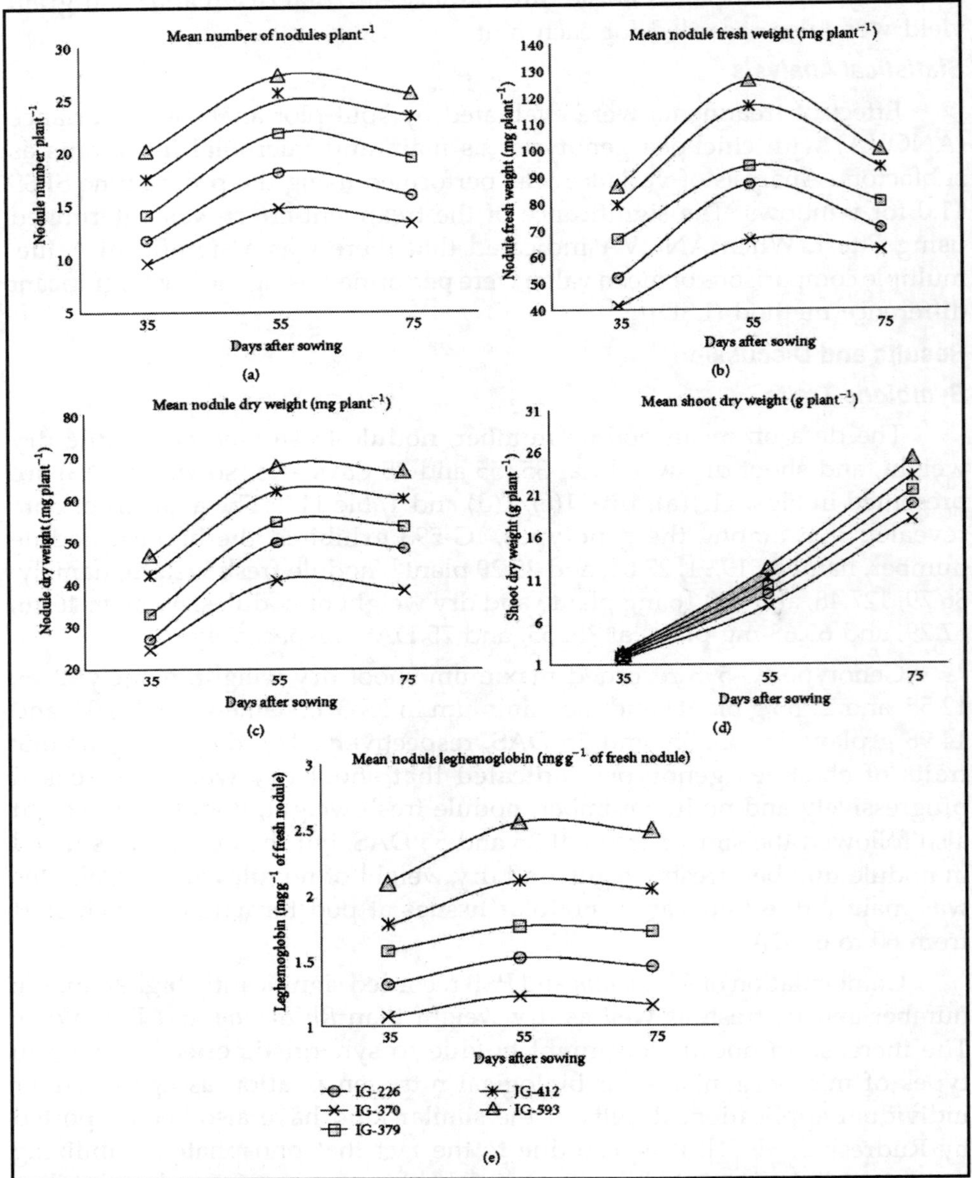

Fig. 11.1: ((a)-(d)) Symbiotic parameters and (e) leghemoglobin content in nodular tissues of chickpea genotypes at different intervals

Table 11.2: Symbiotic parameters and leghemoglobin content in nodular tissues at different intervals

Chickpea Genotypes	Nodule Number $Plant^{-1}$			Nodule Fresh Weight (mg $Plant^{-1}$)			Nodule Dry Weight (mg $Plant^{-1}$)			Shoot Dry Weight (g $Plant^{-1}$)			Nodule Leghemoglobin (mg g^{-1} of Fresh Nodule)		
	Days after sowing			Days after sowing			Days after sowing			Days after sowing			Days after sowing		
	35	55	75	35	55	75	35	55	75	35	55	75	35	55	75
							Chickpea genotype								
IG-226	11.7	18.1	15.8	52.3	87.9	70.8	26.8	49.7	48.1	1.8	9.4	20.2	1.3	1.5	1.5
IG-370	9.5	14.6	13.3	41.2	66.7	63.0	24.5	40.8	38.4	1.7	8.0	18.5	1.1	1.2	1.2
IG-379	14.0	21.7	19.3	67.0	94.8	81.3	32.7	54.3	53.4	2.1	10.4	21.9	1.6	1.8	1.7
JG-412	17.4	24.6	23.3	80.5	117.8	94.2	41.7	61.7	59.9	2.3	11.4	23.6	1.8	2.1	2.0
IG-593	19.9	27.0	25.3	86.8	127.5	100.2	46.2	67.3	65.7	2.6	12.6	25.5	2.1	2.6	2.5
SEm±	1.2	1.2	0.9	2.0	3.1	2.2	0.6	1.3	0.6	0.04	0.3	0.5	0.1	0.7	0.1
LSD (=0 .05)	3.9	3.6	2.8	6.6	10.1	7.3	1.9	4.1	2.0	0.1	1.0	1.7	0.2	0.2	0.3
							Microbial inoculants								
Control	9.4	15.6	14.8	46.2	56.9	54.1	24.3	39.0	38.0	1.9	9.2	16.6	1.2	1.5	1.5
Rhizobium	18.9	25.4	24.7	67.1	120.9	102.1	40.3	64.6	63.1	2.2	10.8	24.6	1.7	2.0	1.9
PSB	10.0	16.8	15.7	54.8	64.6	61.6	26.3	42.1	40.9	2.0	9.6	20.7	1.3	1.5	1.5
Rhizobium + PSB	20.7	27.7	26.7	95.1	144.9	120.4	46.6	74.3	70.5	2.3	11.8	26.5	2.0	2.3	2.3
SFm±	0.6	0.8	0.7	3.1	3.9	2.8	0.8	1.3	1.3	0.05	0.2	0.3	0.04	0.05	0.1
LSD (=0 .05)	1.7	2.2	1.9	9.1	11.2	8.0	2.3	3.7	3.8	0.1	0.4	0.8	0.1	0.1	0.2

PSB: phosphate solubilising bacteria.

Leghemoglobin Content in Root Nodules

The results given in Fig. 11.1(e) and Table 11.2 showed that the leghemoglobin content in chickpea root nodules increased with the advancement of crop age and was maximum at 55 DAS and thereafter decline at 75 DAS. Among the genotypes, IG-593 possessed the highest nodule leghemoglobin of 2.10, 2.55, and 2.47 mg g^{-1} of fresh nodule and lowest 1.07, 1.23, and 1.45 mg g^{-1} of fresh nodule in IG-370 at 35, 55 and 75 DAS, respectively. In the present study, coinoculation of *Rhizobium* and PSB performed better than *Rhizobium* and PSB alone with respect to leghemoglobin content in the nodular tissues of chickpea crop. In case of microbial inoculants, higher leghemoglobin content in nodular tissues was observed in *Rhizobium* + PSB in comparison to their individual inoculation. The better nodulation under chickpea genotype IG "593 might be resulted in higher content of leghemoglobin in nodular tissues. Similarly, higher leghemoglobin content in *Rhizobium* + PSB was mainly due to better root and nodules development [17].

Yield Attributes

The significant differences were found in yield attributing parameters due to genotypes and microbial inoculants, while their interaction effect was non-significant (Table 11.3). Among the genotypes, IG-593 exhibited the highest mean number of branches and pods per plant and seeds per pod, that is, 15.95, 63.96 $plant^{-1}$ and 1.59 pod^{-1}, respectively, and the lowest values were recorded in IG-370, that is, 10.23, 34.71 $plant^{-1}$ and 1.13 pod^{-1}, respectively. It was further noted that among the genotypes, IG-593 produced the tallest plant (42.07 cm), while the genotype IG-370 had shortest plant (30.63 cm). Variation in the above parameters is bound to occur due to difference in genetic makeup and inherited characters in different genotypes. The results corroborate with the findings of Singh *et al.* [18] and Tiwari *et al.* [19].

The data further indicated that IG-593 had highest test weight (333.80 g) followed by JG-412 (249.13 g), IG-379 (191.48 g), IG-370 (158.68 g), and IG-226 (152.34 g). The variation in test weight among the genotypes is likely to occur due to difference in seed size of the individual genotype. A high value of test weight indicated the boldness of seeds, while the lower values indicated small seeds. Large/small seed size of chickpea is basically a genotypic character [19]. In the present study, seed inoculation with *Rhizobium* + PSB significantly increased the plant height, number of branches, number of pods per plant, number of seeds per pod, and 1000 seed weight (test weight) over no inoculation. The higher growth and yield attributes under *Rhizobium* + PSB inoculation were mainly due to more availability of N, P, K, and S in the soil for chickpea plants [20-22]. Moreover, growth promoting substances (phytohormones) are produced by these organisms which further promote plant growth [23-25]. Further, inoculation of *Rhizobium* and PSB alone produced significantly higher number of pods per plant and test weight. These results are in close agreement with Takankhar *et al.* [26] and Khoja *et al.* [27].

Grain and Straw Yield

Critical examination of the data in Table 11.3 revealed that genotype IG-593 produced the highest grain and straw yields (2 286 and 2 728 Kg ha^{-1}) followed by JG-412 (1 995 and 2 291 Kg ha^{-1}) and lowest in IG-370 (1 475 and 1 613 Kg ha^{-1}). The observed variation in seed and straw yields in the present investigation seems to be due to genetic difference in yield potential of different genotypes and also due to variable response of different genotypes to microbial inoculants [19, 28].

Significant differences in grain and straw yields were also recorded due to microbial inoculation. The grain and straw yields increased due to microbial inoculation, and the highest seed and straw yields were obtained in inoculation of *Rhizobium* + PSB, that is, 2 150 and 2 461 Kg ha^{-1}, and the lowest in the case of control, that is, 1 587 and 1 901 Kg ha^{-1}, respectively. The increase in grain and straw yield might be attributed to the increased availability of N and P in soil which resulted in higher growth and development and finally yields [20, 23, 29-31].

Soil Characteristics

Soil pH and EC remain unaffected under different chickpea genotypes and microbial inoculation. However, highest value of soil organic carbon (SOC) was observed under IG-593 (0.53%) and the lowest under IG-370 (0.47%). The significant variations in available N, P, K, and S were also recorded due to chickpea genotypes and microbial inoculation. The highest value of available N (219.25 kg ha^{-1}), available P (12.18 kg ha^{-1}), available K (568.6 kg ha^{-1}), and available S (13.6 kg ha^{-1}) was recorded after harvest of chickpea genotype 1G-593 and the lowest values of available N, P, K and S were recorded in IG-370. In case of microbial inoculation, the highest values of available N (220.3 kg ha^{-1}), available P (14.1 kg ha^{-1}), available K (556.9 kg ha^{-1}), and available S (13.41 kg ha^{-1}) were recorded under inoculation of both *Rhizobium* and PSB; however, the lowest values of available N, P, K, and S were under no-inoculation (control). The variations in available nutrients under different genotype might be due to variations in compatibility between soil microflora and chickpea genotypes. However, *Rhizobium* and PSB inoculation had resulted in better plant growth, nodulation, and rhizospheric environment which finally resulted in more availability of plant nutrients (NPKS) in the soil [28, 32, 33].

Table 11.3: Yield attributes, grain and straw yields of chickpea genotypes

Chickpea Genotypes	Plant Height (cm)	Number of Branches Plant^{-1}	Number of Pods Plant^{-1}	Number of Seeds Pod^{-1}	Test Weight (g)	Mean Yield (Kg ha^{-1})	
						Grain	Straw
		Chickpea genotype					
IG-226	33.4	12.4	38.6	1.25	152.3	1622	1894
IG-370	30.6	10.2	34.7	1.13	158.7	1475	1613
IG-379	34.5	13.3	42.8	1.30	191.5	1922	2199
JG-412	39.0	14.4	48.4	1.33	249.1	1995	2291
IG-593	42.1	16.0	64.0	1.38	333.8	2286	2728
SEm±	1.4	0.3	0.9	0.058	2.0	88	91
LSD (P=0.05)	4.5	0.9	3.0	0.191	6.5	288	299
		Microbial inoculants					
Control	34.1	11.4	37.9	1.1	213.1	1587	1901
Rhizobium	36.7	13.6	48.9	1.3	220.0	1967	2303
PSB	34.2	12.1	43.5	1.3	216.0	1764	2089
Rhizobium + PSB	37.1	16.0	55.7	1.4	220.7	2150	2461
SEm±	0.8	0.3	0.8	0.6	1.4	59	52
LSD (P=0.05)	2.4	0.8	2.2	0.2	4.0	170	152

PSB: phosphate solubilising bacteria.

Table 11.4: Soil fertility as influenced by chickpea genotypes and microbial inoculants

Chickpea Genotypes	pH	EC dS m^{-1}	SOC (%)	Available Nutrients in Soil (kg ha^{-1})				*Rhizobium* Population	PSB Population
				N	P	K	S	(×10^{4} g^{-1} of soil)	(×10^{5} g^{-1} of soil)
				Chickpea genotype					
IG-226	7.75	0.36	0.49	198.5	10.6	545.6	12.5	9.68	4.23
IG-370	7.68	0.35	0.47	192.8	10.4	544.8	12.4	9.29	4.03
IG-379	7.76	0.36	0.49	194.5	11.4	546.4	13.0	9.99	4.42
JG-412	7.79	0.37	0.53	210.3	11.6	547.1	13.4	10.60	4.53
IG-593	7.79	0.38	0.53	219.3	12.2	568.6	13.6	10.99	5.09
SEm±	–	–	0.01	1.5	0.4	1.6	0.4	0.24	0.13
LSD (P=0.05)	NS	NS	0.02	4.8	1.4	5.1	1.2	0.78	0.41
				Microbial inoculants					
Control	7.71	0.48	0.36	193.3	9.1	545.7	12.5	9.37	4.12
Rhizobium	7.76	0.37	0.51	206.8	9.2	552.7	13.0	10.79	4.14
PSB	7.73	0.36	0.48	191.9	12.5	546.7	13.0	9.40	4.77
Rhizobium + PSB	7.81	0.37	0.54	220.3	14.1	556.9	13.4	10.86	4.80
SEm±	–	–	0.01	2.6	0.2	1.9	0.3	0.08	0.03
LSD (P=0.05)	NS	NS	0.02	7.5	0.6	5.5	0.7	0.24	0.10

SOC: soil organic carbon, EC: electrical conductivity. ^{4}g^{-1} of soil.

Initial rhizobial count: 9.56×10^{3}g^{-1} of soil and phosphate solubilizing bacterial (PSB) count: 4.36×10.

Microbial Population

The data on *Rhizobium* and phosphate solubilising bacterial counts are given in Table 11.4. Significant variations in *Rhizobium* and phosphate solubilising bacteria (PSB) was observed due to both chickpea genotypes and microbial inoculation; however, their interactions were non-significant. Among chickpea genotypes, significantly highest *Rhizobium* population was recorded in IG-593 (10.99×10^4 g^{-1} of soil) followed by: JG-412 (10.60×10^4 g^{-1} of soil) and least in IG-370 ($9.29 \times 10^4 g^{-1}$ of soil). Similarly, PSB population was significantly higher in 1G-593 (5.09×10^5 g^{-1} of soil) over rest of genotypes. In case of microbial inoculation, the highest values of *Rhizobinum* (10.86×10^4 g^{-1} of soil) and PSB (4.80×10^5 g^{-1} of soil) were recorded in 1G-593 and lowest under control (no-inculcation). The highest values of microbial counts in 1G-593 might be due to greater compatibility of this genotype with inoculated microbial strains. However, inoculation of both *Rhizobinum* and PSB might have given added advantage over native microbial population [34].

Conclusion

Based on above results, it can be concluded that the chickpea genotype IG-593 is superior over the remaining genotypes with respect to nodulation, yield attributing parameters, nodule leghemoglobin content, and yield under limited irrigation in vertisols of Malwa Region. Use of *Rhizobium* and PSB inoculation had also shown advantage over no-inoculation. Thus, chickpea genotype IG-593 and inoculation of *Rhizobium* and PSB may be recommended to realize higher yield of chickpea in this region.

REFERENCES

1. FAOSTAT, Food and Agriculture Organization of the United Nations, 2010.
2. Government of M.P., *Agricultural Statistics*, Department of Agriculture. Government of M.P., Bhopal, India, 2011.
3. P.C. Jain, P.S. Kushawaha, U.S. Dhakal, H. Khan, and S.M. Trivedi, "Response of Chickpea (*Cicer arietinum* L.) to Phosphorus and Biofertilizer," *Legume Research*, Vol. 22, pp. 241-244, 1999.
4. D.L. Rudresh, M.K. Shivaprakash, and R.D. Prasad, "Effect of Combined Application of *Rhizobium*, Phosphate Solubilizing Bacterium and Trichoderma *spp.* on Growth, Nutrient uptake and Yield of Chickpea (*Cicer aritenium* L.)," *Applied Soil Ecology*, Vol. 28, No. 2, pp. 139-146, 2005.
5. M.S. Khan, A. Zaidi, and P.A. Wani, "Role of Phosphate-sol-ubilizing Microorganisms in Sustainable Agriculture – A Review," *Agronomy for Sustainable Development*, Vol. 27, No. 1, pp. 29-43, 2007.
6. A.C. Gaur, *Phosphate Solubilizing Microorganisms as Biofertilizer*, Omega Scientific Publishers, New Delhi, India, 1990.
7. M.L. Jackson, *Soil Chemical Analysis*, Prentice Hall of India, Pvt. Ltd., New Delhi, India, 1967.

8. A. Walkley and I.A. Black, "An Examination of the Degtjareff Method for Determining Organic Carbon in Soils: Effect of Variations in Digestion Conditions and of Inorganic Soil Constituents," *Soil Science*, Vol. 63, pp. 251-263, 1934.

9. R.H. Bray and L.T. Kurtz, "Determination of Total, Organic and Available Forms of Phosphorous in Soils," *Soil Science*, Vol. 59, pp. 39-45, 1954.

10. L. Chesnin and C.H. Yein, "Turbiditymetric Determination of Available Sulphur in Soil," *Soil Science Society of America Proceedings*, Vol. 15, pp. 149-151, 1951.

11. B. Toomsan, O.P. Rupela, S. Mittal, P.J. Dart, and K.W. Clark, "Counting Cicer-*Rhizobium* using a Plant Infection Technique," *Soil Biology and Biochemistry*, Vol. 16, No. 5, pp. 503-507, 1984.

12. W.V.B. Sundara Rao and M.K. Sinha, "Phosphate Dissolving Organisms in the Soil and Rhizosphere," *Indian Journal of Agricultural Sciences*, Vol. 33, pp. 272-278, 1963.

13. A.F. Beau, "A Method for Hemoglobin in Serum and Urine," *Technical Bulletin of the Registry of Medical Technologists*, Vol. 32, pp. 111-112, 1962.

14 N.S. Subba Rao, *Soil Microorganisms and Plant Growth*, Oxford and IBH Pub. Co. Pvt. Ltd., New Delhi, India, 1986.

15. S.C. Gupta and S.L. Namdeo, "Fertilizer Economy through Composts and Bio-fertilizer in Chickpea," *Annals of Plant and Soil Research*, Vol. 2, pp. 244-246, 2000.

16. J.M. Barea, M.J. Pozo, R. Azcon, and C. Azcon-Aguilar, "Microbial Co-operation in the Rhizosphere," *Journal of Experimental Botany*, Vol. 56, No. 417, pp. 1761-1778, 2005.

17. G.S. Sidhu, N. Singh, and R. Singh, "Symbiotic Nitrogen Fixation by some Summer Legumes in Punjab. Role of Leghemoglobin in Nitrogen Fixation," *Journal of Research, Punjab Agricultural University*, Vol. 4, pp. 244-248, 1967.

18. R.C. Singh, M. Singh, R. Kumar, and D.P. Tomer, "Response of Chickpea (*Cicer arietinum*) Genotypes to Row Spacing and Fertility under Rainfed Conditions," *Indian Journal of Agronomy*, Vol. 39, No. 4, pp. 569-572, 1994.

19. K.P. Tiwari, L.N. Yadav, and U.S. Thakur, "Relative Performance of Gram Varieties under different Dates of Sowing," *Crop Research*, Vol. 11, No. 1, pp. 127-130, 1996.

20. N. Togay, Y. Togay, K.M. Cimrin, and M. Turan, "Effects of *Rhizobium* Inoculation, Sulfur and Phosphorus Applications on Yield, Yield Components and Nutrient uptakes in Chickpea (*Cicer arietinum* L.)," *African Journal of Biotechnology*, Vol. 7, No. 6, pp. 776-782, 2008.

21. R.K. Sharma, S.K. Dubey, R.S. Sharma, and J.P. Tiwari, "Effect of Irrigation Schedules and Fertility Levels of Nodulation Yield and Water use Efficiency in Chickpea (*Cicer arietinum* L.)," *JNKVV Research Journal*, Vol. 28, No. 1-2, pp. 8-10, 1998.

22. A. Namvar, R.S. Sharif i, M. Sedghi, R.A. Zakaria, T. Khandan, and B. Eskandarpour, "Study on the Effects of Organic and Inorganic Nitrogen Fertilizer on Yield, Yield Components, and Nodulation State of Chickpea (*Cicer arietinum* L.)," *Communi-cations in Soil Science and Plant Analysis*, Vol. 42, No. 9, pp. 1097-1109, 2011.

23. R.S. Jat and I.P.S. Ahlawat, "Effect of Vermicompost, Biofertilizer and Phosphorus on Growth, Yield and Nutrient Uptake by Gram (*Cicer arietinum*) and their Residual Effect on Fodder Maize (*Zea mays*)," *Indian Journal of Agricultural Sciences*, Vol. 74, No. 7, pp. 359-361, 2004.

24. M. Geneva, G. Zehirov, E. Djonova, N. Kaloyanova, G. Georgiev, and I. Stancheva, "The Effect of Inoculation of Pea Plants with Mycorrhizal Fungi and *Rhizobium* on Nitrogen and Phosphorus Assimilation," *Plant, Soil and Environment*, Vol. 52, No. 10, pp. 435-440, 2006.

25. H. Ögütçü, Ö.F. Algur, E. Elkoca, and F. Kantar, "The Determination of Symbiotic Effectiveness of *Rhizobium* Strains Isolated from wild Chickpeas Collected from High Altitudes in Erzurum," *Turkish Journal of Agriculture and Forestry*, Vol. 32, No. 4, pp. 241-248, 2008.

26. V.G. Takankhar, S.S. Mane, B.G. Kamble, and B.S. Indulkar, "Grain Quality of Chickpea as Influenced by Phosphorus Fertilization and *Rhizobium* Inoculation," *Journal of the Indian Society of Soil Science*, Vol. 45, No. 2, pp. 394-396, 1997.

27. J.R. Khoja, S.S. Khangarot, A.K. Gupta, and A.K. Kulhari, "Effect of Fertilizer and Biofertilizers on Growth and Yield of Chickpea," *Annals of Plant and Soil Research*, Vol. 4, pp. 357-358, 2002.

28. N.R.N. Reddy and I.P.S. Ahlawat, "Response of Chickpea (*Cicer arietinum*) Genotypes to Irrigation and Fertilizers under late-sown Conditions," *Indian Journal of Agronomy*, Vol. 43, No. 1, pp. 95-101, 1998.

29. K.N. Meena, R.G. Pareek, and R.S. Jat, "Effect of Phosphorus and Biofertilizers on Yield and Quality of Chickpea (*Cicer arietinum* L.)," *Annals of Agricultural Research*, Vol. 22, pp. 388-390, 2001.

30. S.C. Gupta, "Response of gram (*Cicer arietinum*) to types and Method of Microbial Inoculation," *Indian Journal of Agricultural Science*, Vol. 74, No. 2, pp. 73-75, 2004.

31. M. Erman, S. Demir, E. Ocak, . Tufenkçi, F. Oguz, and A. Akkopru, "Effects of *Rhizobium*, Arbuscular Mycorrhiza and Whey Applications on Some Properties in Chickpea (*Cicer arietinum* L.) under Irrigated and Rainfed Conditions 1-Yield, Yield Components, Nodulation and AMF Colonization," *Field Crops Research*, Vol. 122, No. 1, pp. 14-24, 2011.

32. L.K. Jain, P. Singh, and P. Singh, "Growth and Nutrient uptake of Chickpea (*Cicer arietinum* L.) as Influenced by Biofertilizers and Phosphorus Nutrition," *Crop Research*, Vol. 25, pp. 410-413, 2003.

33. Reddy, B. Gopal, and M. Suryanarayan Reddy, "Effect of Organic Manures and Nitrogen Levels on Soil Available Nutrients Status in Maize-Soybean Cropping System," *Journal of the Indian Society of Soil Science*, Vol. 46, pp. 474-476, 1998.

34. J.P. Singh and J.C. Tarafdar, "Rhizospheric Microflora as Influenced by Sulphur Application, Herbicide and *Rhizobium* Inoculation in Summer Mung Bean (*Vigna radiata* L.)," *Journal of the Indian Society of Soil Science*, Vol. 50, pp. 127-130, 2002.

Pages 130-135

INTEGRATED NUTRIENT MANAGEMENT IN CHICKPEA
***Edited by* : Dr. Virendra Kumar and Dr. Nirmal Kumar Katiyar**
***Edition* : 2017**
ISBN : 978-93-5056-872-9
***Published by* : Discovery Publishing House Pvt. Ltd., New Delhi (India)**

12

Effect of Phosphorus and Zinc Nutrition on Yield, Nutrient Uptake and Quality of Chickpea

Devendra Singh
Harendra Singh

ABSTRACT

A field experiment was conducted to study the individual and interactive effect of P and Zn on yield, nutrient content and nutrient uptake of chickpea (Cicer arietinum L.) The grain and straw yields increased significantly with increasing doses of P and Zn. The interaction between P and Zn also had significantly beneficial effect on the yield of chickpea. An increase in P uptake by grain and straw with applied P was recorded but it was decreased at higher level of applied Zn. The content and uptake of Zn in grain and straw increased significantly with increasing levels of Zn. Phosphorus and zinc applied to chickpea significantly increased the protein content in grain and straw.

Keywords: Phosphorus, Zinc, Nutrition, Protein, Chickpea, Economics.

INTRODUCTION

Chickpea (*Cicer arietinum* L.) is a multipurpose pulse crop consumed by the people in different forms *viz;* dal leaves, germinated seed etc. Phosphorus, key nutrient for increasing productivity of pulses, is required for plant growth and root development. Phosphorus deficiency in soils is widespread and crops grown under deficient situation show significant responses to fertilizer P. Zinc is essential for promoting certain metabolic reactions. It is necessary

Department of Agricultural Chemistry, Amar Singh College Lakhaoti, Bulandshahr (U.P.) - 245 407.

for the production of chlorophyll and carbohydrates. Zinc is directly or indirectly required by several enzyme systems, auxin and protein synthesis. Zinc is believed to promote RNA synthesis, which in turn is needed for protein production. At several places normal yield of crops could not be achieved despite judicious use of NPK fertilizers due to deficiency of micronutrients in soil, in general, that of Zn in particular. A favourable balance between phosphorus and zinc should be maintained for optimum growth of plant. Most of the soils of Uttar Pradesh have been rated as deficient in available zinc. Sharma *et al.* (2000) reported antagonistic effect of P levels on Zn nutrition by the crops. The information on Zn and P relationship in an important crop like: chickpea is not adequate, especially in situations where both the interacting nutrients (P and Zn) are deficient in soil. Therefore, the present investigation was carried out to study the effect of P and Zn application on yield, nutrient uptake and quality in chickpea grown in alluvial soils of Uttar Pradesh.

Materials and Methods

A field experiment was conducted during the winter (*rabi*) seasons of 2008-09 and 2009-10 at Amar Singh College, Lakhaoti, Bulandshahr (U.P.). The experimental soil had pH 7.8, EC (1:2) 0.19 dS m^{-1}, organic carbon 3.9 g kg^{-1}, available N 178 kg ha^{-1}, available P 9.8 kg ha^{-1}, available K 195 kg ha^{-1} and DTPA – extractable Zn 0.50 mg kg^{-1}. Four levels of each of P_2O_5 (0, 30, 60 and 90 kg ha^{-1} as DAP) and Zn (0, 2.5, 5 and 10 kg ha^{-1} as Zn) were applied in 16 treatment combinations replicated thrice in randomized block design. A common basal dose of 20 kg N ha^{-1} through Urea and 40 kg K_2O ha^{-1} through muriate of Potash was applied to all the plots. The N present in DAP was adjusted while calculating the amount of N given as basal dressing by Urea. The plot size was 4.5 m × 3.6 m with row spacing of 30 cm × 10 cm. Chickpea var. KPG 59 was shown on 28 and 26 October in 2008 and 2009 and harvested on 21 and 18 March in 2009 and 2010, respectively. Grain and straw samples collected at maturity were analyzed for P content in di acid (HNO_3: $HClO_4$) extract by Vanadomolybdo phosphoric yellow extract was determined by atomic absorption spectrophotometer. Protein in grain and straw was computed by multiplying per cent N content by 6.25.

Results and Discussion

Yield, Protein Content and Economics

Successive and significant increase in P levels up to 60 kg P_2O_5 ha^{-1} resulted in enhanced grain and straw yields of chickpea (Table 12.1). Application of 60 kg P_2O_5 ha^{-1} increased the grain and straw yields significantly by 27.4 and 24.7 per cent, respectively over the control. The higher level of P (90 kg $P_2O_5$$ha^{-1}$) was statistically at par with 60 kg P_2O_5 ha^{-1} in increasing the yield.

The increase in yield of chickpea grain and straw with P application may be due to fact that soil under study was deficient in available P (9.8 kg ha^{-1}). Kumar *et al*. (2009) also observed an increase in yield of chickpea with increasing levels of P on phosphorus deficient soils. The yield of chickpea grain and straw (Table 12.1) increased significantly by 9.8 and 11.4 per cent, respectively with the application of 5 kg Zn ha^{-1}. This might be due to its function as catalyst or stimulant in most of the physiological and metabolic processes. However, the response was better at lower rate (2.5 kg Zn ha^{-1}) application rather than at higher rate. Increase in yield due to application of Zn is quite obvious, as the soil under study was deficient in available zinc (0.5 mg kg^{-1}). Sharma *et al*. (2000) and Singh and Ram (2001) also noted a significant response of legumes to Zn applied to deficient soils.

Table 12.1: Effects of phosphorus and zinc levels on yield, protein content and economics of chickpea (Pooled data)

Treatments	Yield (qha^{-1})		Protein (%)		Net Profit ($Rs\ ha^{-1}$)	Benefit: Cost Ratio
	Grain	Straw	Grain	Straw		
P_2O_5 (kg ha^{-1})						
0	15.40	18.50	20.09	8.99	18572.6	1.18
30	17.23	20.72	20.37	9.34	22035.3	1.34
60	19.63	23.07	20.59	9.55	26748.0	1.57
90	20.22	23.81	20.90	9.71	27457.7	1.56
CD(P=0.05)	0.90	1.40	0.16	0.17	–	–
Zn (kg ha^{-1})						
0	17.02	20.23	20.21	9.18	21372.6	1.28
2.5	18.24	21.74	20.49	9.31	24015.5	1.43
5.0	18.69	22.54	20.55	9.52	25565.8	1.52
10.0	18.26	21.60	20.65	9.62	23859.7	1.41
CD (P=0.05)	0.90	1.40	0.16	0.17	–	–

Protein content in chickpea grain and straw increased significantly with application of phosphorus and zinc individually as well as in combination as compared to control (Table 12.1). The maximum percentage of protein (20.90% in grain and 9.71% in straw) was recorded at 90 kg P_2O_5 ha^{-1}. The response of applied phosphorus with respect to protein contents in chickpea is attributed to more nitrogen fixation in soil. Similar results were reported by Meena *et al*. (2001) in chickpea. Application of increasing doses of zinc resulted in a significant increase in protein content of chickpea over control. The protein content in grain and straw increased from 20.21 to 20.65 and 9.18 to 9.62 with 10 kg Zn ha^{-1}. The increase in protein content due to Zn addition might be attributed to its involvement in N metabolism of plants. The data on monetary advantage (Table 12.1) based on 2 years of experimentation indicated that maximum net return and benefit: cost ratios were obtained with higher dose of P and Zn. This could be ascribed to higher grain yield obtained owing of higher levels of P and Zn.

Table 12.2: Effect of phosphorus and zinc levels on their content and uptake in chickpea (pooled data)

Treatment	P Content (%)		Zn Content (mg kg^{-1})		P Uptake (kg ha^{-1})		Zn Uptake (g ha^{-1})	
	Grain	Straw	Grain	Straw	Grain	Straw	Grain	Straw
P_2O_5 (kg ha^{-1})								
0	0.46	0.21	23.76	20.73	7.1	3.8	36.6	37.6
30	0.50	0.23	23.02	19.91	8.6	4.7	39.7	40.5
60	0.58	0.26	22.99	19.81	11.4	6.0	45.1	44.7
90	0.60	0.27	22.52	19.41	12.1	6.5	45.6	45.1
CD (P=0.05)	0.012	0.007	0.73	0.50	0.65	0.43	3.10	2.50
Zn (kg ha^{-1})								
0	0.51	0.23	19.93	16.91	8.7	4.6	34.0	34.2
2.5	0.55	0.25	21.52	20.31	10.1	5.5	39.3	44.0
5.0	0.51	0.25	24.23	21.42	9.6	5.5	46.0	48.3
10.0	0.49	0.23	26.60	23.15	9.0	5.0	48.6	49.5
CD (P=0.05)	0.012	0.007	0.73	0.50	0.65	0.43	3.10	2.50

Content and Uptake of Nutrients

Phosphorus content of grain and straw of chickpea increased significantly with increasing doses of P (Table 12.2) which may be attributes to deeper root growth by phosphorus, resulting in higher content of P in the crop. Application of lower levels of zinc increased the P content in grain and straw over control. The maximum Values of P content in grain and straw were recorded with 2.5kg Zn ha^{-1}. Application of 10 kg Zn ha^{-1} tended to decrease the P content in grain and straw and this reduction in P content was significant over 5 kg Zn ha^{-1}. This reduction in P content may be due to hindrance caused by increased concentration of zinc in the absorption and translocation of P from the roots to the above ground parts. Singh and Manohar (1982) also reported similar results. The highest uptake of P was recorded at 90 kg P_2O_5 ha^{-1} and lowest in the control. Among various levels of P, the higher level could probably maintain the available P status in soil to facilitate its uptake at an optimum level. This increase in P uptake may be attributed to higher P content as well as grain and straw yields with higher dose of P. The results are in conformity with the findings of Kanwar and Paliyal (2002).

Application of 2.5 kg Zn ha^{-1} tended to increase the P uptake by chickpea grain and straw significantly over the control. Phosphorus uptake by chickpea decreased at higher level of Zn (5 and 10 kg Zn ha^{-1}) over 2.5 kg Zn ha^{-1}. The results indicate an antagonistic relationship between P and Zn nutrition of chickpea.A significant increase in the Zn content of grain and straw of chickpea with a corresponding increase in the Zn dose was observed (Table 12.2). Application of 10 kg Zn ha^{-1} increased the zinc content by 6.6 mg kg^{-1} and that of straw by 6.2 mg kg^{-1} over control. Similar results were reported by Singh and Ram (2001). Zinc content of grain and straw of chickpea decreased significantly as the dose of P increased. This decrease in Zn content at an increased P level may be due to the depressive effect of P on Zn. The reduction in Zn content may be ascribed to antagonistic effect of P on Zn absorption by the plants. Similar observations with added phosphorus were reported by Singh and Ram (2001). The uptake of zinc by chickpea grain and straw increased significantly with increasing levels of zinc over the control due to increase in yield and zinc content as a result of zinc application. The uptake of zinc was also influenced significantly by P application. Uptake of zinc by chickpea crop increased significantly with phosphorus addition up to 90 kg P_2O_5 ha^{-1}. The higher levels (60 and 90 kg P_2O_5 ha^{-1}) of P were at par in respect of zinc uptake by chickpea. Similar results were also reported by Sharma *et al.* (2000). Maximum values of Zn uptake by grain and straw were obtained with 90 kg P_2O_5 ha^{-1}. On the other hand, lower values of Zn uptake by grain and straw were recorded under control.

Table 12.3: Interaction effect of phosphorus and zinc levels on grain and straw yield of chickpea (pooled data)

P_2O_5 (kg ha^{-1})	Zn Levels (kg ha^{-1})			
	0	2.5	5.0	10
	Grain yield (q ha^{-1})			
0	14.42	15.26	16.02	15.89
30	16.27	17.40	18.17	17.07
60	18.23	19.73	20.48	20.08
90	19.18	20.56	21.18	19.98
CD (P=0.05)		2.10		
	Straw yield (q ha^{-1})			
0	17.17	18.64	19.43	18.76
30	19.81	20.94	21.69	20.48
60	21.43	23.28	24.05	23.52
90	22.51	24.11	25.00	23.65
CD (P=0.05)		2.55		

Interaction

The interaction effect of P and Zn was significant for grain and straw yield (Table 12.3). The maximum grain and straw yields were obtained under 90 kg P_2O_5 + 5 kg Zn ha^{-1} treatment. Application of 60 kg P_2O_5 + 5 kg Zn ha^{-1} proved at par to 90 kg P_2O_5 + 5 kg Zn ha^{-1} in respect of grain and straw production. Protein content also improved with P and Zn application. This favourable effect of P and Zn combination may be because addition of Zn with P might have maintained a favourable balance between P and Zn in the chickpea plant for optimum growth. Satyajit *et al.* (2003) also reported response of chickpea to P and Zn. In can be concluded that combination of 60 kg P_2O_5 + 5 kg Zn ha^{-1} would be sufficient to get higher yields of chickpea.

REFERENCES

Jackson, M.L. (1973). *Soil Chemical Analysis.* Prentice Hall of India Private Limited, New Delhi.

Kanwar, Kamla and Paliyal, S.S. (2002). Influence of Phosphorus Management and Organic Manuring on uptake and Yield of Chickpea *(Cicer arietinum).* Annals of Agricultural Research New Series 23(4): 642-645.

Kumar, R., Singh, N.B. and Pal, S. (2004). Effect of Phosphorus, Sulphur and Rhizobium Inoculation on Yield, Nodulation and Nutrients uptake in Chickpea. *Annals of Plant and Soil Research* 6(2): 131-133.

Kumar, V., Dwivedi, K.N. and Tiwari, D.D. (2009). Effect of Phosphorus and Iron on Yield and Mineral Nutrition in Chickpea. *Annals of Plant and Soil Research* 11(1): 16-18.

Meena, K.N., Pareek, R.G. and Jat, R.S. (2001). Effect of Phosphorus and Biofertilizers on Yield and Quality of Chickpea *(Cicer arietinum L.). Annals of Agricultural Research New Series* 22(3): 388-390.

Satyajit, Pathak, Namdeo, K.N., Chakrawarti, V.K. and Tiwari, R.K. (2003). Effect of Biofertilizers, Diammonium Phosphate and Zinc Sulphate on Nutrient Contents and Uptake of Chickpea *(Cicer arietinum L.). Crop Research Hisar* 26(1): 47-52.

Sharma, R.S., Om Prakash and Singh, B.P. (2000). Response of Mothbean Genotypes to Phosphorus and Row Spacing under Semi-arid Conditions. *Annals of Plant and Soil Research* 2(2):240-243.

Singh, A.K. and Ram, H. (2001). Effect of Phosphorus and Zinc on Yield and Quality of Mungbean. *Annals of Plant and Soil Research* 3(2): 307-309.

Singh, G., and Manohar, R.S. (1982). Study on the uptake of Nitrogen and Phosphorus by Green Gram and Quality of Crops as Affected by Phosphorus by Levels and Foliar Spray of H_2SO_4 and Micronutrients. *Indian Journal of Agriculture Research* 16(4): 219-222.

Pages 136-144

INTEGRATED NUTRIENT MANAGEMENT IN CHICKPEA
Edited by **: Dr. Virendra Kumar** and **Dr. Nirmal Kumar Katiyar**
Edition **: 2017**
ISBN : 978-93-5056-872-9
Published by **: Discovery Publishing House Pvt. Ltd., New Delhi (India)**

13

Nutrient Uptake and Yield of Chickpea (*Cicer arietinum* L.) Inoculated with Plant Growth-Promoting Rhizobacteria

Asad Rokhzadi[1]*
Vafa Toashih[2]

ABSTRACT

This research was carried out to evaluate the effects of single and combined inoculation with plant growth-promoting rhizobacteria from four genera including: Azospirillum, Azotobacter, Mesorhizobium and Pseudomonas on nutrient uptake, growth and yield of chickpea plants under field conditions. Nodulation and nutrient concentration in shoots were significantly affected by the treatments at the beginning of flowering stage. The maximum dry weight of root nodules was recorded by applying the combined inoculation with Azospirillum spp. + Azotobacter chroococcum 5 + Mesorhizobium ciceri SWRI7 + Pseudomonas fluorescens P21. All inoculants were statistically superior over uninoculated control with respect to nitrogen concentration of shoots. The treatments containing Azospirillum + Azotobacter significantly improved phosphorus concentration in shoots. Grain yield, biomass dry weight and nitrogen and phosphorus uptake of grains were statistically improved by applying every inoculation treatment in comparison with control plants. Group comparisons between treatments showed that the occurance of Azospirillum or Azotobacter inoculants in the treatment composition caused an expressive improvement in grain yield and plant biomass. In conclusion, application of every inoculation treatment

1. Department of Agronomy and Plant Breeding, Faculty of Agriculture and Natural Resources, Islamic Azad University, Sanandaj Branch, Iran. *E-mail: asadrokh@yahoo.com
2. Soil and Water Research Institute, Agricultural and Natural Resources Research Center of Kurdistan, Iran.

studied here, especially treatments which contained Azospirillum or Azotobacter may stimulate growth and yield of chickpea as compared with uninoculated plants.

Keywords: Azospirillum, Azotobacter, *Cicer arietinum* L., Mesorhizobium, Plant Growth-promoting Rhizobacteria, Pseudomonas.

Abbreviations: CFU-colony forming units; DAS-days after sowing; PGPR-plant growth promoting rhizobacteria.

INTRODUCTION

Plant growth promoting rhizobacteria (PGPR) represent a wide variety of soil bacteria which, when grown in association with a host plant, result in stimulation of growth of their host plant (Vessey, 2003). Several mechanisms have been suggested by which PGPR can promote plant growth, including: phytohormone production, N_2 fixation, stimulation of nutrient uptake and biocontrol of pathogenic microorganisms (Kloepper *et al.* 1981; Rodriguez and Fraga, 1999; Sindhu *et al.* 1999; Benizri *et al.* 2001; Persello-Cartieaux *et al.* 2003; Somers *et al.* 2004). Many different genera of plant growth promoting rhizobacteria such as: *Azospirillum, Azotobacter, Bacillus, Enterobacter* and *Pseudomonas* have been used as biofertilizers for economically important crops. Seed inoculation with a combination of beneficial microorganisms including rhizobia, PGPR and PSB (Phosphate Solubilizing Bacteria) have been shown to increase crop growth and productivity (Dashti *et al.* 1998; Rodelas *et al.* 1999; Chebotar *et al.* 2001; Sindhu *et al.* 2002; Zaidi *et al.* 2003; Rudresh *et al.* 2005). However little is known about the response of chickpea to combined inoculation with rhizobium and plant growth promoting rhizobacteria under field conditions. Chickpea (*Cicer arietinum* L.) is one of the major pulse crops in the world and provides high quality protein for the people in South, West and East Asia and North Africa. It is also used as feed for livestock and has a significant role in farming systems (Singh, 1997). In Iran chickpea is the most important grain legume and improving it's productivity is a necessity. Hence the present study was conducted to evaluate the effects of single and combined inoculations with strains of bacteria from genera *Mesorhizobium, Azospirillum, Azotobacter* and *Pseudomonas* on nutrient uptake, growth and yield of chickpea under field conditions.

Materials and Methods

Experimental Site

This experiment was carried out at the agricultural research station of Saral (35° 432 N and 47° 82 E with an altitude of 2100 m) in Kurdistan, Iran, during the cropping season of 2005-06 in rainfed conditions. The long-term rates of average temperature and annual precipitation in the region are 7.9°C and 393.6 mm respectively. The total precipitation during 2005-06 was 305.8 mm. Some of the soil properties were: sand 35.3 per cent, silt 38.7 per cent, clay 26 per cent, pH 7.5, OC 0.89 per cent, total N 0.076 per cent, available P and K, 8.7 and 409.3 ppm respectively. All plots of experimental field treated with 30 kg nitrogen ha^{-1} in urea form according to soil tests before sowing.

Bacterial Strains

The bacterial cultures used in this study were obtained from the soil biology department, Soil and Water Research Institute (SWRI), ministry of agriculture, Tehran, Iran. The strains included: *Mesorhizobium ciceri* strain SWRI7 (1×10^7 CFU mL^{-1} carrier), *Pseudomonas fluorescens* strain P21 (5×10^7 CFU mL^{-1} carrier), *Azotobacter chroococcum* strain 5 (2.5×10^9 CFU mL^{-1} carrier) and *Azospirillum* spp. (5×10^8 CFU mL^{-1} carrier). *Azospirillum* culture contained a combination of *Azospirillum brasilense* (strain OF) and *Azospirillum lipoferum* (strain 21) at an equal ratio.

Table 13.1: Root nodules dry weight and concentration of nitrogen and phosphorus in shoots of chickpea in response to inoculation with plant growth-promoting rhizobacteria at the flowering stage

Treatments	Nodule Dry Weight (mg Plant^{-1})	N Concentration (%)	P Concentration (%)
1. Uninoculated	33.37 d	2.96 f	0.280 e
2. *Azos.*	40.02 b-d	3.18 e	0.287 e
3. *Azot.*	44.62 b-d	3.51 ab	0.303 de
4. *M.*	53.35 b-d	3.47 a-c	0.297 de
5. *P.*	53.38 b-d	3.32 b-e	0.293 de
6. *Azos.+Azot.*	35.77 cd	3.46 a-c	0.390 ab
7. *Azos.+M.*	45.78 b-d	3.43 a-d	0.320 c-e
8. *Azos.+P.*	52.28 b-d	3.45 a-c	0.353 b-d
9. *Azot.+M.*	52.70 b-d	3.31 c-e	0.300 de
10. *Azot.+P.*	32.64 d	3.40 b-d	0.280 e
11. *M.+P.*	34.41 cd	3.33 b-e	0.283 e
12. *Azos.+Azot.+M.*	60.54 b	3.30 c-e	0.417 a
13. *Azos.+Azot.+P.*	40.77 b-d	3.63 a	0.370 a-c
14. *Azos.+M.+P.*	54.49 bc	3.46 a-c	0.310 de
15. *Azot.+M.+P.*	50.16 b-d	3.23 de	0.280 e
16. *Azos.+Azot.+M.+P.*	83.29 a	3.37 b-e	0.283 e
Selected group comparisons			
Comparison 1			**
Comparison 2			NS
Comparison 3			NS
Comparison 4			NS
Comparison 5			**

Azos: *Azospirillum*, *Azot*: *Azotobacter*, *M*: *Mesorhizobium*, *P*: *Pseudomonas*, Values followed by the same letters in a column are not significantly different at $P < 0.05$ according to Duncan's multiple range test. Comparison 1: *Azospirillum*-cotaining *vs.* non-*Azospirillum*-containing treatments. Comparison 2: *Azotobacter*-containing *vs.* non-*Azotobacter*-containing treatments. Comparison 3: *Mesorhizobium*-containing *vs.* non-*Mesorhizobium*-containing treatments. Comparison 4: *Pseudomonas*-containing *vs.* non-*Pseudomonas*-containing treatments. Comparison 5: *Azospirillum* + *Azotobacter*-containing *vs.* non-*A Azospirillum+Azotobacter*-containing treatments.

** Significant at the 0.01 probability level, NS: not significant.

Experimental Design and Treatments

The layout of the trial was a randomized complete block design (RCBD) with 3 replications and 16 treatments included: (1) Uninoculated control (2) *Azospirillum* (3) *Azotobacter* (4) *Mesorhizobium* (5) *Pseudomonas* (6) *Azospirillum* + *Azotobacter* (7) *Azospirillum* + *Mesorhizobium* (8) *Azospirillum* + *Pseudomonas* (9) *Azotobacter* + *Mesorhizobium* (10) *Azotobacter* + *Pseudomonas* (11) *Mesorhizobium* + *Pseudomonas* (12) *Azospirillum* + *Azotobacter* + *Mesorhizobium* (13) *Azospirillum* + *Azotobacter* + *Pseudomonas* (14) *Azospirillum* + *Mesorhizobium* + *Pseudomonas* (15) *Azotobacter* + *Mesorhizobium* + *Pseudomonas* (16) *Azospirillum* + *Azotobacter* + *Mesorhizobium* + *Pseudomonas.* Each plot contained 6 rows of 5 m length with 30 cm inter-row spacing and 10 cm between plants in each row.

Seed Inoculation and Sowing

Seeds of chickpea (*Cicer arietinum* L.) cv. Pirooz (a desi type cultivar) were mixed with 1 per cent gum arabic as adhesive agent and then inoculation was performed at the rate of 2 mL bacterial inoculant suspension per 100 g seeds. Then the inoculated seeds were dried under shed (to avoid direct sunshine) and sowing was immediately performed by hand. In order to prevent cross infection between treatments, the uninoculated control plots were sown beforehand and about other plots new sterile medical gloves were used for sowing each plot.

Sampling and Data Collection

At the beginning of flowering stage (74 days after sowing) the whole plants located in an area of 1.2 m^2 from the central four rows of each plot were carefully uprooted. Roots were washed through slow running tap water to remove adhering soil particles. Nodules were precisely separated from roots, dried and weighed. Then the shoots were oven dried at 65°C for 48 h and nitrogen and phosphorus concentration of shoots was determined in the laboratory of Soil and Water Research Institute, Sanandaj, Iran. At maturity, a 2.4 m^2 area of unsampled four central rows of each plot was hand-harvested. The plants were air dried and biomass dry weight, grain yield, nitrogen and phosphorus contents in grain samples were determined.

Statistical Analysis

The data were subjected to analysis of variance (ANOVA), and comparison among treatment means was performed by Duncan's multiple range test (at $P < 0.05$) using MSTAT-C software (Version 2.10). About some of the recorded parameters, group comparisons between treatments were made.

Table 13.2: Inoculation effects of plant growth-promoting rhizobacteria on grain yield, biomass dry weight and nitrogen and phosphorus uptake by grains

Treatments	Grain Yield (kg ha^{-1})		Biomass (kg ha^{-1})		N Yield (kg ha^{-1})		P Yield (kg ha^{-1})	
1. Uninoculated	543.9	i	1082.3	f	14.49	e	2.088	d
2. *Azos.*	826.8	b-f	1609.3	b-d	27.85	ab	3.252	a-c
3. *Azot.*	797.1	b-g	1549.4	b-d	28.60	a	3.168	a-c
4. *M.*	772.5	d-h	1514.4	b-e	27.05	a-d	2.890	bc
5. *P.*	739.3	gh	1445.8	de	22.17	cd	2.747	c
6. *Azos.+Azot.*	877.2	ab	1695.8	a-c	27.05	a-c	3.459	ab
7. *Azos.+M.*	751.8	e-h	1493.1	c-e	24.53	a-d	2.869	bc
8. *Azos.+P.*	781.1	c-g	1509.6	b-e	20.32	d	3.132	a-c
9. *Azot.+M.*	835.3	a-e	1629.4	b-d	27.53	a-c	3.142	a-c
10. *Azot.+P.*	697.5	h	1427.8	de	21.97	cd	2.963	bc
11. *M.+P.*	689.9	h	1340.8	e	22.96	b-d	3.017	a-c
12. *Azos.+Azot.+M.*	818.6	b-g	1621.8	b-d	25.40	a-d	3.147	a-c
13. *Azos.+Azot.+P.*	910.6	a	1845.8	a	29.78	a	3.606	a
14. *Azos.+M.+P.*	864.0	a-c	1705.6	ab	26.60	a-c	3.277	a-c
15. *Azot.+M.+P.*	847.5	a-d	1665.3	abc	25.28	a-d	3.151	a-c
16. *Azos.+Azot.+M.+P.*	743.3	f-h	1442.8	de	22.10	cd	3.016	a-c
Selected group comparisons								
Comparison 1	**	**						
Comparison 2	**	**						
Comparison 3	NS	NS						
Comparison 4	NS	NS						

Azos: *Azospirillum*, *Azot*: *Azotobacter*, *M*: *Mesorhizobium*, *P*: *Pseudomonas*, Values followed by the same letters in a column are not significantly different at $P < 0.05$ according to Duncan's multiple range test. Comparison 1: *Azospirillum*-cotaining *vs.* non-*Azospirillum*-containing treatments. Comparison 2: *Azotobacter*-containing *vs.* non-*Azotobacter*-containing treatments. Comparison 3: *Mesorhizobium*-containing *vs.* non-*Mesorhizobium*-containing treatments. Comparison 4: *Pseudomonas*-containing *vs.* non-*Pseudomonas*-containing treatments. ** Significant at the 0.01 probability level, NS: not significant.

Results

Data analysis at the beginning of flowering stage (74 DAS) showed that inoculation treatments significantly affected nodule dry weight and the concentration of nitrogen and phosphorus in shoots (Table 13.1). Maximum dry weight of root nodules per plant was recorded by applying the combined inoculation of *Azospirillum* spp. + *Azotobacter chroococcum* 5 + *Mesorhizobium ciceri* SWRI7 + *Pseudomonas fluorescens* P21 (Table 13.1). All inoculants were statistically superior over uninoculated control with respect to nitrogen concentration of shoots. The highest rates of phosphorus concentration in shoots were recorded by the treatments of number 12 (*Azospirillum* spp. + *Azotobacter chroococcum* 5 + *Mesorhizobium ciceri* SWRI 7), number 6 (*Azospirillum* spp. + *Azotobacter chroococcum* 5) and number 13 (*Azospirillum* spp. + *Azotobacter chroococcum* 5 + *Pseudomonas fluorescens* P 21) respectively (Table 13.1). These inoculation treatments contain *Azospirillum* and *Azotobacter* strains in their combinations, suggesting that *Azospirillum* and *Azotobacter* jointly may have a role in promoting phosphorus uptake by plant. Therefore a group comparison between *Azospirillum* + *Azotobacter*-containing treatments *vs.* non-*Azospirillum* + *Azotobacter*-containing treatments was performed with respect to phosphorus concentration of shoots, as a result this comparison was significant ($P < 0.01$), demonstrating that treatments containing *Azospirillum* + *Azotobacter* significantly improved phosphorus concentration in shoot (Table 13.1). Furthermore group comparison analyses showed that *Azospirillum*-containing treatments statistically enhanced phosphorus concentration of shoots in comparison with other treatments, even though the comparison of *Azotobacter*-containing treatments vs. other treatments was not significant (Table 13.1).

The mentioned contrast analyses revealed that *Azospirillum* had the main role in improving phosphorus uptake in plant, besides *Azotobacter* had an auxiliary role in this respect. Grain yield and biomass dry weight of chickpea plants were significantly affected by inoculation treatments. Grain yield ranged from 543.9 kg ha $^{-1}$ in uninoculated control to 910.6 kg ha^{-1} in triple inoculation with *Azospirillum* spp., *Azotobacter chroococcum* 5 and *Pseudomonas fluorescens* P21. Plant biomass ranged from 1082.3 kg ha^{-1} in control to 1845.8 kg ha^{-1} in combined inoculation with *Azospirillum* spp., *Azotobacter chroococcum* 5 and *Pseudomonas fluorescens* P21 (Table 13.2).

The uninoculated control treatment was statistically alone in a class with respect to grain yield and biomass. Therefore application of any bacterial treatments resulted a significant improvement in grain yield and plant biomass as compared with control (Table 13.2). Group comparisons between treatments showed that the occurance of *Azospirillum* or *Azotobacter* inoculants in the treatment composition caused an expressive improvement in grain yield and plant biomass (Table 13.2). The total nitrogen and phosphorus yield of grains followed a similar trend to grain yield. The lowest rates of total N and P uptake by grain were recorded in control plants which significantly differed from all inoculation treatments, showing that treating the plant with any inoculation treatments caused the elevation of N and P uptake in grains.

Discussion

The observed promotion in root nodulation of plant in this study could be attributed to the cumulative effects of these rhizobacteria. Similar results were obtained by Wani *et al.* (2007). They showed that multiple inoculation with *Mesorhizobium ciceri* and phosphate-solubilizing rhizobacteria increased the nodule number and biomass per plant. The lowest rate of N concentration in shoots at the flowering stage was shown in control plants that was in a class alone, in other words the application of all bacterial inoculants studied in this experiment resulted in significant promotion of N concentration in shoots as compared with uninoculated control. This is in agreement with the results of Wani *et al.* (2007). In this study the presence of *Azospirillum* in treatment composition played an important role in improving P concentration in shoots at the flowering stage that was similar to the findings of other authors (Lin *et al.* 1983; Dobbelaere *et al.* 2001). Grain yield, biomass and N and P uptake by grains were significantly improved by applying all inoculant compositions in comparison with control plants. Moreover, the presence of *Azospirillum* or *Azotobacter* in the composition of inoculant stimulated the growth and yield of chickpea in this study. *Azospirillum* is one of the best characterized genera among associative plant growth-promoting rhizobacteria and the bacterial strains of this genus are able to exert beneficial effects on plant growth and yield of many agronomic crops (Okon and Vanderleyden, 1997; Steenhoudt and Vanderleyden, 2000). *Azotobacter* spp. are free-living and nitrogen fixing bacteria which under appropriate conditions can enhance plant development and promote the crop yield (Rodelas *et al.* 1999). Stimulation of crop performance by *Azotobacter* inoculation has also been reported by other workers. For example Narula *et al.* (2005a, b) declared that inoculation of wheat and cotton by various *Azotobacter* strains resulted in significant improvement in crop yield and growth parameters under field conditions. The enhancement of nutrient uptake by plant, following the inoculation with rhizobacteria has been illustrated in many experiments (Zaidi *et al.* 2003; Rudresh *et al.* 2005; Wu *et al.* 2005; Wani *et al.* 2007). Under conditions similar to present experiment the application of every inoculation treatment studied here, especially treatments which contained *Azospirillum* or *Azotobacter* may stimulate growth and yield of chickpea in comparison with uninoculated plants.

REFERENCES

Benizri E., Baudoin E., Guckert A. (2001). Root Colonization by Inoculated Plant Growth-Promoting Rhizobacteria. *Biocontrol Sci Techn* 11: 557-574.

Chebotar V.K., Asis Jr C.A., Akao S. (2001). Production of Growth-promoting Substances and High Colonization Ability of Rhizobacteria Enhance the Nitrogen Fixation of Soybean when Coinoculated with *Bradyrhizobium japonicum*. *Biol Fert Soils* 34: 427-432.

Dashti N., Zhang F., Hynes R., Smith D.L. (1998). Plant Growth-promoting Rhizobacteria Accelerate Nodulation and Increase Nitrogen Fixation Activity by Field Grown Soybean [*Glycine max* (L) Merr.] under Short Season Conditions. *Plant Soil* 200: 205-213.

Dobbelaere S., Croonenborghs A., Thys A., Ptacek D., Vanderleyden J., Dutto P., Labandera-Gonzalez C., Caballero-Mellado J., Aguirre J.F., Kapulnik Y., Brener S., Burdman S., Kadouri D., Sarig S., Okon Y. (2001). Responses of Agronomically Important Crops to Inoculation with *Azospirillum. Aust J Plant Physiol* 28: 871-879.

Kloepper J.W., Schroth MN (1981). Plant Growth-promoting Rhizobacteria and Plant Growth under Gnotobiotic Conditions. *Phytopathol* 71: 642-644.

Lin W., Okon Y., Hardy R.W.F. (1983). Enhanced Mineral Uptake by *Zea mays* and *Sorghum bicolor* Roots Inoculated with *Azospirillum brasilense. Appl Environ Microbiol* 45 (6): 1775-1779.

Narula N., Kumar V., Singh B., Bhatia R., Lakshminarayana K. (2005a). Impact of Biofertilizers on Grain Yield in Spring wheat under Varying Fertility Conditions and Wheat-cotton Rotation. *Arch Agron Soil Sci* 51 (1):79-89.

Narula N., Saharan B.S., Kumar V., Bhatia R., Bishnoi L.K., Lather P.B.S., Lakshminarayana K. (2005b). Impact of the use of Biofertilizers on Cotton (*Gossypium hirsutum*) Crop Under Irrigated Agro-ecosystem. *Arch Agron Soil Sci* 51 (1): 69-77.

Okon Y., Vanderleyden J. (1997). Root-Associated *Azospirillum* Species can Stimulate Plants. *ASM News* 63: 364-370.

Persello-Cartieaux F., Nussaume L., Robaglia C. (2003). Tales from the Underground: Molecular Plant-Rhizobacteria Interactions. *Plant Cell Environ* 26: 189-199.

Rodelas B., Gonzalez-Lopez J., Pozo C., Salmeron V., Martinez-Toledo M.V. (1999). Response of Faba bean (*Vicia faba* L.) to Combined Inoculation with *Azotobacter* and *Rhizobium leguminosarum* bv. *viceae. App Soil Ecol* 12: 51-59.

Rodriguez H., Fraga R. (1999). Phosphate Solubilizing Bacteria and their Role in Plant Growth Promotion. *Biotechnol Adv* 17: 319-339.

Rudresh D.L., Shivaprakash M.K., Prasad R.D. (2005). Effect of Combined Application of *Rhizobium*, Phosphate Solubilizing Bacterium and *Trichoderma spp.* on Growth, Nutrient uptake and Yield of Chickpea (*Cicer arietinum* L.). *Appl Soil Ecol* 28: 139-146.

Sindhu S.S., Gupta S.K., Dadarwal K.R. (1999). Antagonistic Effect of *Pseudomonas spp.*, on Pathogenic Fungi and Enhancement of Growth of Green Gram (*Vigna radiata*). *Biol Fert Soils* 29: 62-68.

Sindhu S.S., Suneja S., Goel A.K., Parmar N., Dadarwal K.R. (2002). Plant Growth Promoting Effects of *Pseudomonas sp.* on Coinoculation with *Mesorhizobium sp. Cicer* Strain under Sterile and Wilt Sick Soil Conditions. *Appl Soil Ecol* 19: 57-64.

Singh K.B. (1997). Chickpea (*Cicer arietinum* L.). Field Crop Res 53: 161-170.

Somers E., Vanderleyden J., Srinivasan M. (2004). Rhizosphere Bacterial Signaling: A Love Parade Beneath our Feet. *Crit Rev Microbiol* 30: 205-240.

Steenhoudt O., Vanderleyden J. (2000). *Azospirillum,* A Free-living Nitrogen-fixing Bacterium Closely Associated with Grasses: Genetic, Biochemical and Ecological Aspects. *FEMS Microbiol Rev* 24: 487-506.

Vessey J.K. (2003). Plant Growth Promoting Rhizobacteria as Biofertilizers. *Plant Soil* 255: 571-586.

Wani P.A., Khan M.S., Zaidi A. (2007). Synergistic Effects of the Inoculation with Nitrogen-Fixing and Phosphate-Solubilizing Rhizobacteria on the Performance of Field-Grown chickpea. *J. Plant Nutr Soil Sci* 170 (2): 283-287.

Wu S.C., Cao Z.H., Li Z.G., Cheurg K.C., Wong M.H. (2005). Effects of Biofertilizer Containing N-fixer, P and K Solubilizers and AM Fungi on Maize Growth: A Greenhouse Trial. Geoderma 125: 155-166.

Zaidi A., Khan M.S., Amil M. (2003). Interactive Effect of Rhizotrophic Microorganisms on Yield and Nutrient Uptake of Chickpea (*Cicer arietinum* L.). *Eur J. Agron* 19: 15-21.

Pages 145-160

INTEGRATED NUTRIENT MANAGEMENT IN CHICKPEA
Edited by **: Dr. Virendra Kumar** and **Dr. Nirmal Kumar Katiyar**
Edition **: 2017**
ISBN : 978-93-5056-872-9
Published by **: Discovery Publishing House Pvt. Ltd., New Delhi (India)**

14

Chickpea (*Cicer arietinum* L.) Response to Zinc, Boron and Molybdenum Application under Field Conditions

J.B. Valenciano*
J.A. Boto
V. Marcelo

ABSTRACT

In Spain-Europe's leading chickpea producing country-chickpea (Cicer arietinum) is mainly cultivated on non-irrigated soils with low native fertility. This study was carried out from 2006-08 in the province of León, Spain, under acid soil field conditions, with the aim of determining whether the application of zinc (Zn), boron (B) and molybdenum (Mo) improved chickpea growth and yield on acid soils. A split-split-plot design with three replications was used. Chickpea responded only to the Zn and Mo applications. At maturity, plants fertilized with Zn and with Mo had a greater total dry matter production and seed yield, mainly due to an increment in pod dry matter. For Zn, the highest yield was obtained with 2 mg Zn per plant (6.80 g plant^{-1}), whereas for Mo the highest yield was obtained with 1 mg Mo per plant (6.73 g plant^{-1}). Interaction was observed between B and Mo, interpreted as indicating that Mo can counteract the effect of B application.

Keywords: Acid Soil, Dry Matter, Kabuli Type Chickpea, Micronutrients, Yield Components.

INTRODUCTION

Spain is the main chickpea (*Cicer arietinum* L.) producing country in Europe, with 20,832 ha of land under chickpea cultivation in 2008 (Ministerio

Department of Agrarian Engineering and Sciences, University of León, León, Spain.
*E-mail: joseb.valenciano@unileon.es

de Medio Ambiente y Medio Rural y Marino, 2010). Despite the importance of this crop, few studies have analysed the application of micronutrients to chickpea, and Knights *et al.* (2007) have suggested that the lack of public investment in research, breeding and technology transfer may have contributed to the significant decline in chickpea cultivation in Europe. Chickpea is mainly cultivated on non-irrigated soils, and water stress often affects both productivity and yield stability (Kurdali 1996). Non-irrigated soils are generally impoverished, with low native fertility. Although chickpea is a rustic plant, a limited moisture supply together with mineral nutrient deficiencies and/or imbalances in the soil are considered major environmental stresses leading to yield loss in chickpea (Khan 1998; Ali *et al.* 2000). Plant nutrient availability depends, among other factors, on texture, on organic matter content and especially on soil pH. Micronutrients contribute substantially to achieving higher production through their effects on the plant itself, their role in the symbiotic nitrogen-fixing process, where micro-nutrient deficiencies can limit nitrogen fixation by legume-rhizobium symbiosis, and their influence on effective uptake of the principal and secondary nutrients.

Zinc (Zn) is the main micronutrient limiting chickpea productivity, boron (B) may cause yield losses of up to 100 per cent (Ahlawat *et al.* 2007) and molybdenum (Mo) presents low availability in acidic soils. With the exception of Mo, micro-nutrient availability is greatest in the very slightly-to-medium acid range. In general, each tonne of chickpea grain removes 38 g of Zn, and it has been estimated that 35 g of B and 1.5 g of Mo are also removed from the soil (Ahlawat *et al.* 2007).

Zn deficiency is common in the chickpea-growing regions of the world and is perhaps the most widespread of micronutrient deficiencies (Roy *et al.* 2006; Ahlawat *et al.* 2007). Chickpea is generally considered sensitive to Zn deficiency (Khan 1998); more so, for example, than cereal and oil seeds (Tiwari and Pathak 1982). The consequences of Zn deficiency include reduced yield and a delay in crop maturity. Furthermore, Zn deficiency reduces water use, water use efficiency (Khan *et al.* 2004), nodulation and nitrogen fixation (Shukla and Yadav 1982; Ahlawat *et al.* 2007), which further contributes to a decrease in crop yield. Critical Zn concentrations in soils vary from 0.48 2.5 mg kg^{-1}, depending on soil type (Ahlawat *et al.* 2007), and according to Ankerman and Large (1974), soils have low Zn availability when there is less than 1.1 mg kg^{-1} of Zn (DTPA extraction). Zn solubility decreases markedly above pH 6.0 6.5 (Sims 2000) and thus Zn deficiencies can be encountered in neutral to alkaline soils (Roy *et al.* 2006). Zn uptake is positively correlated with the amount of organic matter in the soil and negatively correlated with phosphorus (P) concentration in the soil (Sillanpää 1972; Hamilton *et al.* 1993; Ahlawat *et al.* 2007). Soils with more sand and less organic matter produce lower yields due to poor utilization of Zn (Singh and Ram 1996).

Although B deficiency limits chickpea productivity less than Zn deficiency (Ahlawat *et al.* 2007), it has been shown to have a significant limiting effect on chickpea yield in some regions with acid soil conditions (Srivastava *et al.* 1997). B application is most important when B concentration in soil is below 0.3 mg kg^{-1} (Ahlawat *et al.* 2007), and crop response to B application is higher in chickpea than in some cereals (Wankhade *et al.* 1996). B deficiency causes flower drop and, consequently, poor podding in chickpeas (Srivastava *et al.* 1997) and poor yields. According to Ankerman and Large (1974), soils have low B availability when B concentration is below 0.6 mg kg^{-1} (hot water extraction), whereas according to Sillanpää (1972), the deficiency limit may be around 0.5 mg kg^{-1}, depending on conditions, extraction time and the soil. B deficiency can be caused by high soil pH, and availability decreases at a pH above 6.5 7.0 (Sims 2000) on highly leached sandy soils or on low organic matter soils.

Mo deficiency is common in acidic soils. Total Mo content varies from 0.2 5.0 mg kg^{-1} (Sims 2000) but Mo in soil is largely unavailable, with less than 0.2 mg kg^{-1} generally being reported as soluble Mo (Sillanpää 1972). According to Ankerman and Large (1974), soils have low Mo availability when Mo concentration in the soil is below 0.11 mg kg^{-1} (ammonium acid oxalate). In Mo-deficient chickpea, the flowers produced are fewer in number, smaller in size and many of them fail to open or to mature, leading to lower seed yield (Ahlawat *et al.* 2007). Mo is directly related to N fixation by legumes (Roy *et al.* 2006) and Mo availability increases as the soil pH approaches neutrality (pH 7.0) or goes higher (Sims 2000); it is lower in the very slightly-to-medium acid range. Mo deficiency is common on very acidic soils, especially with crops that are very sensitive to low concentrations of Mo, such as: legumes (Sims 2000). High phosphate levels are positively correlated with Mo deficiency.

Foliar and soil application of micronutrients is effective in some cases (Ali *et al.* 2000; Roy *et al.* 2006). However, Zn, B and Mo application results are controversial according to reports in the literature (Yanni 1992; Bhuiyan *et al.* 1997; Braga and Vieira 1998; Ali *et al.* 2000; Johnson *et al.* 2005; Johansen *et al.* 2007; Shil *et al.* 2007). Under pot conditions with acidic soils at high moisture availability, Zn and B soil and Mo foliar applications increased chickpea total dry matter and improved seed yield (Valenciano *et al.* 2009; 2010). However, nutrient interactions in annual crops affect yield, and these interactions can be positive, negative or neutral (Fageria *et al.* 1997). Soil, plant and climatic factors can influence interaction; under pot conditions with acidic soils at high moisture availability, Zn application was more efficient when it was applied in conjunction with B and Mo (Valenciano *et al.* 2010).

This study was conducted to determine the effect of Zn and B soil applications and Mo foliar application on growth and seed yield of a Kabuli chickpea under field conditions on acidic soils. The possible interactions of these micro-nutrients were also studied.

Material and Methods

Site Characteristics

Three experimental fields were established in the province of León (Spain), between 2006 and 2008, using a Kabuli chickpea ecotype (cv. Pedrosillano) and different micronutrient applications. The seed of this variety is small (1000-seed weight, 340 g) cream, rounded and smooth.

The plots were located in Ribas de la Val-duerna (León, Spain) (42°18.5′N, 5°57.1′W). Wheat had been the previous crop on all plots. The experimental fields were not fertilized for the present experiment, and the main physical and chemical properties of the soils used are listed in Table 14.1. The experiments were conducted using acidic soils, which presented a medium availability of Zn and a very low to high availability of B according to Ankerman and Large (1974), and high total Mo availability according to Gupta (1997). Weather-related parameters for this area during the experimental period are shown in Fig. 14.1.

Table 14.1: Main physical and chemical characteristics of soils used in the experiments, with local names

	Soil (Local Name) - Year		
	Sotico - 2006	Housa - 2007	Era - 2008
Texture (Bouyoucos densimeter)	Loam	Loam	Loam
Organic matter (Walkley-Black) (g kg^{-1})	2.1	2.3	2.3
pH (1:2.5, water)	5.6	5.9	6.2
EC (1:5, water) (dS m^{-1})	medium acid 0.06	medium acid 0.13	slight acid 0.06
Calcium carbonate (Bernard calcimeter) (g kg^{-1})	Negligible	Negligible	Negligible
P (Olsen) (mg kg^{-1})	31.6	26.1	8.5
K (1 N NH_4 Ac) ($cmol_c$ kg^{-1})	0.55	0.15	0.19
Ca (1 N NH_4 Ac) ($cmol_c$ kg^{-1})	3.07	4.43	4.63
Mg (1 N NH_4 Ac) ($cmol_c$ kg^{-1})	0.59	0.73	0.92
Na (1 N NH_4 Ac) ($cmol_c$ kg^{-1})	0.09	0.02	0.06
Mn (DTPA) (mg kg^{-1})	9.79	17.50	16.59
Fe (DTPA) (mg kg^{-1})	105.0	160.0	83.7
Cu (DTPA) (mg kg^{-1})	1.12	1.38	1.38
Zn (DTPA) (mg kg^{-1})	1.26	2.03	1.53
B (hot water) (mg kg^{-1})	1.95	0.15	0.40
Mo (nitric acid digestion) (mg kg^{-1})	1.76	2.32	0.61

EC electrical conductivity.

DTPA diethyl triamine penta-acetic acid.

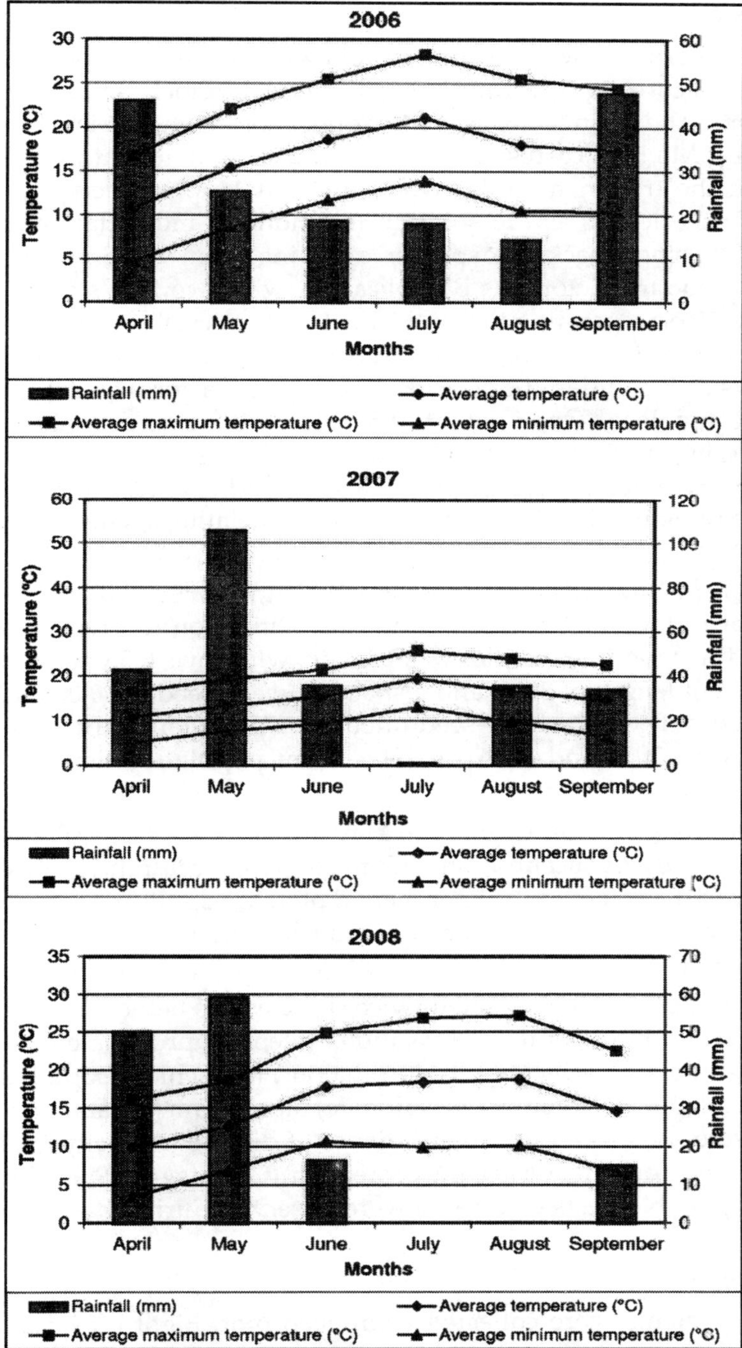

Fig. 14.1: Climatic conditions at Ribas de la Valduerna (León, Spain) during the experimental period (*Source*: Meteorological Station, Sugar Refinery, La Bañeza, Spain)

Experimental Design

The experiment was carried out following a statistical pattern of split-split-plots according to a randomized complete block design, with three replications. The main factor was Mo application, with two levels of Mo, *i.e.* 0 and 241 g Mo ha^{-1} (corresponding to 0 and 1 mg $plant^{-1}$ at establishment), for which the treatment codes were Mo_0 and Mo_1, respectively. Mo was applied to the leaves as Mo solution (ammonium molybdate and sodium molybdate) using a backpack sprayer, applying 0.4 m^3 of spraying solution/ha. The secondary factor was B application, with two levels of B, *i.e.* 0 and 241 g B ha^{-1} (corresponding to 0 and 1 mg $plant^{-1}$ at establishment), for which the treatment codes were B_0 and B_1, respectively. B was applied to the soil in plant rows as B solution (boric acid). The tertiary factor was Zn application, with five levels of Zn, *i.e.* 0, 120.5, 241.0, 482.0 and 964.0 g Zn ha^{-1} (corresponding to 0, 0.5, 1, 2 and 4 mg $plant^{-1}$ at establishment), for which the treatment codes were Zn_0, $Zn_{0.5}$, Zn_1, Zn_2 and Zn_4, respectively. Zn was applied to the soil in plant rows as Zn chelate (chelating agents: DTPA, EDTA and HEDTA).

Conventional tillage was used for land preparation, including mouldboard ploughing and vibrating tine cultivation to prepare a suitable seedbed. The experimental plot was 82.5 m^2, with rows 0.55 m apart (5 rows per plot), plot length of 30 m and a space between seeds of 0.068 m. Sowing was carried out with a single-seed pneumatic precision planter on 20 April 2006, 22 April 2007 and 30 April 2008. Plant population density was 24.1 plants/m^2.

Three weeks after emergence (6 May in 2006, 4 May in 2007 and 17 May in 2008), the five Zn concentrations and the two B concentrations were applied separately to the soil of each experimental plot. Mo applications were carried out by spraying each experimental plot at 30 days after emergence (Bhanavase and Patil 1994).

The trial plots were irrigated twice, 1.5 2 weeks before and 1.5 2 weeks after flowering, using a furrow irrigation system (approximately 30 L m^{-2} of water was applied each time). Chlorothalonil (tetrachloroisophthalonitrile) and quinosol (8-hydroxyquinoline sulphate) plus thiram (tetramethyl-thiuram sulfide) were used to reduce the incidence of disease (Ascochyta blight and root rots) and for chickpea plant protection (Ondategui 1996) throughout the crop cycle. No pests or disease were observed during the experimental period.

Data Collection

Eighty plants were collected from each plot. Eight effective areas in each plot were randomly selected and then, from each of these areas, 10 consecutive plants bearing productive pods were hand-harvested at seed maturity (10 August in 2006, 4 August in 2007 and 11 August in 2008). Each plant was extracted manually with an agricultural tool. Plants were cut at ground level to separate the roots from the stems. Roots, stems with leaves (leaf-stems) and pods including seeds were separated, oven-dried at 80°C to a constant weight to allow correction of data to absolute dry weight, and weighed. Data were recorded for the following characteristics:

- *Dry weight (DW) data*: DW data were recorded for the 80 harvested plants and this was used to calculate indices of DW partitioning: root weight ratio (RWR root DW/total DW); leaf-stem weight ratio (LSWR leaf-stem DW/total DW); pod weight ratio (PWR pod DW/total DW); and harvest index (HI seed DW/total DW).
- *Number of pods per plant*: this was determined from the 80 harvested plants.
- *Number of seeds per pod*: this was determined from the 80 harvested plants.
- *Dry seed weight (g)*: this was determined from a sample of 1000 chickpea seeds.
- Grain yield (g plant^{-1}) was calculated from the yield components.

Data Analyses

Combined analysis of variance was performed using the routines of SPSS version 15.0.1. Mo application, B application, Zn application and environment were considered to be fixed effects. Means comparison was based on the Tukey test ($P<0.01$ and $P<0.05$) (Steel and Torrie 1986). Different correlations were also calculated and a regression analysis was performed.

Results and Discussion

The symptoms of Zn, B and Mo deficiencies (Roy *et al.* 2006) were not observed in any of the sub-subplots; however, there were significant differences between the treatments for Zn soil application and for Mo foliar application.

There were highly significant differences between environments for dry matter (DM) production (Table 14.2), for yield and for yield components (Table 14.3). This indicates the strong influence of the environment on chickpea performance, which has also been reported by other authors (Singh and Sandhu 2006). Environmental conditions during experiments affected plant response differently. At maturity, DM production was highest in Era-2008 (18.46 g plant^{-1}) and all yield components also improved in Era-2008; therefore the highest yield was obtained from Era-2008 (7.19 g plant^{-1}) (Fig. 14.2). Valenciano *et al.* (2010) reported similar results in pot assays. These differences could mainly be explained by the different soil pH values.

In Era-2008, the pH value was higher than 6 and according to Ondategui (1996) and Ahlawat *et al.* (2007), chickpea grows better in pH conditions ranging from 6 to 9. In addition, the high level of phosphorus in the Sotico-2006 and Housa-2007 soils may have limited the yields due to its antagonistic effect on other nutrients, according to Sillanpää (1972), Ankerman and Large (1974) and Hamilton *et al.* (1993). Temperature had less influence since it was not critical (Nielsen 2001), and was similarover the 3 years. In contrast, Sotico-2006 produced the highest HI; in Era-2008, total DW increased more than yield, which resulted in a lower HI (Fig. 14.2), although DW in Era-2008 increased mostly in pod DW. Although drought reduces chickpea growth (Gunes *et al.* 2007), soil moisture contributed little to differences between years in the present study. During the sowing-establishment period, soil moisture was not critical as rainfall was satisfactory. The greatest differences in rainfall occurred during the flowering-maturity period, but two supplementary irrigations (Pacucci *et al.* 2006) were applied during this period to compensate for moisture differences.

Table 14.2: Effects of concentration of Zn, B and Mo applicat.ons on dry matter production of chickpea plants at maturity, indicating significance of analysis of variance and co-efficient of variation (CV)

	Root DW (g Plant^{-1})	Leaf-stem DW (g Plant^{-1})	Pod (Including Seeds) DW (g Plant^{-1})	Total DW (g Plant^{-1})	HI (%)
Environment (E)	P<50.01	P<50.01	P<50.01	P<50.01	P<50.01
Zinc application (Zn)	P<50.01	P<50.01	P<50.01	P<50.01	NS
Zn_0	0.50	4.27	6.03	10.79	44.27
$Zn_{0.5}$	0.53	5.00	7.19	12.71	44.30
Zn_1	0.59	5.49	8.68	14.76	46.90
Zn_2	0.59	5.56	8.82	14.97	46.20
Zn_4	0.62	5.47	8.44	14.53	45.79
Boron application (B)	NS	NS	NS	NS	NS
B_0	0.56	5.05	7.49	13.10	45.37
B_1	0.57	5.26	8.17	14.01	45.62
Molybdenum application (Mo)	P<50.05	NS	P<50.01	P<50.01	P<50.01
Mo_0	0.54	4.91	6.92	12.37	43.99
Mo_1	0.59	5.40	8.75	14.74	46.99
Interactions					
Zn × B	NS	NS	NS	NS	NS
Zn × Mo	NS	NS	NS	NS	NS
B × Mo	NS	NS	P<50.01	P<50.01	NS
Zn × B × Mo	NS	NS	NS	NS	NS
CV (%)	40.1	59.7	53.1	50.4	20.7

DW dry weight, HI harvest index, NS not significant.

Table 14.3: Mean yield components and seed yield of the main treatment, indicating significance of analysis of variance and co-efficient of variation (CV)

	Yield Components			
	Pods Plant^{-1}	Seeds Pod^{-1}	1000-Seed Weight (g)	Yield (g Plant^{-1})
Environment (E)	P<50.01	P<50.01	P<50.01	P<50.01
Zinc application (Zn)	P<50.01	NS	NS	P<50.01
Zn_0	14.29	1.11	289.76	4.69
$Zn_{0.5}$	16.84	1.13	288.18	5.67
Zn_1	20.63	1.10	291.54	6.65
Zn_2	20.65	1.10	293.19	6.80
Zn_4	20.10	1.09	296.58	6.55
Boron application (B)	NS	NS	NS	NS
B_0	17.99	1.11	288.93	5.80
B_1	19.02	1.10	294.77	6.30
Molybdenum application (Mo)	P<50.01	NS	NS	P<50.01
Mo_0	16.44	1.11	288.65	5.37
Mo_1	20.57	1.10	295.04	6.73
Interactions				
Zn × B	NS	NS	NS	NS
Zn × Mo	NS	NS	NS	NS
B × Mo	P<50.01	NS	NS	P<50.01
Zn × B × Mo	NS	NS	NS	NS
CV (%)	47.4	6.0	9.6	52.4

NS not significant.

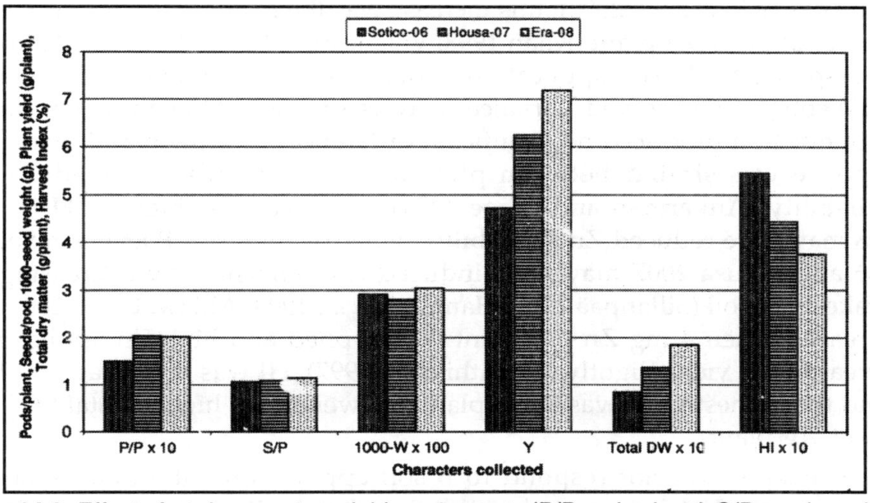

Fig. 14.2: Effect of environment on yield components (P/P pods plant^{-1}; S/P seeds pod^{-1}; 1000-W = 1000-seed weight in g), yield (Y = g plant^{-1}), total dry weight (total DW = g plant^{-1}) and harvest index (HI)

Chickpea responded to the Zn soil applications even though Zn availability is higher at this pH range (Ankerman and Large 1974; Roy *et al.* 2006); however, a high P soil concentration can reduce Zn uptake (Sillanpää 1972; Hamilton *et al.* 1993; Ahlawat *et al.* 2007). Brennan *et al.* (2001) reported that the relative response of chickpea to Zn application is greater than that of other crops. As with other leguminous crops, Zn application resulted in more vegetative growth on acid soil (Singh *et al.* 1992), leading to higher DM production and greater yield (Tables 14.2 and 14.3). Zn soil application increased chickpea growth (Khan *et al.* 2000) and thus at maturity plants fertilized with Zn had a greater total DW (Brennan *et al.* 2001), mainly due to increased pod DW per plant. In addition, Zn application increased root DW (Ahlawat *et al.* 2007) and leaf-stem DW, although in pot assays these characteristics were not affected (Valenciano *et al.* 2009; 2010), indicating that pot cultivation may limit growth, especially root growth. Treatments influenced DW partitioning between plant organs. A relationship between Zn soil application and relative DW of different chickpea plant organs was established (Fig. 14.3); LSWR decreased to 2.4 g plant^{-1}, whereas PWR increased to 2.4 g plant^{-1}. The least number of pods per plant (14.29 pods plant^{-1}) and the lowest yield were obtained with Zn_0 (4.69 g plant^{-1}). Zn soil applications increased chickpea yield (Brennan *et al.* 2001), but this increase only occurred up to Zn_2 (6.80 g plant^{-1}), whereas the Zn_4 treatments reduced maximum yield (Tripathi *et al.* 1997). Valenciano *et al.* (2009; 2010) obtained similar results in the same environments but under pot conditions at high moisture availability; they also recorded differences for 1000-seed weight. Zn soil application increased yield (Khan *et al.* 2000) and, as with the common bean (Valenciano *et al.* 2007), this increase was the result of an increase in the number of pods per plant (Khan 1998; Valenciano *et al.* 2009; 2010). Although the response to Zn soil application varied with environment, as Loneragan and Webb (1993) observed, variance analysis established that the environment Zn interaction produced no significant differences in growth and yield. The response was similar between plots because all soils had medium Zn availability (Ankerman and Large 1974). However, the higher pH in Era-2008 may have reduced Zn availability, whereas high soil P levels in Sotico-2006 and Housa-2007 may have induced Zn deficiency by decreasing Zn uptake from soil (Sillanpää 1972; Hamilton *et al.* 1993; Ahlawat *et al.* 2007). HI decreased when 4 mg Zn per plant was applied and high Zn applications decreased the yield slightly (Tripathi *et al.* 1997). HI was higher at 1 g plant^{-1}, and the highest yield was at 2 g plant^{-1}; however, the highest total DW was also at 2 g plant^{-1}.

Chickpea did not respond to B soil application, although in similar environments, Valenciano *et al.* (2010) found a significant response to B soil application in pot assays. This could be explained by soil moisture status; in pot assays, the soil moisture was maintained near field capacity, whereas in field conditions, limited irrigation was used. This may indicate that chickpea response to nutrient application varies according to soil moisture content (Sekhon and Singh 2007) or that chickpea plants in field conditions have access to higher soil volume, enabling them to meet their moisture needs. According to the literature, chickpea responds to B soil application in B deficient soils (Wankhade *et al.* 1996; Roy *et al.* 2006; Ahlawat *et al.* 2007; Shil *et al.* 2007). Consequently, significant interaction between soils and B application was expected due to the difference in B availability in the soils, which was low in some of them, such as: Housa-2007 (Ankerman and Large 1974). However, no response was observed in any of the environments. B soil application did not cause either toxicity or a reduction in yield, perhaps because the doses used were not very high (Panwar *et al.* 1998), since high rates can cause a reduction in yield, especially in dry conditions (Ahlawat *et al.* 2007). Although Ali and Mishra (2001) did find a significant response, they carried out foliar rather than soil applications.

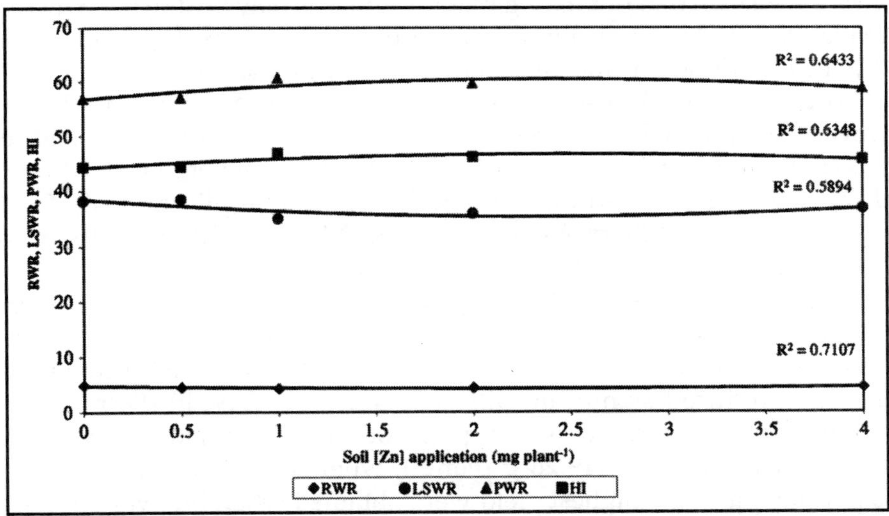

Fig. 14.3: Relationships between zinc soil application and relative dry matter production of different chickpea plant organs. RWR root weight ratio, LSWR leaf-stem weight ratio, PWR pod weight ratio and HI harvest index

Chickpea responded to Mo foliar application (Ali and Mishra 2001), which might be explained by a decrease in availability due to reduced soil pH (Ankerman and Large 1974). As with other leguminous crops, Mo application resulted in greater DM production on acidic soil (Singh *et al.* 1992). Mo foliar application affected chickpea growth (Table 14.2), and at maturity plants fertilized with Mo had a greater total DM production (Bhanavase and Patil 1994); according to Johansen *et al.* (2007), lack of Mo causes a reduction in growth. An increased Mo supply led to a corresponding increase in DM production, primarily in the number of pods (including seeds), and Ahlawat *et al.* (2007) have indicated that Mo application increases the number of flowers. Leaf-stem DW was not affected by Mo application. Treatments influenced DW partitioning between plant organs, except for RWR, and LSWR was highest at Mo_0 (38.77), whereas PWR was highest at Mo_1 (60.72). In addition, chickpea yield characteristics were affected by Mo application (Table 14.3), a finding that has also been reported by Shil *et al.* (2007). There were highly significant differences for Mo foliar application with regard to the number of pods per plant and yield but, contrary to pot assays (Valenciano *et al.* 2010), the number of seeds per pod was not affected. The least number of pods per plant (16.44 pods plant^{-1}) was obtained without Mo treatment. Bozoglu *et al.* (2007) reported contrary results, obtaining a decrease in pods per plant with Mo application, but their experiments were carried out with neutral pH soil where Mo availability is higher. As with the pot assays (Valenciano *et al.* 2010), the highest yield was obtained when Mo application was carried out (6.73 g plant^{-1}), and this may be due to an increase in availability and/or possibly an increase in N_2 fixation (Deo and Kothari 2002), since nodulation improved (Yanni 1992; Bhanavase and Patil 1994). Singh and Singh (1994) also recorded yield increases with Mo application. However, Braga and Vieira (1998) did not find an increment in yield, but they carried out Mo application later (57 60 days after emergence). Although total Mo was high, according to Gupta (1997), the application of Mo still increased chickpea yield, probably due to low Mo availability resulting from low soil pH (Sillanpää 1972; Sims 2000; Ahlawat *et al.* 2007); total Mo soil content apparently does not always represent the amount available to plants. As Mo application increased seed production, its application resulted in an increased HI (6.8%). Variance analysis established that the environment Mo interaction produced significant differences in total DW, in the number of pods per plant and in yield. The highest total DW was obtained when Mo was applied in Era-2008 (19.26 g plant^{-1}), whereas the highest number of pods per plant and the highest yield were obtained when Mo was applied in Housa-2007, with 26.06 pod plant^{-1} and 8.10 g plant^{-1}, respectively. Different soil pH levels could explain this interaction since, according to Ankerman and Large (1974), soil pH is the most influential factor affecting Mo availability, whereas differences in phosphate levels have less influence. Although organic matter also influences Mo availability because it helps prevent leaching (Wichard *et al.* 2009), organic matter levels were very similar in all three soils.

These interaction results are contrary to those reported by Valenciano *et al.* (2010) for pot assays with acidic soils. The only significant interactions found in the present study were between B and Mo applications, an effect that was not reported by Valenciano *et al.* (2010). For total DW there was a highly significant interaction between B and Mo; the highest total DW was obtained with B_1 and Mo_1 (16.20 g plant^{-1}) and the lowest with B_1 and Mo_0 (11.81g plant^{-1}). Shil *et al.* (2007) also reported finding an interaction between B and Mo, for plant height. There was also a highly significant interaction between B and Mo for pod DW, where the highest pod DW was obtained with B_1 and Mo_1 (9.91 g plant^{-1}), and the lowest with B_1 and Mo_0 (6.44 g plant^{-1}). This finding can be interpreted as indicating that Mo can counteract the effect of B application. There was no interaction between Zn B or between Zn Mo, as reported by Valenciano *et al.* (2010) for pot assays. There was a highly significant B Mo interaction as regards the number of pods per plant and seed yield. The highest number of pods per plant (22.73 pods plant^{-1}) and the highest seed yield (7.61 g plant^{-1}) were obtained with B_1 and Mo_1 treatments. The lowest number of pods per plant (15.30 pods plant^{-1}) and the lowest seed yield (4.99 g plant^{-1}) were obtained with B_1 and Mo_0 treatments. Shil *et al.* (2007) also detected an interaction between B and Mo, and in their study they found that the combined application of B and Mo produced better results than single applications. There was no interaction between Zn B, between Zn Mo, or between the three micronutrients, as reported by Valenciano *et al.* (2010) for pot assays.

According to Bhatia *et al.* (1993) and Omar and Singh (1997), total DW is highly correlated with seed yield (0.892). HI showed a low significant positive correlation with the number of pods per plant (0.210), although this was the yield component that exhibited the highest positive correlation with HI, a finding that has also been reported by Bhatia *et al.* (1993). The number of pods per plant was the most influential yield component, and the one most closely correlated with seed yield (0.969) (Maiti and Wesche-Ebeling 2001), but was also the most variable component (Bhatia *et al.* 1993). The number of seeds per pod was the least variable yield component, and the average for seeds per pod obtained in this study fell within the mean range reported in the literature (Khanna-Chopra and Sinha 1987).

Conclusions

This study shows that Zn soil and Mo foliar applications in acidic soils increase total DM and seed yield, primarily due to an increase in the number of pods per plant. High levels of Zn can cause a reduction in yield. Mo foliar applications improve the harvest index. Finally, the number of pods per plant is the most influential yield component, and the one that is most closely correlated with seed yield. Zn soil and Mo foliar applications can increase the yield of Kabuli chickpea cultivated in medium-acid soils with limited irrigation.

REFERENCES

Ahlawat I.P.S., Gangaiah B., Ashraf Zadid M. (2007). Nutrient Management in Chickpea. In: Yadav S.S., Redden R., Chen W., Sharma B eds. Chickpea Breeding and Management. Wallingford, Oxon, UK, CAB International. pp. 213-232.

Ali M., Dahan R., Mishra J.P., Saxena N.P. (2000). Towards the more Efficient use of Water and Nutrients in Food. In: Knight R ed. Linking Research and Marketing Opportunities for Pulses in the 21st Century. Proceedings of the Third International Food Legumes Research Conference. Adelaide, Australia, 22 26 September. Dordrecht, The Netherlands, Kluwer Academic Publishers. pp. 355-368.

Ali M., Mishra J.P. (2001). Effect of Foliar Nutrition of Boron and Molybdenum on Chickpea. *Indian Journal of Pulses Research* 14 (1): 41-43.

Ankerman D., Large R. (1974). Soil and Plant Analysis. New York, USA, A and L Agricultural Laboratories, Inc.

Bhanavase D.B., Patil P.L. (1994). Effects of Molybdenum on Nodulation in Gram. *Journal of Maharashtra Agricultural Universities* 19 (1): 127-129.

Bhatia V.S., Singh B.N., Lal S. (1993). Variability and Interrelationship of Yield and its Attributes in Chickpea. *Indian Journal of Pulses Research* 6 (1): 1 5.

Braga N.R., Vieira C. (1998). Efeito da inoculação com Bradyrhizobium sp., Nitrogenio e Micronutrientes no Rendimento do grão-de-bico. *Bragantia* 57 (2): 349-353.

Brennan R.F., Bolland M.D.A., Siddique KHM (2001). Responses of Cool-season Grain Legumes and Wheat to Soil-Applied Zinc. *Journal of Plant Nutrition* 24 (4 5): 727-741.

Bhuiyan M.A.H., Khanam D., Rahman M.H.H., Hossain A.K.M. (1997). Influence of Rhizobium inoculum, Molybdenum and Boron on Chickpea (*Cicer arietinum* L.) in Grey Terrace Soil of Bangladesh. *Annals of Bangladesh Agriculture* 7 (2): 119-126.

Bozoglu H., Ozcelik H., Mut Z., Pesken E. (2007). Response of Chickpea (*Cicer arietinum* L.) to Zinc and Molybdenum Fertilization. *Bangladesh Journal of Botany* 36 (2): 145-149.

Deo C., Kothari M.L. (2002). Effect of Modes and Levels of Molybdenum Application on Grain Yield Protein Content and Nodulation of Chickpea Grown on Loamy Sand Soil. *Communications in Soil Science and Plant Analysis* 33 (15 18): 2905-2915.

Fageria NK, Baligar V.C., Jones C.A. (1997). Growth and Mineral Nutrition of Field Crops. New York, USA, M Deker.

Gunes A., Inal A., Adak M.S., Alpaslan M., Bagci E.G., Erol T., Pilbeam D.J. (2007). Mineral Nutrition of Wheat, Chickpea and Lentil as Affected by Mixed Cropping and Soil Moisture. *Nutrient Cycling in Agroecosystems* 78 (1): 83-96.

Gupta U.C. (1997). Molybdenum in Agriculture. Cambridge, UK, Cambridge University Press.

Hamilton M.A., Westermann D.T., James D.W. (1993). Factors Affecting Zinc Uptake in Cropping Systems. *Soil Science Society of America Journal* 57 (5): 1310-1315.

Johansen C., Musa A.M., Kumar Rao J.V.D.K., Harris D., Ali M.Y., Shahidullah A.K.M., Lauren J.G. (2007). Correcting Molybdenum Deficiency of Chickpea in the High Barind Tract of Bangladesh. *Journal of Plant Nutrition and Soil Science* 170 (6): 752-761.

Johnson S.E., Lauren J.G., Welch R.M., Duxbury J.M. (2005). A Comparison of the Effects of Micronutrient Seed Priming and Soil Fertilization on the Mineral Nutrition of Chickpea (*Cicer arietinum*), Lentil (Lens culinaris) Rice (Oriza sativa) and Wheat (*Triticum aestivum*) in Nepal. *Experimental Agriculture* 41 (4): 427-448.

Khan H.R. (1998). Response of Chickpea (*Cicer arietinum*) to Zinc Supply and Water Deficits. PhD. thesis, Department of Plant Science. Glen Osmond, Australia, University of Adelaide.

Khan H.R., McDonald G.K., Rengel Z. (2000). Response of Chickpea Genotypes to Zinc Fertilization under Filed Conditions in *South Australia and Pakistan. Journal of Plant Nutrition* 23 (10): 1517-1531.

Khan H.R., McDonald G.K., Rengel Z (2004). Zinc Fertilization and Water Stress Affects Plant Water Relations, Stomatal Conductance and Osmotic Adjustment in Chickpea (*Cicer arietinum*). *Plant and Soil* 267 (1 2): 271-284.

Khanna-Chopra R., Sinha S.K. (1987). Chickpea: Physiological Aspect of Growth and Yield. In: Saxena MC, Singh KB eds. The chickpea. Wallingford, Oxon, UK, CAB International. pp. 163-189.

Knights E.J., Açikgöz N., Warkentin T., Bejiga G., Yadav S.S., Sandhu J.S. (2007). Area, Production and Distribution. In: Yadav S.S., Redden R., Chen W., Sharma B. eds. Chickpea Breeding and Management. Wallingford, Oxon, UK, CAB International. pp. 167-178.

Kurdali F. (1996). Nitrogen and Phosphorus Assimilation, Mobilization and Partitioning in Rainfed Chickpea (*Cicer arietinum* L.). *Field Crops Research.* 47 (2 3): 81-92.

Loneragan J.F., Webb M.J. (1993). Interactions between Zinc and other Nutrients Affecting the Growth of Plants. In: Robson AD Zinc in Soils and Plants. Dordrecht, The Netherlands, Kluwer Academic Publishers. pp. 45-57.

Maiti R.K., Wesche-Ebeling P. (2001). Vegetative and Reproductive Growth and Productivity. In: Maiti R., Wesche-Ebeling P eds. Advances in Chickpea Science. Enfield, NH, USA, Science Publishers. pp. 67-104.

Ministerio de Medio Ambiente y Medio Rural y Marino (2010). Anuario de estadística 2009. Madrid, Ministerio de Medio Ambiente y Medio Rural y Marino.

Nielsen D.C. (2001). Production Functions for Chickpea, Field pea and Lentil in the Central Great Plains. *Agronomy Journal* 93 (3): 563-569.

Omar M., Singh K.B. (1997). Increasing Seed Yield in Chickpea by Increased Biomass Yield. International Chickpea and Pigeonpea Newsletter 4: 14.

Ondategui J. (1996). El garbanzo In: El cultivo de las leguminosas de grano en Castilla y León. Valladolid, Spain, Junta de Castilla y León. pp. 357-398.

Pacucci G., Troccoli C., Leoni B. (2006). Effect of Supplementary Irrigation on Yield of Chickpea Genotypes in a Mediterranean Climate. Agricultural Engineering International 8: Manuscript LW 04: 005.

Panwar B.S., Gupta S.P., Kala R. (1998). Responses to Boron in Pearl Millet and Chickpea in a pot Experiment with a Non-Calcareous Soil in India. *Acta Agronomica Hungarica* 46 (4): 335-340.

Roy R.N., Finck A., Blair G.J., Tandon H.L.S. (2006). Plant Nutrition for Food Security. A Guide for Integrated Mutrient Management. FAO Fertilizer and Plant Nutrition Bulletin 16. Rome, Italy, Food and Agriculture Organization of the United Nations.

Sekhon H.S., Singh G. (2007). Irrigation Management in Chickpea. In: Yadav S.S., Redden R., Chen W., Sharma B eds. Chickpea Breeding and Management. Wallingford, Oxon, UK, CAB International. pp. 246-267.

Shil N.C., Noor S., Hossain M.A. (2007). Effects of Boron and Molybdenum on the Yield of Chickpea. *Journal of Agriculture and Rural Development* (Gazipur) 5 (1 2): 17-24.

Sillanpää M. (1972). Trace Elements in Soils and Agriculture. Rome, Italy, Food and Agriculture Organization of the United Nations.

Sims T.T. (2000). Soil Fertility Evaluation. In: Summer ME Handbook of Soil Science. Boca Raton, Florida, USA, CRC Press. pp. 113-154.

Singh M., Ram N. (1996). Effect of Soil Enrichment with Zinc on Crop Yields and Its Replenishment in Mollisols of Northern India. *Agrochimica* 40 (1): 19-24.

Singh A., Sandhu J.S. (2006). Genotype Environment Interaction in Chickpea. Crop Improvement 33 (1): 67-69.

Singh V., Singh G.P. (1994). Effect of Applied Potassium and Molybdenum on Yield and Composition of Chickpea. *Journal of Potassium Research* 10 (4): 411 414.

Singh A., Singh B.B., Patel C.S. (1992). Response of Vegetable pea (*Pisum sativum*) to Zinc, Boron and Molybdenum in an Acidi Alsifol of Meghalaya. *Indian Journal of Agronomy* 37 (3): 615-616.

Srivastava S.P., Yadav C.R., Rego T.J., Johansen C., Saxena N.P. (1997). Diagnosis and Alleviation of Boron Deficiency Causing Flower and Pod Abortion in Chickpea (*Cicer arietinum* L.) in Nepal. In: Bell RW, Rerkasem B eds. Boron in Soils and Plants, Developments in Plant and Soil Sciences, 76. Dordrecht, The Netherlands, Kluwer Academic Publishers. pp. 95-99.

Steel RGD, Torrie JH (1986). Bioestadística: Principios y Procedimientos. México DF, México, McGraw Hill.

Shukla U.C., Yadav O.P. (1982). Effect of Phosphorus and Zinc on Nodulation and Nitrogen Fixation in Chickpea (*Cicer arietinum* L.). *Plant and Soil* 65 (2): 239-248.

Tiwari N.K., Pathak A.N. (1982). Studies of the Zinc Requirements of Different Crops. *Experimental Agriculture* 18 (4): 393-398.

Tripathi H.C., Singh R.S., Misra V.K. (1997). Response of Gram (*Cicer arietinum*) to Sulphur and Zinc Fertilization. *Indian Journal of Agricultural Sciences* 67 (11): 541-542.

Valenciano J.B., Miguélez-Frade M.M., Marcelo V., Reinoso B. (2007). Response of Irrigated Common Bean (Phaseolus vulgaris) Yield to Foliar Zinc Application in Spain. *New Zealand Journal of Crop and Horticultural Science* 35 (3): 325-330.

Valenciano J.B., Miguélez-Frade M.M., Marcelo V. (2009). Response of Chickpea (*Cicer arietinum*) to Soil Zinc Application. *Spanish Journal of Agricultural Research* 7 (4): 952-956.

Valenciano J.B., Marcelo V., Boto J.A. (2010). Response of Chickpea (*Cicer arietinum*) Yield to Micronutrient Application Under Pot Conditions in Spain. *Spanish Journal of Agricultural Research* 8 (3): 797-807.

Wankhade S.G., Dakhore R.C., Wanjari S.S., Patil D.B., Potdukhe N.R., Ingle R.W. (1996). Response of Crops to Micronutrients. *Indian Journal of Agricultural Research* 30 (3 4): 164-168.

Wichard T., Mishra B., Myneni S.C.B., Bellenger J.P., Kraepiel A.M.L. (2009). Storage and Bioavailability of Molybdenum in Soils Increased by Organic Matter Complexation. *Nature Geoscience* 2 (9): 625-629.

Yanni Y.G. (1992). Performance of Chickpea, Lentil and Lupin Nodulated with Indigenous or Inoculated Rhizobia Micropartners Under Nitrogen, Boron, Cobalt and Molybdenum Fertilization Schedules. *World Journal of Microbiology and Biotechnology* 8 (6): 607-613.

Pages 161-173

INTEGRATED NUTRIENT MANAGEMENT IN CHICKPEA
***Edited by* : Dr. Virendra Kumar** and **Dr. Nirmal Kumar Katiyar**
***Edition* : 2017**
ISBN : 978-93-5056-872-9
***Published by* : Discovery Publishing House Pvt. Ltd., New Delhi (India)**

15

Effectiveness of Micronutrient Application and Rhizobium Inoculation on Growth and Yield of Chickpea

Shrila Das*, Navneet Pareek
K.P. Raverkar, R. Chandra
Aditya Kaustav[1]

ABSTRACT

The field investigation was carried out to improve the inoculated Rhizobium efficiency by applying different micronutrients on nodulation, growth and uptake of N and P and yield of chickpea during Rabi seasons of 2006-07 at the Crop Research Centre, G.B. Pant University of Agriculture and Technology, Pantnagar. Fourteen treatments consisting combinations of micronutrients viz; Zinc, Boron and Molybdenum, with and without Rhizobium sp., inoculation, were laid out in randomized block design (RBD) in triplicates. Rhizobium sp., inoculation gave significant increases of 33.72, 26.11 and 4.56 per cent in nodule dry weight and 15.59, 14.25 and 1.90 per cent in plant dry weight at 45, 75 and 120 DAS, respectively. Among the two levels of $ZnSO_4$, 25 kg $ZnSO_4$/ha was found superior to 10 kg $ZnSO_4$/ha for different studied parameters. Application of 10 kg Borax/ha was found better than 5 kg Borax/ha for chickpea. Seed treatment of Mo with 0.5 kg Na_2MoO_4/ha was found sufficient to meet the crop need. Rhizobium inoculation in combination with different micronutrients recorded higher nodulation, plant dry weight, grain and straw yield and uptake of N and P than the treatments of only micronutrients or Rhizobium alone. The highest nodule dry weight of 235, 616 and

Department of Soil Science, College of Agriculture, G.B. Pant University of Agriculture and Technology, Pantnagar, Uttarakhand, India.
1. Division of Sample Survey, IASRI, Pusa Campus, New Delhi, India.
*E-mail: shrila34040@gmail.com

1476 mg/plant was recorded with treatment of 5 kg Borax/ha + Rhizobium at 45, 75 and 120 DAS, respectively. The treatment with 0.5 kg Na_2MoO_4/ha + Rhizobium gave the highest plant dry weight of 4.22, 9.12 and 11.35 g/plant at 45, 75 and 120 DAS, respectively. The highest grain yield of 2977 kg/ha and straw yield (7111 kg/ha) was recorded due to inoculation with Rhizobium + 10 kg Borax/ha and Rhizobium + 5 kg Borax/ha, respectively. Significant variations in total N and P uptake due to Rhizobium inoculation and application of micronutrients were also observed and it varied from 122.83 kg/ha and 10.67 kg/ha in uninoculated control to 203.90 kg/ha and 22.02 kg/ha in 5 kg Borax/ha + Rhizobium, respectively.

Keywords: Boron, Chickpea, Grain, Molybdenum, Nodulation, Rhizobium, Straw, Yield, Zinc.

Chickpea (*Cicer arietinum* L.), a grain legume, play essential role in ensuring nutritional security and environmental safety, as they have inbuilt mechanism to fix atmospheric di-nitrogen. Besides legume – *Rhizobium* symbiosis is an important facet of symbiotic nitrogen fixation which is exploited to benefit agriculture and its sustainability (Brahmaprakash and Sahu, 2012). Therefore, its cultivation is gaining importance not only in India, but also all over the world because of its nutritional benefits. Chickpea grain provides about 18-22 per cent protein, 4-10 per cent fat and 52-70 per cent carbohydrate (Ali and Kumar, 2003).

Rhizobium nodulating chickpea is highly specific in infectivity and do not show affinity with any member of known cross inoculation groups. Survey of root nodulation status in chickpea crop at 2482 farmer's field carried out under AICRP on pulses, indicated good nodulation only at 12.5 per cent locations, while 54.8 per cent and 31.4 per cent locations showed poor and moderate nodulation, respectively (Pareek and Chandra, 2003). Response to inoculation and efficiency of inoculation varies with the strains of *Rhizobium*, plant genotype and environmental conditions (Vincent, 1974). These situations suggest the need of inoculation for establishment of effective strains of *Rhizobium* in soil to cause adequate infection in chickpea for good nodulation, N_2-fixation and growth of the crop (Choudhary *et al.* 2005).

Mineral nutrient deficiencies limit nitrogen fixation by the legume-*Rhizobium* symbiosis, resulting in low legume yields. Adequate supply of nutrients including micronutrients is also essential for proliferation and survival of *Rhizobium* in soil and establishment of effective associations. Several reports indicated the positive effects of micronutrient application on nodulation and nitrogen fixation (O'Hara *et al.* 1988). Nutrient limitations to legume production result from deficiencies of not only major nutrients but also micronutrients such as: molybdenum (Mo), zinc (Zn), and boron (B) (Bhuiyan *et al.* Boron (B) and Molybdenum (Mo) are the most important 1999). However, the effect depends on the micronutrient status and effectiveness of *Rhizobium* strain in the soil. Zinc (Zn), micronutrients, as they perform several physiological functions in the plant to cause adequate infection for good nodulation, wherever deficient under intensive cultivation of legumes as it N_2-fixation and growth of the crop. Several study indicated that there is a necessity of application of micronutrients is directly involved in biological nitrogen fixation through nitrogenase enzyme activity (Gupta and Sahu, 2012). The present paper communicates the impact of different micronutrients application on efficacy of introduced chickpea rhizobia.

Materials and Methods

A field experiment during *Rabi* seasons of 2006-07 was carried out to find out the effect of different micronutrients *viz;* Zinc, Boron and Molybdenum, with and without *Rhizobium* sp., inoculation on nodulation, growth, uptake of N and P and yield of chickpea at the Crop Research Centre, G.B. Pant University of Agriculture and Technology, Pantnagar. The experimental field soil was sandy loam having pH 6.92, available N and P of 163.07 and 12.33 kg/ha and 0.84, 1.33 and 0.30 mg/kg available Zn, B and Mo, respectively.

Fourteen treatments consisting combinations of different micronutrients (Zinc, Boron, Molybdenum), with and without *Rhizobium* sp., inoculation, were laid out in randomized block design (RBD) in triplicates to evaluate the response of chickpea to micronutrients and *Rhizobium* sp., (strain LN-7007) inoculation.

The sowing of seed was carried out using 100 kg/ha seed rate of chickpea (Cultivar 'Pant G-186') with net plot size 1.8 m × 3.0 m. Seeds were treated with the respective *Rhizobium* sp. (LN-7007) inoculants by following the standard procedure. Zinc sulphate and Borax, as a source of zinc (Zn) and boron (B), respectively were applied in the soil according to the selected concentration in their respective plots whereas, for molybdenum (Mo) application, first seed was treated with sodium molybdate salt and then inoculated with *Rhizobium* sp., using carboxyl methyl cellulose (CMC) as adhesive. The treated seeds were sown immediately in pre-opened furrows at 3-4 cm depth. A uniform basal dose of nitrogen (20 kg/ha) and phosphorus (40 kg P_2O_5/ha) were applied as per treatment through urea and SSP, respectively, in furrow prior to seed sowing. No potash was added. The recommended agronomic practices were followed throughout experiment for raising the crop.

For different observations samples of soil and plant were taken before and after sowing and after harvest of crop, like collection of soil samples (0-15 cm depth), processing of collected soil samples, analysis of processed samples for their physico-chemical properties, collection of plant samples at different intervals *viz;* 45, 70 and 120 DAS (for counting of nodules, nodule and plant dry weight). Grain and straw yield were also observed at maturity and both grain and straw samples of chickpea collected from each plot at harvest for yield and N, P uptake.

The obtained experimental data were statistically analyzed by applying analysis of variance (ANOVA) technique (Panse and Sukhatme, 1978). The differences among treatments were compared by applying 'F' test of significance at 5 per cent level of probability.

Results and Discussion

Effect of Rhizobium Inoculation

Inoculation of *Rhizobium* sp., improved the nodule number and their dry weights at different intervals (Fig. 15.1). The numbers of nodules were higher by 14.28, 9.14 and 4.85 per cent and nodule dry weight by 33.72, 26.11 and 4.56 per cent due to inoculation with *Rhizobium* at 45, 75 and 120 DAS, respectively over the uninoculated control. *Rhizobium* sp., inoculation also gave numerical increases of 1.90 to 15.59 per cent in plant dry weight at different intervals (Fig. 15.1). The non-significant response of *Rhizobium* sp., inoculation could be because of high population of native rhizobia nodulating chickpea in soil because of its cultivation from time immortal.

Table 15.1: Effect of *Rhizobium* sp., inoculation and application of micro-nutrient(s) on total N and P uptake (kg/ha) and grain and straw yield (kg/ha) of Chickpea

Treatment	Total N Uptake	Total P Uptake	Grain Yield	Straw Yield
Uninoculated Control	122.83	10.67	2033	5497
Rhizobium	161.09	15.18	2606	5602
10 kg $ZnSO_4$/ha	149.26	14.47	2379	6064
25 kg $ZnSO_4$/ha	154.01	14.61	2444	6074
10 kg $ZnSO_4$/ha + *Rhizobium*	181.34	17.74	2555	6271
25 kg $ZnSO_4$/ha + *Rhizobium*	190.12	17.74	2583	6101
5 kg Borax/ha	140.87	14.21	2277	5666
10 kg Borax/ha	146.87	15.34	2453	5805
5 kg Borax/ha + *Rhizobium*	203.90	22.02	2826	7111
10 kg Borax/ha + *Rhizobium*	202.18	21.49	2977	6244
0.5 kg Na_2MoO_4/ha	140.04	13.39	2231	6348
1.0 kg Na_2MoO_4/ha	137.23	15.33	2299	5663
0.5 kg Na_2MoO_4/ha + *Rhizobium*	187.33	18.41	2647	6166
1.0 kg Na_2MoO_4/ha + *Rhizobium*	176.80	16.46	2609	5759
C.D. at 5 %	31.95	2.85	4.60	NS

The high population of native rhizobia probably did not allow the inoculated rhizobia to increase nodule number in soil. Similar findings were also obtained by Pareek and Chandra (2003), Choudhary *et al.* (2005) and Gupta (2006). Inoculation of *Rhizobium* significantly increased 21.98, 1.87, 23.75 and 29.71 per cent grain yield, straw yield, total N and P uptake by over uninoculated control, respectively (Table 15.1). It could be attributed to competitiveness and effectiveness of introduced strain of rhizobia, which might have fixed higher amount of atmospheric nitrogen over the native rhizobia. Similar results were reported and supported by Khurana and Dudeja (1997) and Pareek and Chandra (2003), Gupta (1998) and Gupta (2006). Similar response of *Rhizobium* sp., inoculation in chickpea in terms of yield has also been reported by Bharti *et al.* (2002).

Effect of Micronutrient Application

Zinc application alone

Among the two different grades of Zn alone *i.e.* 10 and 25 kg $ZnSO_4$/ha applied, treatment 25 kg $ZnSO_4$/ha gave better results than the treatment 10 kg $ZnSO_4$/ha. Results were corroborated with the findings of Ahlawat *et al.* (2007).

Application of zinc produced more nodule number of 5.21, 4.85 and 9.14 per cent with 10 kg $ZnSO_4$/ha and 2.43, 9.14, and 13.05 per cent with 25 kg $ZnSO_4$/ha over the uninoculated control at 45, 75 and 120 DAS, respectively (Fig. 15.1). Results corroborated with Yadav and Shukla (1983) who reported that number of nodule in chickpea increased with increasing Zn application up to 7.5 µg/g soils. Misra *et al.* (2002) also observed an increase of 55 per cent in root nodulation with application of 20 mg Zn/kg soil. They further reported that application of Zn also favoured the nodule dry weight. Increase in nodule dry weight ranged from 2.75 to 16.87 per cent with 10 kg $ZnSO_4$/ha and 4.27 to 32.82 per cent 25 kg $ZnSO_4$/ha was observed over the uninoculated control at different intervals, respectively. Similar results were observed and explained by Ahlawat *et al.* (2007), that the fertilization of Zn enhanced root growth, nodulation and nodule dry weight. Application of zinc at both levels increased plant dry weight by 23.38, 3.43 and 0.12 per cent with 10 kg $ZnSO_4$/ha and 27.82, 7.22 and 4.75 per cent with 25 kg $ZnSO_4$/ha application over the uninoculated control at 45, 75 and 120 DAS, respectively. Yadav and Shukla (1983) also found increased dry matter yield of chickpea with increasing Zn application up to 10 µg/g soil. Similarly, Choudhary *et al.* (1990) reported that final plant height and dry matter yield were affected significantly following soaking seeds in $ZnSO_4$ solution resulted higher yield.

Both the level of applied zinc were at par for total N uptake and recorded increase of 17.70 per cent with 10 kg $ZnSO_4$/ha and 20.24 per cent with 25 kg $ZnSO_4$/ha application over uninoculated control (Table 15.1). Similarly, Both

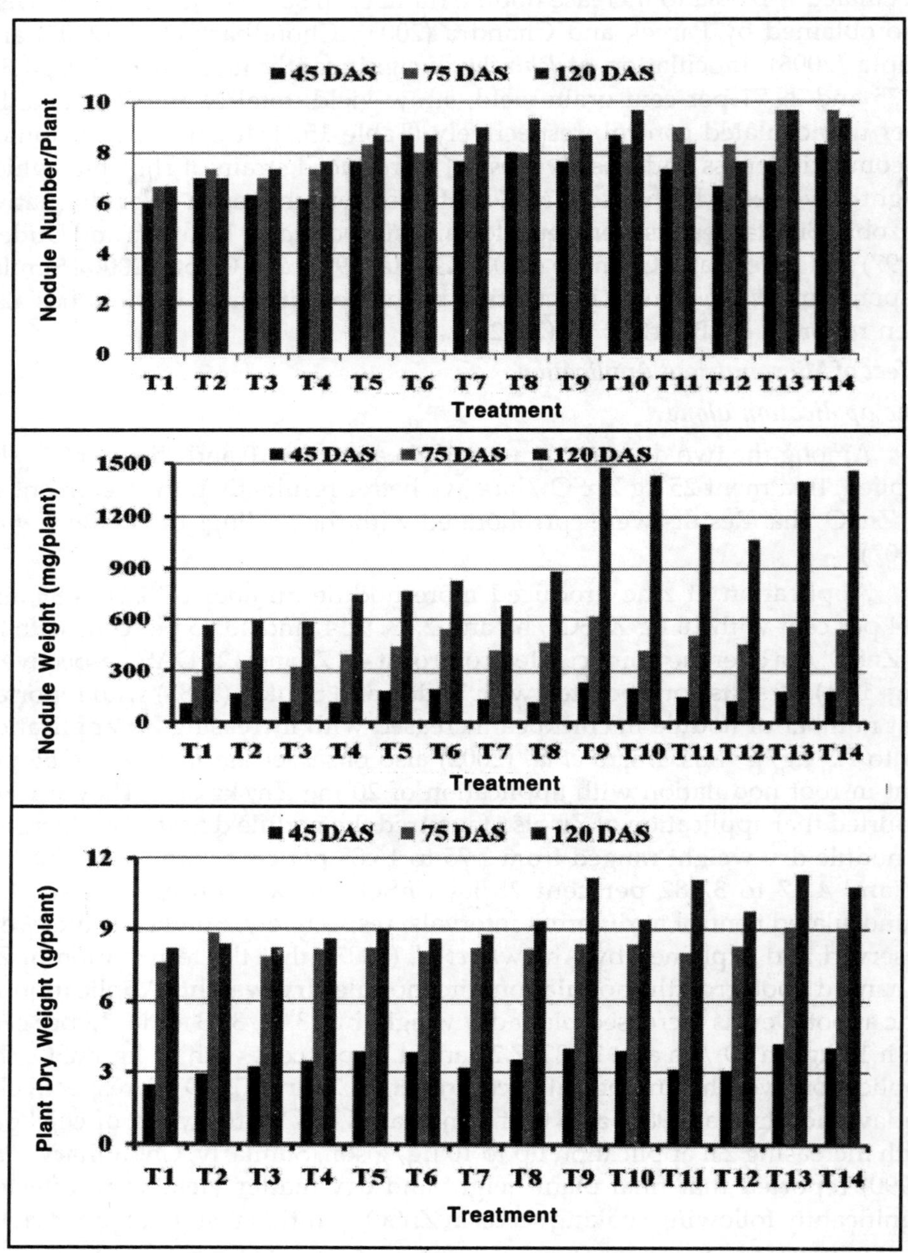

Fig. 15.1: Effect of *Rhizobium* sp. inoculation and micronutrient(s) application on nodule number, nodule dry weight and plant dry weight at 45, 75 and 120 DAS

the levels of applied zinc were at par in respect of total P uptake, however, its application resulted in increase of 26.26 and 26.96 per cent with 10 and 25 kg $ZnSO_4$/ha over uninoculated control, respectively. This could be attributed to enhanced supply of Zn in soil leading to better plant growth, nodulation and N_2-fixation. Ahlawat *et al.* (2007) reported significant response upto 25 kg $ZnSO_4$/ha application in improving yield of chickpea. However, 10 kg $ZnSO_4$/ha seems to be the optimum in most of the chickpea growing areas.

Grain yields due to Zn application were numerically higher by 14.54 per cent with 10 kg $ZnSO_4$/ha and 16.81 per cent with 25 kg $ZnSO_4$/ha application over uninoculated control (Table 15.1). Similarly, straw yield due to both level of Zn application were numerically higher by 9.35 and 9.49 per cent with 10 and 25 kg $ZnSO_4$ /ha application over the uninoculated control, respectively. Increase in grain and straw yield due to application of micronutrient could be due to adequate supply of these nutrients. Similar, results were also reported by Sawires (2001) and Choudhary *et al.* (1990).

Combined application of Zinc with Rhizobium sp

Combined application of *Rhizobium* sp., with Zn found better than *Rhizobium* and Zn alone.

Inoculation of *Rhizobium* in combination with 10 and 25 kg $ZnSO_4$/ha gave 8.61 to 19.16 per cent and 8.37 to 19.16 per cent more nodule number and 8.15 to 22.71 per cent and 12.88 to 33.33 per cent more nodule dry weight over the *Rhizobium* alone at different intervals, respectively (Fig. 15.1). The results are in agreement with Singh *et al.* (2004) who reported increased nodule number and nodule dry weight due to inoculation with *Rhizobium* + Zn, because of their positive effect on nodulation and N_2-fixation. Combined inoculation of *Rhizobium* with 10 and 25 kg $ZnSO_4$/ha gave 6.88 to 24.16 per cent and 2.67 to 23.17 per more plant dry weight over the *Rhizobium* alone at different intervals, respectively. These results are in the close proximity with the data reported by Singh *et al.* (2004) who also observed that inoculation of *Rhizobium* and application of micronutrients gave more plant dry weight than *Rhizobium* alone.

Similarly, Micronutrient zinc application at the rate of 10 and 25 kg $ZnSO_4$/ha in combination with *Rhizobium* resulted in 11.16 and 15.26 per cent more total N uptake and similar of 14.43 per cent more total P uptake over the *Rhizobium* alone, respectively (Table 15.1). In a pot culture experiment Singh *et al.* (1984) found that application of *Rhizobium* and Zn in chickpea increased N content and uptake.

Grain yield due to *Rhizobium* inoculation with both levels of Zn application were numerically higher by 20.43 per cent with 10 kg $ZnSO_4$/ha and 21.29 per cent with 25 kg $ZnSO_4$/ha over *Rhizobium* alone (Table 15.1). Similarly, straw yield due to Zn application was also found numerically higher with 10 and 25 kg $ZnSO_4$/ha over *Rhizobium* alone. Singh *et al.* (2004) further reported that the content and uptake of Zn, N and P, irrespective of *Rhizobium*, increased significantly with the addition of micronutrients individually or in combination over control.

Boron Application Alone

In legume B also apparently plays a structural role by maintaining the integrity of cell wall and membranes (Bolanos *et al.* 1996). Soil application of B at the rate of 5 and 10 kg Borax/ha produced 20.00 to 26.00 and 16.75 to 28.61 per cent more nodule number than the uninoculated control at different intervals (Fig. 15.1). Bolanos *et al.* (1996) suggested that B plays an important role in mediating cell-surface interactions that lead to endocytosis of rhizobia by host cells and hence to the correct establishment of the symbiosis between legume and *Rhizobium*. Similarly, B alone applied at the rate of 5 and 10 kg Borax/ha produced 16.91 to 36.05 and 4.27 to 42.54 per cent more nodule dry weight than the uninoculated control at different intervals, respectively. These results corroborates with the findings of Bolanos *et al.* (1996); Rahman *et al.* (1999); O'Hara (2001). Similarly, B alone applied at 5 and 10 kg Borax/ha produced 6.48 to 22.00 and 7.22 to 30.05 per cent more plant dry weight than the uninoculated control at different intervals. These results are in agreement with Bolanos *et al.* (1996); Rahman *et al.* (1999); O'Hara, (2001).

Non-significant improvements were observed when B alone applied at the rate of 5 and 10 kg Borax/ha resulting in 12.80 and 16.36 per cent more N uptake over the uninoculated control, respectively. Similar result was also found in case of total P uptake registering nonsignificant increase of 24.91 and 30.44 per cent in total P uptake over the uninoculated control, with the treatments of 5 and 10 kg Borax/ha respectively (Table 15.1). Similar response has been reported by Bolanos *et al.* (1996).

Grain yield due to both level of B application were numerically higher by 10.71 per cent with 5 kg Borax/ha and 2.98 per cent with 10 kg Borax/ha application over uninoculated control (Table 15.1). Straw yield due to B application was numerically higher by 17.12 per cent with 5 kg Borax/ha and 5.30 per cent with 10 kg Borax/ha application over uninoculated control. Similarly, Sakal *et al.* (1998) reported increased grain yield up to 750 kg/ha due to 2 kg B/ha fertilization with an agronomic efficiency of 375 kg grain/kg B. Numerical increase in the yield may be attributed due to proper nutrition of Boron, which play an important role in hormone synthesis and translocation, carbohydrate metabolism and DNA synthesis and probably contributes to additional growth and yield (Kalyani *et al.* 1993).

Combined Application of Boron with Rhizobium

Rhizobium inoculation along with different B levels also favoured the nodule number registering 8.61 to 19.16 and 20.04 to 31.05 per cent more nodule number and 28.08 to 59.72 and 14.28 to 58.60 per cent more nodule dry weight with 5 kg and 10 kg Borax/ha over the *Rhizobium* alone at different intervals, respectively (Fig 15.1). Application of *Rhizobium* in combination with micronutrients probably facilitated more root infection and increased the metabolic activity of chickpea. These results are in agreement with Solaiman (1999). Bharti *et al.* (2002) also reported that the number and dry weight of nodules increased with *Rhizobium* inoculation along with B application in chickpea. *Rhizobium* inoculation with different B levels also favoured the plant dry weight and application of 5 kg and 10 kg Borax/ha registered 25.04 to 26.61 and 11.0 to 25.12 per cent more plant dry weight over the *Rhizobium* alone at different intervals. Solaiman (1999) also reported increased plant dry weight with *Rhizobium* inoculation along with B application.

Rhizobium inoculation in combination with both the B levels of 5 and 10 kg Borax/ha favoured the total N uptake (kg/ha) by 20.99 and 20.32 per cent and total P uptake registering 31.06 and 29.36 per cent over the *Rhizobium* inoculation alone, respectively (Table 15.1). Similar response has also been reported by Bharti *et al.* (2002) who reported that inoculation of *Rhizobium* with different levels of B had positive effect on the yield, dry weight and nutrients uptake of chickpea. Results were also in agreement with Singh *et al.* (2004). Singh and coworkers suggested that combined application of *Rhizobium* and different levels of B improved the dry matter production and yield of chickpea. This may be due to the presence of B could change the affinity with which the bacterial cell surface interacts with peribacteroid membrane glycocalyx relative to its interaction with intercellular plant matrix glycoprotein. Thus B plays an important role in establishment of the symbiosis between host and *Rhizobium*.

Grain yield due to *Rhizobium* inoculation with B application was numerically higher by 7.78 per cent with 5 kg Borax/ha and 12.46 per cent with 10 kg Borax/ha over *Rhizobium* alone (Table 15.1). Similarly straw yield due to both the levels of B application were numerically higher by 21.22 per cent with 5 kg Borax/ha and 10.28 per cent with 10 kg Borax/ha over *Rhizobium* alone. Similar results were also reported by Bharti *et al.* (2002).

Molybdenum Application Alone

Mo application at both the levels (*i.e.* 0.5 kg Na_2MoO_4/ha and 1.0 kg Na_2MoO_4/ha) increased nodule number ranging from 18.14 to 26.00 per cent with 0.5 kg Na_2MoO_4/ha and 9.90 to 20.00 per cent with 1.0 kg Na_2MoO_4/ha over the uninoculated control at different intervals (Fig. 15.1). Such increase in nodule number due to Mo application was also reported by Islam *et al.* (1995); could be associated with an increase in nitrate reductase and nitrogenase activities, as Mo is an essential part of these enzymes. Chandra and Kothari (2002) revealed that the application of Mo with increasing doses significantly increased number of nodules/plant. Application of 0.5 kg Na_2MoO_4/ha and 1.0 kg Na_2MoO_4/ha also registered 25.33, 47.11 and 50.99 per cent and 11.11, 41.28 and 46.69 per cent more nodule dry weight over uninoculated control at 45, 75 and 120 DAS, respectively. It suggests that application of Mo allowed synthesis of more nodule tissue due to better supply of Mo from soil to plants and also by maintaining supply of essential metabolites to the nodules (Jongruaysup *et al.* 1993). Similar results were reported by Chahal *et al.* (1976), who treated pea with molybdenum (30µ g/ L) and achieved significantly higher nodule number as well as nodule leghaemoglobin content compared to untreated treatments. Application of Mo at both levels increased plant dry weight ranging from 5.95 to 25.94 per cent with 0.5 kg Na_2MoO_4/ha and 8.89 to 15.95 per cent with 1.0 kg Na_2MoO_4/ ha application over the uninoculated control at different intervals. Such increase in plant dry weight due to Mo application was also reported by Chandra and Kothari (2002). They revealed that the application of Mo with increasing doses significantly increased plant dry weight.

Applications of 0.5 kg Na_2MoO_4 /ha was found slightly better than 1.0 kg Na_2MoO_4/ha registering 12.28 per cent more N uptake than the uninoculated control. However, application of 1.0 kg Na_2MoO_4/ha was found better than 0.5 kg Na_2MoO_4/ha registering 30.39 per cent more P uptake than the uninoculated control. Kumar *et al.* (2005) also reported that application of 1.0 kg Mo/ha, which was at par with 1.5 kg Mo/ha, significantly enhanced all the yield attributing characters, yield and quality characters of chickpea over the control and 0.5 kg Mo/ha. The N and P content in seeds, haulms and their total uptake and protein content in seeds increased significantly upto application of 1.0 kg Mo/ha over 0.5 kg Mo/ha. Similar response has also been reported by Brodrick *et al.* (1992). This could be due to better availability of N due to increased N_2-fixation or better root development that might have allowed more absorption of plant nutrients from soil.

Grain yield due to both level of Mo application were numerically higher by 8.87 per cent with 0.5 kg Na_2MoO_4/ha and 11.57 per cent with 1.0 kg $NaMoO_4$/ha over uninoculated control (Table 15.1). Similarly, straw yield was numerically higher by 13.40 per cent with 0.5 kg Na_2MoO_4/ha and 2.93 per cent with 1.0 kg Na_2MoO_4/ha over uninoculated control. Chandra and Kothari (2002) also reported beneficial effect of the application of Mo with increasing doses on the grain yield, protein content of grain and available N content. Similar results were also reported by Chahal *et al.* (1976), who observed significantly higher yields of green mass and dry matter, compared to untreated treatments by treating pea with molybdenum (30µ g/L).

Combined application of Molybdenum with Rhizobium

Seed inoculation with *Rhizobium* and application of 0.5 kg Na_2MoO_4/ha was found better by producing 8.61, 31.05 and 31.05 per cent more nodule number and 5.58, 35.25 and 57.71 per cent more nodule dry weight over the *Rhizobium* alone at 45, 75 and 120 DAS, respectively (Fig. 15.1). However, Mudholkar and Ahlawat (1979) reported that response of Mo was greater when applied along with P and *Rhizobium* inoculation. *Rhizobium* inoculation with different Mo levels favoured the plant dry weight. Application of Mo 0.5 kg and 1.0 kg per ha registered increase of 3.07 to 30.09 and 2.75 to 38.2 per cent over the *Rhizobium* alone at different intervals. These results are in agreement with Brkiæ *et al.* (2004), reported more plant dry weight with *Rhizobium* inoculation + Mo application than *Rhizobium* alone.

Seed inoculation of *Rhizobium* showed better impact with 0.5 kg Na_2MoO_4/ha by producing 14.00 per cent more N uptake by grain and straw over the *Rhizobium* alone and 5.62 per cent more over 1.0 kg Na_2MoO_4/ha + *Rhizobium* application and accumulating 17.54 per cent more total P uptake over the *Rhizobium* alone and 10.60 per cent more over 1.0 kg Na_2MoO_4/ ha + *Rhizobium* application (Table 1). Similar response has also been reported by Brkiæ *et al.* (2004).

Grain yield due to *Rhizobium* inoculation with Mo application was numerically higher by 1.54 per cent with 0.5 kg Na_2MoO_4/ ha and 0.11 per cent with 1.0 kg Na_2MoO_4/ha over *Rhizobium* alone (Table 15.1). Similarly, straw yield was numerically higher by 9.14 per cent with 0.5 kg Na_2MoO_4/ ha and 2.72 per cent with 1.0 kg Na_2MoO_4/ha over *Rhizobium* alone. Pal (1986) has also reported that Seed inoculation in combination with 60 kg P_2O_5+1.5 kg Sodium Molybdate/ha gave the highest yields of chickpea. These improvements in plant dry weight, grain and straw yield, N, P and micronutrients content and uptake in chickpea may be because of their synergistic interaction with inoculated and native rhizobia nodulating chickpea by helping in survival in rhizosphere, root colonization, root hair infection and efficiency of N_2-fixation.

It could be concluded from the study that mineral nutrient deficiencies are limiting legume nitrogen fixation and yield. Besides nutrients application of micronutrients at optimum doses is necessary to harness the maximum benefits of N_2-fixation for achieving maximum productivity of pulse crops. A dose of 25 kg $ZnSO_4$/ha and 5 kg Borax/ha and seed treatment with 0.5 kg $NaMoO_4$/ha and *Rhizobium* was found optimum for chickpea growth, yield, residual soil fertility under *Tarai* conditions. To ensure full benefit from N_2-fixation by legume symbioses, successful management strategies should consider the whole legume-*Rhizobium* system and selection for improved inoculants and not only the host plant.

REFERENCES

Ahlawat, IPS., Gangaiah, B., and Singh, O. (2007). Effect of Fertilizer and Stover Management on Productivity and Soil Fertility in Chickpea (*Cicer arietinum*) – Maize (*Zea mays*) Cropping System. *Indian Journal of Agricultural Sciences* 75: 400-403.

Ali., and Kumar. (2003). Chickpea Research in India: An Overview. *In: Chickpea Research in India* (Ali, M.; Shiv Kumar and Singh, N.B. Eds.). IIPR, pp. 13.

Bharti, N., Murtuza, M., and Singh, A.P. (2002). Effect of Boron-*Rhizobium* Relationship on Yield, Nitrogen and Boron Nutrition of Chickpea. *Journal of Research of Birsa Agricultural University*. 14:175-179.

Bhuiyan, M., Khanam, D., and Ali, M. (1999). Chickpea Root Nodulation and Yield as Affected by Micronutrient Application and *Rhizobium* Inoculation. *International Chickpea Pegionpea Newsletter*. 6 : 28-29.

Bolanos, L., Brewin, N.J., and Bonilla, I. (1996). Effect of boron on *Rhizobium*-legume cell-surface Interaction and Nodule Development. *Plant Physiology*. 110: 1249-1258.

Brahmaprakash, G.P., and Sahu, P.K. (2012). Biofertilizers for Sustainability. *Journal of the Indian Institute of Science*. 92 (1):37-62.

Brkiæ, S., Milakoviæ, Z., Kristek, A., and Antunoviæ, M. (2004). Pea Yield and Its Quality Depending on Inoculation, Nitrogen and Molybdenum Fertilization. *Plant Soil and Environment*. 50: 39-45.

Brodrick, S.J. and Giller, K.E. (1992). Root nodules Efficient Scavengers of Molybdenum for N_2 Fixation. *Journal of Experimental Botony*. 42 : 679-686.

Chahal, V.P.S., Gupta, R.P., and Pandher, M.S. (1976). Inoculate and Get More Yields of Gram. *Programming Farming*. 13: 24-25.

Chandra, D., and Kothari, M.L. (2002). Effect of Modes and Nodulation of Chickpea Grown on Loamy Sand Soil. *Communication of Soil Science and Plant Analysis*. 33:2905-2915.

Choudhary, A.U., and Muhammad, N. (1990). Effect of Micronutrients on Nodulation and Seed Yield of Chickpea (*Cicer arietinum* L.). *Journal of Agricultural Research*. 28:139-147. Choudhary, L. M., Kulthe, K.S., Baig, M.F.N., Dhuppe, M.V., and More, S.S. (2005). Effect of *Rhizobium* Isolates on Nodulation and Growth of Chickpea. *Journal of Soils and Crops*. 15: 323-327.

Gupta, S.C. (2006). Effect of Combined Inoculation on Nodulation Nutrient Uptake and Yield of Chickpea in Vertisol. *Journal of Indian Society of Soil Science*. 54 : 251-254.

Gupta, S.C., and Sahu, S. (2012). Response of Chickpea to Micronutrients and Biofertilizers in Vertisol. Legume Research - *An International Journal*. 35 (3):248-251.

Islam, M.A., Saha, U.K., Islam, M.S., and Saha, R.R. (1995). Fertilizing Chickpea for Yield with Special Emphasis on Boron and Molybdenum in Grey Flood Plain Soils of Bangladesh. *Annals of Bangladesh Agriculture*. 5:43-49.

Jongruaysup, S., O'Hara, G.W., Bell, R.W., and Dell, B. (1993). Effect of Molybdenum Deficiency on Noduole Intiation, Development and N_2-fixation in Black Gran (*Vigna mungo* L. Hepper). *Plant and Soil*. 156 : 345-348.

Khurana, A.L., and Dudeja S.S. (1997). Biological Nitrogen Fixation Technology for Pulse Production in India. Indian Institute of Pulse Research, Kanpur, India. pp. 18.

Kumar, B.S.D., Berggren, I., and Martensson, A.M. (2005). Potential for Improving pea Production by Co-inoculation with Florescent *Pseudomonas* and *Rhizobium*. *Plant and Soil*. 229: 25-34.

Misra, S.K., Upadhyay, R.M., and Tiwari, V.N. (2002). Effect of Salt and Zinc on Nodulation Leghaemoglobin and Nitrogen Content of Rabi legumes. *Indian Journal of Pulses Research*. 15 : 145-148.

Mudholkar, N.J., and Ahlawat, I.P.S. (1979). Response of Bengal Gram to Nitrogen, Phosphorus and Molybdenum. *Indian Journal of Agronomy*. 24 : 61-65.

O'Hara, G.W. (2001). Nutritional Constraints on Root Nodule Bacteria Affecting Symbiotic N_2-fixation: A Review. *Australian Journal of Experimental Agriculture*. 41:417-433.

O'Hara, G.W., Boonkerd, N., and Dilworth, J. (1988). Mineral Constraints to Nitrogen Fixation. *Plant and Soil*. 5 : 93-110.

Pal, A.K. (1986). Interaction of *Rhizobium* Inoculation with Phosphate and Molybdenum Application on Chickpea (*Cicer arietinum* L.) at Rainfed Condition. *Environment and Ecology*. 4:642-647.

Panse, V.G., and Sukhatme, P.V. (1978). Statistical Methods for Agricultural Workers. I.C.A.R., New Delhi.

Pareek, R.P., and Chandra, R. (2003). Chickpea: Microbiology and Nitrogen Fixation. In: Chickpea Research in India (Eds. Ali, M.; Shiv Kumar and Singh, N.B.). IIPR, pp. 167-193.

Rahman, M.H.H., Arima, Y., and Watanabe, K.H. (1999). Adequate Range of Boron Nutrition is more Restricted for Root Nodule Development that for Plant Growth on Young Soybean Plant. *Soil Science and Plant Nutrition*. 45 : 287-296.

Ratna Kalyani, R., Sree Devi, V., Satyanarayana, N.V., and Madhava Rao, K.V. (1993). Effect of Foliar Application of Boron on crop Growth and Yield of Pigeonpea (*Cajanus cajan* L. Millsp.). *Indian Journal of Plant Physiology*. 36(4):223-226.

Sakal, R., Sinha, R.B., Singh, A.P., and Bhogal, N.S. (1998). Responses of some Rabi Pulses to B, Zn and S Application in Farmers Fields. *Fertilizer News*. 43 : 39-43.

Sawires, E.S. (2001). Effect of Phosphorus Fertilization and Micronutrients on Yield and Yield Components of Chickpea (*Cicer arietinum* L.). *Annals of Agricultural Science*. 46(1) : 155-164.

Singh, B., Laura, R.D., and Gupta, V.K. (1984). Influence of Molybdenum, Zinc and *Rhizobium* Inoculation on Dry Matter Yield and Nitrogen Content in Chickpea. *International Journal of Tropical Agriculture*. 2 : 159-165.

Singh, M., Chaudhary, S.R., Sharma, S.R., and Rathore, M.S. (2004). Effect of Some Micronutrients on Content and Uptake by Chickpea. *Agricultural Science Digest*. 24 : 268-270.

Solaiman, A.R.M. (1999). Influence of *Rhizobium* Inoculant, Nitrogen and Boron on Nodulation, Dry Weight and Grain Yield of Chickpea. *Annals of Bangladesh Agriculture*. 9 : 75-84.

Vincent, J.M. (1974). Root Nodule Symbiosis with *Rhizobium*. *In*: "The biology of Nitrogen Fixation" (Eds. Quispal, A.,). North Holland Publishing Company, Amsterdam. pp. 265-341.

Yadav, O.P. and Shukla, U.C. (1983). Effect of Zinc on Nodulation and Nitrogen Fixation in Chickpea. *Journal of Agricultural Science*. 101:559-563.

Pages 174-177

INTEGRATED NUTRIENT MANAGEMENT IN CHICKPEA
Edited by : **Dr. Virendra Kumar** and **Dr. Nirmal Kumar Katiyar**
Edition : **2017**
ISBN : 978-93-5056-872-9
Published by : **Discovery Publishing House Pvt. Ltd., New Delhi (India)**

16

Yield and Quality of Chickpea as Affected by Rhizobium Inoculation

Shivendra Kumar Vishwakarma
Pratibha Singh, R.P. Singh
R.N. Kewat

In India, chickpea is the premier pulse crop occupying 7.10 million hectares area and contributing 5.75 million tonnes to the national pulse basket. Pulse or legume grains, being an important source of vegetable proteins, are easily digestable under normal condition, possess good cooking quality and also helps in decreasing the blood cholesterol level as compared to animal proteins, the consumption of which causes atherosclerosis (Khanna and Gupta, 1988). Pulses containing high protein content (20-30%) are enormously utilised in covering widespread protein-calorie-malnutrition problem of the underdeveloped and developing countries including India also. Rhizobium is a soil bacteria, which has a close association with the roots of higher plants. Rhizobium culture is low cost technology for increasing the yield. In India, the cost of fertilizers is very high and they are not easily available at the time of sowing and other cultural practices of the crop. Due to the importance of rhizobium bacterium in nitrogen fixation process, the present investigation has been conduced to observe the influence of this bacteria on quality parameters of chickpea.

The field experiment was conducted at Students Instructional Farm of Narendra Deva University of Agriculture and Technology, Kumarganj,

Department of Biochemistry, N.D. University of Agriculture and Technology, Faizabad, U.P. 224 229.

Faizabad during the *Rabi* season, 2007-08. Eight treatment combinations (Table 16.1) were replicated four times in randomized block design. Four prominent tested varieties were sown on 29 October, 2007. The row to row and plant to plant spacing were kept 30 cm and 10 cm respectively. The seeds were sown at the rate of 70 kg ha^{-1}. Fertilizers NPK were applied @ 20:50:25 kg ha^{-1}. *Rhizobium* was applied @ 200 g/10 kg seeds. After harvesting, the produce of each plot was collected and weighed separately. For the determination of dal-husk ratio, the hundred seeds were collected randomly from each plot and their weight was recorded on balance. The husk of each seed was removed manually and weighed on same balance. Lastly the weight of dal and husk were noted and calculated their ratio. Protein content in chickpea was estimated by Lowery *et al.* (1951) using folinciocalteau's reagent. Methionine content was analysed by the method as described by the Horn *et al.* (1946). Tryptophan content was estimated by the method given by Spice and Chamber (1949). The seed yield ranged from 18.29 to 22.26 q/ha. Maximum seed yield (22.60 q ha^{-1}) was recorded in Udai variety and the lowest seed yield (18.29 q/ha) in Avarodhi variety after the Rhizobium inoculation. Rhizobium increased the capacity of nitrogen fixation by the crop. The result shows a very close relationship between nitrogen metabolism and increasing nitrogen levels. A relationship between enzyme and nitrogen, there is a general agreement that increase in nitrate level enhanced the nitrate reductase activity. This is the reason to increase the rate of photosynthesis by increasing the enzyme activity of carbonic anhydrase which is an important enzyme governing the role of photosynthesis in plants.

Table 16.1: Seed yield, test weight and dal husk ratio of chickpea seeds is affected by *Rhizobium* inoculation

Varieties	Seed Yield (q/ha)		Test Weight (g)		Dal Husk Ratio	
	Control	*Rhizobium*	Control	*Rhizobium*	Control	*Rhizobium*
Radhey	16.43	21.41	300.10	312.80	76.30	101.80
Avarodhi	14.60	18.29	130.81	140.92	87.80	90.80
Udai	17.34	22.26	216.92	226.40	104.90	117.80
K-850	17.75	21.55	317.30	333.90	150.40	171.40
CD at 5%	V=0.494, R=0.403, V×R=0.698		V=0.569, R=0.465, V×R=0.805		V=0.013, R=0.011, V×R=0.019	

The test weight as influenced by Rhizobium inoculation was in the range of 140.92 to 333.90 g. The highest test weight (333.90 g) was recorded in K-850 variety and lowest (140.92 g) in Avarodhi variety. The magnitude of increase was being proportional to level of Rhizobium treatment. Rhizobium treatment increased the quality of carbohydrate that is assimilated by different plant parts and translocating to the developing grains in plants (Mishra and Dixit, 1988). It may be a possible reason for higher value of test weight of chickpea. The results are well supported with the finding of Singh (1985) in chickpea. Rhizobium treatment enhanced the dal-husk ratio. Maximum dal-husk ratio (171:40) was recorded in K-850 variety and minimum (90:80) in Avarodhi variety. Protein content in inoculated seed ranged between 23.31 and 24.50 per cent. Highest protein content (24.50%) was noticed in K-850 variety followed by the Avarodhi (24.48%) and Udai (23.89%) Rhizobium inoculation favours the nitrogen pool of the soil which are converted into organic nitrogenous compounds *viz;* amino acids, protein and nucleic acids.

Table 16.2: Protein, methionine and tryptophan content of chickpea seeds after the *Rhizobium* inoculation

Varieties	Protein (%)		Methionine (g/100g Protein)		Tryptophan (g/100g Protein)	
	Control	*Rhizobium*	Control	*Rhizobium*	Control	*Rhizobium*
Radhey	21.51	23.31	0.077	0.073	0.16	0.15
Avarodhi	22.06	24.48	0.086	0.082	0.15	0.15
Udai	21.12	23.89	0.084	0.071	0.15	0.15
K-850	22.86	24.50	0.082	0.079	0.16	0.16
CD at 5%	V=0.38, R=0.31, V×R=0.53		V=NS, R=NS, V×R=NS		V=NS, R=NS, V×R=NS	

Rhizobium treatment influenced the methionine content and highest amount of methionine (0.082 g/100 g protein) was present in Avarodhi variety and lowest (0.071 g/100 g protein) in Udai variety. Highest amount of (0.16 g/100 g protein) was recorded in Avarodhi variety whereas, lowest tryptophan content (0.15 g/100 g protein) in variety Radhey. After Rhizobium inoculation, amino acid variation is reported due to higher peroxidase enzyme activity, which favours low methionine and tryptophan by synthesis (Kushwaha and Srivastava, 1978). The percentage of protein increased while methionine and tryptophan content tended to decrease. There was a negative correlation between methionine and protein content. The results showed that seed yield, test weight and dal husk ratio of chickpea seeds were significantly increased with *Rhizobium* treatments. Highest seed yield was noticed in Udai variety (22.26 q/ha) and lowest in Awarodhi (18.29 q/ha) variety with *Rhizobium* inoculation. Highest test weight (333.90 g) and dal : husk ratio (171:40) was recorded in K-850 variety. Significant improvement in protein content in chickpea seed was recorded but the essential amino acids tryptophan and methionine were slightly decreased. Protein (24.48%) and methionine (0.082 g/100g protein) contents were noticed maximum in Avarodhi variety while, tryptophan content (0.16 g/100g protein) was found highest in K-850 variety. Hence it may be concluded that *Rhizobium* inoculation improved the quality and quantity of chickpea.

REFERENCES

Horn, J.M.; Jones, O.B. and Blum, A.E. (1946). Calorimetric Determination of Methionine in Protein and Foods. *Journal of Biological Chemistry,* 1 (16) : 313.

Khanna, P.K. and Gupta, S.K. (1988). Medicinal Value of Chickpea, *Annals of Agricultural Research,* 25 (6): 214-216.

Kushwaha, P.D. and Srivastava, G.P. (1978). Effect of N., P. and Rhizobium Inoculation on the Biochemical Evaluation of Mungbean. *Indian Journal of Agriculture Chemistry,* 11(1): 42-48.

Lowery, O.H.; Rosebrough, N.J.; Far, A.L. and Randal, R.J. (1951). Protein Measurement with the Follin Phenol Reagent. *Journal of Biological Chemistry,* 193: 265-275.

Mishra, S.K. and Dixit, J.P. (1988). Effect of Rhizobium on Root Nodulation, Protein Production and Nutrient Uptake in Cowpea. *Annals of Agricultural Research,* 24 (1): 139-144.

Singh, G. (1985). Arbuscular Mycorrhiza in Association with Rhizobium Species Improves Nodulation, N_2 fixation and N utilization. *Microbial Research.* 151 (1): 87-92.

Spice, J.T. and Chamber, D.C. (1949). Chemical Determination of Tryptophan in Protein. *Analytical Chemistry,* 21 (3): 1249.

Subramanian, A. and Rodhaprishara, J. (1981). Effect of Foliar Spray on Black Gram (Pulse Crop). *Pulses News Letter.* 1 (4): L-39.

Pages 178-185

INTEGRATED NUTRIENT MANAGEMENT IN CHICKPEA
Edited by : **Dr. Virendra Kumar** and **Dr. Nirmal Kumar Katiyar**
Edition : **2017**
ISBN : **978-93-5056-872-9**
Published by : **Discovery Publishing House Pvt. Ltd., New Delhi (India)**

17

Response of Chickpea (*Cicer Kabulium*) to Different Methods of P Application, Bio-inoculants and Micronutrients

Shalu Ann Abraham
Thomas Abraham

ABSTRACT

Field experiments were conducted during the rabi seasons of 2003-04 and 2004-05 at Allahabad, Uttar Pradesh, to evaluate the effect of different methods of P application, bio-inoculants and micronutrients (Mo+B) on growth and yield of kabuli chickpea (Cicer kabulium) var. Pragati. The experiments were laid out in split-split plot design with three replications. Main plot consisted of four different methods of P application, sub-plots consisted of bio-inoculants and sub-sub-plots comprised of micronutrients. The experimental results revealed that Band placement (basal) recorded significantly higher dry weight (30.04g plant^{-1}), pods plant^{-1} (47.95), pod yield (12.01g plant^{-1}), seed weight plant^{-1} (13.09g) and seed yield (35.03qha^{-1}). Among the bio-inoculants, the performance of dual inoculation of Trichoderma + PSB was the best having recorded significantly superior growth, yield attributes and yield. Increase in grain yield in Trichoderma + PSB was 10.75 per cent and 12.79 per cent over single inoculation of Trichoderma and PSB. Application of molybdenum + boron also significantly influenced nodulation (23.1 and 32.9 at 60 and 80 DAS), dry weight (32.0g plant^{-1}), yield attributes and yield (32.72 q ha^{-1}).

Keywords: Phosphorus, Band Placement, Trichoderma, PSB, Molybdenum, Boron, Chickpea.

Department of Agronomy Allahabad Agricultural Institute-Deemed University, Allahabad - 211 007, India.

INTRODUCTION

Chickpea is a major *rabi* pulse crop and is largely grown in marginal and sub marginal lands of semi-arid and arid tropics, which are characterised by poor fertility status and moisture stress. With an estimated global production of 9.7 million tonnes in 2008-09, chickpea is grown in about 50 countries around the world covering an area of 11 million ha with an average global productivity of 881 kg ha^{-1}. India is the leading producer of chickpea contributing to about 70 per cent of the world's chickpea production. There has been a steady increase in the area under chickpea from 6.71 million ha in 2004-05 to 7.85 million ha in 2008-09 but the production shows variation owing to several factors such as: poor fertility status of the soil, rainfall pattern and disease incidence. During 2008-09 the chickpea production was about 7 million tonnes with average productivity of 894 kg ha^{-1}. Improving soil fertility is one of the most common tactics to increase agricultural production. Maintaining high levels of available Nitrogen and phosphorus, the two most limiting nutrients in soils, is a major challenge to ecologists and land managers. Phosphorus is essential for normal growth and development but most of the P applied is rapidly fixed to unavailable forms and accounts for low P use efficiency. Band placement of P reduces contact with the soil and results in less fixation than broadcast application. The availability of soil phosphorus is largely controlled by biologically mediated processes such as: mineralization and immobilization rates. The use of PSB has opened new vistas of phosphorus nutrition Mukherjee and Rai (2000). An alternative approach for the use of PSB as microbial inoculants is the use of mixed cultures or co-inoculation with biocontrol fungi *Trichoderma* spp. *Trichoderma* spp., are not only known for their ability to act as biocontrol agents against plant pathogens like: *Fusarium oxysporium,* which cause Fusarium wilt in chickpea but also increase root growth, solubilize various plant nutrients, increasing P recovery and hence increasing crop production. Increased removal of micronutrients as a consequence of adoption of high yielding varieties and intensive cropping together with a shift towards high analysis NPK fertilizers has declined the level of micronutrients in soil than required for normal productivity of crops. Application of boron and molybdenum favors better growth and nitrogen assimilation with higher nodulation, which in turn results into enhanced growth. Keeping this in view, the field experiment was conducted to study the effect of different methods of P application, bio-inoculants and micronutrients on growth and yield of chickpea.

Materials and Methods

A field experiment was conducted during the *rabi* seasons of 2003-04 and 2004-05 at Crop Research Farm, Allahabad Agricultural Institute-Deemed University, Allahabad. The soil of the experimental site was sandy loam with pH 7.4, organic carbon 0.72 per cent, available P_2O_5 17.14 kg ha^{-1} and K_2O 156.2 kg ha^{-1}. The experiment was laid out in split split plot design replicated thrice. The main plots comprised of four methods of P application [Broadcast (basal), Broadcast (basal + top dressing of P), Band placement (Basal), Band placement (Basal + top dressing of P), sub-plots consisted of bio-inoculants (*Trichoderma*, PSB, *Trichoderma* + PSB), whereas sub-sub-plots consisted of micronutrients (molybdenum, boron, molybdenum + boron). Kabuli chickpea variety 'Pragati' was used for the experiment using a seed rate of 75 kg ha^{-1}. Sowing was carried out on 5th November during both the years. Uniform dose of N@ 20 kg ha^{-1} in the form of urea and K_2O@60 kg ha^{-1} in the form of muriate of potash were applied to all the treatments as a basal dose, P_2O_5@ 60kg ha^{-1} in the form of single super phosphate was applied in a single dose and split dose (3/4th as basal and 1/4th as top dressing one month after sowing) according to the treatments. *Rhizobium* inoculation was administered as a blanket treatment. *Trichoderma* @ 10g kg^{-1} seed and PSB @20g kg^{-1} seed were used according to the treatments. Micronutrients *viz;* molybdenum@ 1 kg ha^{-1}in the form of ammonium molybdate and boron @ 5 kg ha^{-1}in the form of Borax were applied as basal dressing along with the fertilizers according to the treatments. For band placement of the fertilizers furrows of 6cm depth were made and fertilizers and micronutrients were placed in these furrows in a band raising the depth to 4 cm. Various growth attributes were recorded at different stages of growth. The chickpea crop was harvested at full maturity stage and yield attributes and yield were recorded following normal standard procedures.

Results and Discussion

Plant Growth

(i) *Nodulation:* Effect of different treatments on nodule number was observed at 60 and 80 days after sowing. Perusal of data in Table 17.1 shows that different methods of P application had no significant effect on nodulation whereas bio-inoculants and micronutrients significantly increased nodulation. Dual inoculation of *Trichoderma* + PSB was found to be significantly superior over single inoculation of PSB and *Trichoderma* which might be due to more availability of P to plant that may stimulate formation of more nodules. Also phosphorus solubilizing micro-organisms have synergistic effect on the population of *Bradyrhizobium* sp., *cicer* that lead to increased nodulation. These results are in close conformity with the findings of Gaur (1987), Dubey and Agarwal (1999) and Chaudhary *et al.* (1973).

Combined application of Mo +B significantly influenced nodulation at 60 and 80 DAS in comparison to sole application of Mo or B. Boron plays an important role in nodule formation in legumes and molybdenum also being an essential component of enzyme nitrate reductase favored better enzymatic activity, thereby resulting into higher nodulation (Tisdale *et al.* 2002). Similar results were also reported by (Ali and Mishra, 2001).

(ii) *Dry Matter Production:* The treatments exerted a distinct effect on dry matter production. Among the different methods of P application dry matter accumulation was significantly higher with band placement (basal) method of P application. This may be attributed to the fact that broadcast method of P application on soils with a high capacity to fix phosphorus results in less fertilizer efficiency whereas band application has less potential for fixation due to concentration of phosphorus fertilizers in a smaller volume (Tisdale *et al.* 2002).

Among the bio-inoculants dual inoculation of *Trichoderma* + PSB recorded higher dry matter accumulation. In the first year (2003-04) dry matter accumulation under single inoculation with PSB was recorded at par values with *Trichoderma* + PSB. The increase in dry matter accumulation may be attributed to better availability and uptake of nutrients by plants due to combined inoculation of *Trichoderma* + PSB (Rudresh *et al.* 2004).

Combined application of Mo + B significantly influenced dry matter accumulation.

Coupled effect of Mo + B may be ascribed to enhanced nitrogen availability through more nitrogen fixation causing vigorous plant growth. The results are in conformity with Bhuiyan *et al.* 1999.

Yield and Yield Attributes

The different methods of P application significantly affected the yield and yield parameters *viz;* pods plant^{-1}, pod yield and seed weight plant^{-1}. Band placement (basal) method of P application recorded significantly higher yield attributes and yield. However during the first year broadcast (basal) and broadcast (basal + top dressing of P) recorded at par values with band placement (basal) for pod yield and during the second year band placement (basal + top dressing of P) recorded at par values with band placement (basal). The increase in yield attributes under band placement (basal) may be ascribed to greater availability of phosphorus in soil environment and their increased absorption by the roots and their transportation towards above ground parts which helped in various metabolic activities and hence resulted in greater yield attributes. Superiority of band placement was probably due to a combination of higher available soil moisture and greater probability of roots exposed to the fertilizers. Parihar, (1990) also reported the beneficial effect of phosphorus on the yield attributes. Similar results were also reported by Tiwari and Tripathi, (1995) and Sarkar *et al.* (1995). Thiyagarajan *et al.* (2003) also reported the enhanced efficiency of applied as well as native phosphorus due to band placement of phosphatic fertilizers. Higher seed yield might be attributed to cumulative effect of increased yield attributes.

Table 17.1: Effect of different methods of P application, bio-inoculants and micronutrients on nodulation and dry weight of chickpea

Treatments	No. of Nodules at 60 DAS			No. of Nodules at 80 DAS			Dry Weight (g plant^{-1})		
	2003-04	2004-05	Pooled Mean	2003-04	2004-05	Pooled Mean	2003-04	2004-05	Pooled Mean
Methods of P application									
Broadcast(Basal)	21.0	22.5	21.8	31.7	32.0	31.9	25.90	27.81	26.85
Broadcast(Basal + Topdressing of P)	20.9	23.5	22.2	31.4	33.3	32.4	25.8	27.70	26.75
Band placement (Basal)	20.4	23.6	21.9	32.3	33.0	32.6	28.87	31.28	30.04
Band placement (Basal + top dressing of P)	20.7	21.7	21.2	31.4	32.8	31.8	28.65	30.88	29.95
SEd±	1.05	0.88	0.88	1.01	1.03	0.82	0.4	0.5	0.47
CD (P=0.05)	NS	NS	NS	NS	NS	NS	1.1	1.2	1.16
Bio-inoculants									
Trichoderma	17.0	21.6	19.9	26.8	28.9	27.6	25.48	27.43	26.46
PSB	20.2	21.9	21.0	30.3	31.5	30.9	27.75	29.66	28.83
Trichoderma + PSB	25.1	25.0	25.1	38.0	37.9	37.9	28.65	31.16	29.91
SEd±	0.69	0.60	0.39	0.60	1.04	0.53	0.5	0.5	0.46
CD (P=0.05)	1.46	1.27	0.82	1.28	2.21	1.11	1.0	1.0	0.98
Micronutrients									
Molybdenum	18.1	22.6	20.4	30.5	31.7	31.1	26.28	28.41	27.34
Boron	21.4	22.5	21.9	32.1	32.7	32.4	24.60	26.85	25.85
Molybdenum + Boron	22.8	23.3	23.1	32.4	34.0	32.9	31.01	32.98	32.00
SEd±	0.79	0.65	0.53	0.73	0.60	0.48	0.4	0.4	0.40
CD (P=0.05)	1.60	1.30	1.08	1.47	1.22	0.96	0.8	0.9	0.81

Table 17.2: Effect of different methods of P application, bio-inoculants and micronutrients on yield and yield attributes of chickpea

Treatments	No. of Pods Plant^{-1}			Pod Yield (g Plant^{-1})			Seed Weight Plant^{-1}(g)			Seed Yield (q ha^{-1})		
	2003-04	2004-05	Pooled Mean	2003-04	2004-05	Pooled Mean	2003-04	2004-05	Pooled Mean	2003-04	2004-05	Pooled Mean
Methods of P application												
Broadcast (Basal)	43.56	44.10	43.83	11.14	11.19	11.16	11.52	10.99	11.26	29.56	32.39	30.97
Broadcast (Basal+ Topdressing of P)	41.35	41.79	41.57	11.38	11.56	11.47	11.43	11.22	11.33	27.35	29.75	28.55
Band placement (Basal)	47.81	48.08	47.95	11.52	12.49	12.01	12.83	13.34	13.09	33.81	36.25	35.03
Band placement (Basal + top dressing of P)	43.59	44.11	43.85	10.13	12.12	11.13	11.79	11.13	11.46	29.59	32.50	31.05
SEd±	0.50	0.59	0.54	0.3	0.3	0.2	0.2	0.7	0.39	0.50	0.76	0.60
CD (P=0.05)	1.22	1.45	1.32	0.8	0.8	0.5	0.5	1.8	1.95	1.22	1.85	1.46
Bio-inoculants												
Trichoderma	43.15	43.60	43.38	10.72	11.53	11.12	11.53	11.91	11.72	29.15	31.83	30.49
PSB	42.74	43.38	43.06	10.62	10.63	10.63	11.10	10.29	10.69	28.74	31.15	29.94
Trichoderma +PSB	46.35	46.58	46.46	11.79	13.36	12.58	13.06	12.82	12.94	32.35	35.19	33.77
SEd±	0.37	0.49	0.42	0.4	0.4	0.3	0.3	0.5	0.23	0.37	0.52	0.40
CD (P=0.05)	0.78	1.05	0.90	0.8	0.8	0.6	0.7	1.0	0.49	0.78	1.09	0.85
Micronutrients												
Molybdenum	44.14	44.52	44.33	10.16	11.40	10.78	11.33	10.68	11.01	30.14	32.54	31.34
Boron	42.81	43.11	42.96	10.77	11.61	11.19	11.88	11.16	11.52	28.81	31.49	30.15
Molybdenum + Boron	45.29	45.94	45.62	12.20	12.51	12.35	12.46	13.18	12.82	31.29	34.14	32.72
SEd±	0.41	0.45	0.42	0.6	0.5	0.4	0.3	0.6	0.31	0.41	0.52	0.45
CD (P=0.05)	0.82	0.92	0.85	1.2	0.9	0.8	0.6	1.2	0.63	0.82	1.05	0.90

Dual inoculation of *Trichoderma* + PSB significantly affected the yield attributes *viz;* pods plant^{-1}, pod yield and seed weight plant^{-1} and seed yield over single inoculation of *Trichoderma* or PSB. Root colonization by *Trichoderma* spp enhanced root growth and development, crop productivity, resistance to abiotic stresses and the uptake and use of nutrients (Harman *et al.* 2004). *Trichoderma* spp with their ability to increase plant growth and development due to enhanced root development and deeper rooting in presence of PSB have a synergistic effect and help in more solubilisation of insoluble inorganic phosphorus resulting in higher yield and yield attributes (Rudresh *et al.* 2005). The increase in yield might have also resulted due to significant improvement in yield attributing characters as a result of development of more number of root nodules in the presence of increased phosphorus availability (Chundawat *et al.* 1976 and Patel *et al.* 1987).

Combined application of Mo + B showed significantly positive influence on number of pods plant^{-1}, pod yield, seed weight plant^{-1} and seed yield. Application Mo + B favored better root growth and nitrogen assimilation with higher nodulation which in consequence resulted into better growth and development of sink size (number of pods plant^{-1}) and ultimately higher seed yield. These results fall in line with the findings of Ali and Mishra (2001).

It is concluded that band placement method of P application enhances the efficiency of applied and native P resulting in higher growth and yield. The present findings also indicate that dual inoculation of PSB + *Trichoderma* and combined application of Molybdenum and Boron has a great effect in enhancing the uptake of nutrients by the chickpea crop for its normal metabolic activities resulting in higher growth and yield.

REFERENCES

Ali, Masood and Mishra, J.P. (2001). Effect of Foliar Nutrition of Boron and Molybdenum on Chickpea. *Indian J. Pulses Res.* 14(1): 41-43.

Bhuiyan, A.H., Khanam, D. and Ali, M.Y. (1999). Chickpea Root Nodulation and Yield as Affected by Micronutrient Application and *Rhizobium* Inoculation. *Intern. Chickpea and Pigeonpea Newsletter*. 6 : 28-29.

Chaudhary, S.L., Ram, Sewa and Giri, G. (1973). Effect of Phosphorus, Nitrogen and Inoculation on Root Nodulation and Yield of Gram. *Indian J. Agron.* 30: 290-291.

Chundawat, G.S., Sharma, R.B. and Shekawat, G.S. (1976). Effect of Nitrogen, Phosphorus and Bacterial Fertilization on Growth and Yield of Gram in Rajasthan. *Indian J. Agron.* 12(1): 127-130.

Dubey, S.K. and Agarwal, S. (1999). Effect of Phosphate Solubilizing Microorganisms as Single and Composite Inoculants on Rainfed Soybean (Glycine max) in Vertisol. *Indian J. Agric. Sci.* 69 (8): 611-613.

Gaur, A.C. (1987). Phosphate Solubilizing Biofertilizers in Crop Productivity and their Interaction with VAM. Paper Presented at the National Workshop on Mycorrhizae, 13-15 March, School of Life Sciences, Jawaharlal Nehru University, New Delhi.

Harman, G.E., Howell, C.R., Viterbo, A., Chet, I. and Lorito, M. (2004). Trichoderma Species-Opportunistic, Avirulent Plant Symbionts. *Nature Reviews/Microbiol.* 2: 43-56.

Mukherjee, P.K. and Rai, R.K. (2000). Effect of Vesicular Arbuscular Mycorrhizae and Phosphate Solubilizing Bacteria on Growth, Yield and Phosphorus Uptake by Wheat (*Triticum aestivum*) and Chickpea (*Cicer arietinum*). *Indian J. Agron.* 45(3): 602-607.

Parihar, S.S. (1990). Yield and Water use of Chickpea (*Cicer arietinum*) as Influenced by Irrigation and Phosphorus. - 2014 *Indian J. Agron.* 35(3): 251-257.

Patel, R.G., Joshi, R.S. and Raman, R. (1987). Effect of Water Stagnation and Nitrogen on Growth and Yield of 4-Aug Chickpea. *Indian J. Agron.* 32(1): 12-14.

Rudresh, D.L., Shivaprakash, M.K. and Prasad, R.D. (2004). Effect of Combined Application of *Rhizobium*, Phosphate Solubilizing Bacterium and *Trichoderma* spp., on Growth, Nutrient uptake and Yield of Chickpea (*Cicer arietinum*). *Applied Soil Ecol.*. 28: 139-146.

Rudresh, D.L., Shivaprakash, M.K. and Prasad, R.D. (2005). Tricalcium Phosphate Solubilizing Abilities of *Trichoderma* spp., in Relation to P uptake and Growth and Yield Parameters of Chickpea (*Cicer arietinum* L.). *Canadian J. Microbiol.* 51(3): 217-222.

Sarkar, R.K., Shit, N. and Chakraborthy, A. (1995). Response of Chickpea (*Cicer arietinum*) to Levels of Phosphorus in Downloaded Rainfed Upland of Chota Nagpur plateau. *Indian J. Agron.* 40 (2): 309-311.

Thiyagarajan, T.M., Backiyavathy, M.R. and Savathri R. (2003). Nutrient Management for Pulses – A Review. *Agric. Rev.* 24(1): 40-48.

Tisdale, L.S., Nelson, L.W., Beaton, D.J. and Havlin, L.J. (2002). Elements Required in Plant Nutrition. In : Soil Fertility and Fertilizers. (5th Edition). Prentice Hall of India. New Delhi - pp. 67, 72, 486-488.

Tiwari, O.P. and Tripathi, R.S. (1995). Effect of Planting date, Irrigation and Phosphorus on Nodulation of Chickpea (*Cicer arietinum.*) Grown on clay and Loam Soil. *Indian J. Agron.* 40(3): 513-515.

INTEGRATED NUTRIENT MANAGEMENT IN CHICKPEA
Edited by : **Dr. Virendra Kumar** and **Dr. Nirmal Kumar Katiyar**
***Edition* : 2017**
ISBN : 978-93-5056-872-9
***Published by* : Discovery Publishing House Pvt. Ltd., New Delhi (India)**

18

Productivity and Profitability of Chickpea as Influenced by FYM, Sulphur and Zinc under Rainfed Condition of Central India

Vaishali Sharma
H.S. Kushwaha

ABSTRACT

A field experiment was conducted on chickpea during winter season of 2004-05 and 2005-06 on sandy loam soil at Chitrakoot, Satna (M.P.), to find out appropriate dose of FYM, sulphur and zinc for enhancing the productivity of chickpea under rainfed situation. Application of 10 t FYM alongwith recommended dose of fertilizers produced significantly higher seed and straw yields over without FYM mainly due to improvement in branched/plant, nodulation activity, seeds/plant and heavy seeds. Similarily, chickpea responded to the application of S and Zn upto 20 and 5 kg, respectively in term of growth, nodulation and seed yield of chickpea. Application of 10 t FYM, 20 kg S and 5 kg Zn ha^{-1} was remunerative in terms of net monetatory returns and return/rupee invested.

INTRODUCTION

Chickpea (*Cicer arietinum* L.), is a prime pulse crop of India largely concentrated on marginal and sub-marginal lands which are deficient for several nutrients (Rao *et al.* 2002). Majority of farmers hardly use any manure or fertilizers in chickpea cultivation. However, there is possibility of raising the productivity by judicious use of manure and fertilizers. Organic matter like: FYM has supplied available nutrients to the plants provided favourable

Department of Natural Resource Management, Mahatma Gandhi Chitrakoot Gramodaya Vishwavidyalaya, Chitrakoot, Satna (M.P.) 485 780.
Email: kushwaha_hs@rediffinaiLeom

soil environment and increase water holding capacity of soil for longer time. Sulphur influences plant growth, nodulation and yield attributes, by regulating the metabolic and enzymatic processes and affecting the availability of nutrient by the soil pH. Its significance is more pronounced in pulse crops, which are deficient in sulphur containing amino acids like: methionine and cystiene. Zinc involves in synthesis of protein, indole acetic acid, chlorophyll forrnation, carbohydrate metabolism and biosynthesis of plant harmonss. Hence, present study was undertaken to assess the appropriate doses of FYM, sulphur and zinc for enhancing the productivity of chickpea under rainfed situation.

Materials and Methods

A field experiment was conducted during the rainy season (kharif) of 2004-05 and 2005-06 at Agricultural Research farm of Mahatma Gandhi Chitrakoot Gramodaya Vishwavidyalaya, Chitrakoot, Satna (MP). The soil was sandy loam in texture with pH 6.78 and organic carbon 1.4 g kg^{-1} and 164, 9.1, 255 and 14.6 kg^{-1} available N, P, K and S ha^{-1}, respectively and 1.56 mg kg^{-1} available Zn. Twelve treatments comprised with 2 levels of FYM (0, 10 t ha^{-1}), 3 levels of S (0, 20, 40 kg ha^{-1}), and 2 levels of zinc (0, 5 kg ha^{-1}) were tested in factorial randomized block design with 3 replications. Seeds were treated with Rhizobium and phosphate solublizing bacteria (PSB) *i.e.*, *Pseudomonas* sp., culture 20 and 40 g kg seed by using 100 kg seed ha^{-1}. The seeds of chickpea 'Radhe' was sown on 20 October, 2004 and 15 October, 2005 and respective crop was harvested on 12 March, 2005 and 9 March, 2006. The row and plant spacing of 30 cm. and 15 cm. was maintained, respectively by thinning at 20 day stage of crop. Farmyard manure was prepared in Rajoula Agricultural Farm by use of goat dung and urine. Sulphur and zinc were applied through elemental sulphur (LR grade) and zinc dust (LR grade) respectively. The sulphur and zinc as per treatments were applied at sowing. An uniform dose of 20 kg N, 50 kg P_20_5 and 30 kg K_20 ha^{-1} were given through urea, diammonium phosphate and muriate of potash, respectively to all the experimental plots. The weeds were controlled by two hand weedings first at 30 days and second on 50 days after sowing. The termite of the experimental plot was controlled by one spraying of chloropyriphos 1500 ml ha^{-1} at 35 days stage. Crop growth *viz;* plant height, leaves/plant, plant and root dry weight were recorded at 65 days crop stages.

Results and Discussion

Growth Parameters

Growth Parameters *viz;* trifoliate leaves, plant and root dry weight of chickpea were recorded significantly higher under FYM 10 t FYM ha^{-1} as compared with control. However, plant height, plant dry matter and root dry weight were marginally enhanced due to 10 t FYM ha^{-1} application than that of control treatment. Such improvement in growth parameters might be due to the proper mixing of FYM in soil which had supplied available nutrients to plants that resulted in better growth parameters of chickpea. Sulphur application significantly enhanced plant height upto 40 kg S ha^{-1} but its value statistically at par with sulphur 20 kg S ha^{-1} while, trifoliate leaves/plant and plant dry matter/plant significantly increased upto 20 kg S ha^{-1} application. Further addition of sulphur *i.e.* 40 kg S ha^{-1} could not reach upto level of significance. An improvement in plant growth parameters by such increment doses of S might be because of its role in formation of amino acids *viz;* cystein, cystine, methoinine and synthesis of protein, vitamin and chlorophyll. Addition of 5 kg Zn ha^{-1} gave significantly higher plant dry weight however; plant height, trifoliate leaves, shoot dry weight and root dry weight were remarkably increased in application to zinc of 5 kg Zn ha^{-1}. This increase with the application of zinc was possibly due to its increment in synthesis of IAA and metabolism of auxin. Singh and Singh (1995) also reported the similar results.

Nodulation

Nodule formation and their dry weight were remarkably enhanced due to application of 10 t FYM ha^{-1} at 65 days. However, at 50 days stages, nodule dry weight was recorded significantly more over no FYM addition. Such increase in nodules/plant and nodules dry weight owing to improvement of soil environment, which enhanced proliferous root system, resulting more nodule formation of roots. The rapid multiplication of Rhizobium bacteria under FYM formed more number of nodules.

Nodules formation significantly improved due to application of sulphur up to 20 kg ha^{-1}.

Table 18.1: Effect of FYM, S and Zn level on growth and yield attributes of chickpea (mean of 2 years

Treatments	Plant Heights (cm)	Trifoliate Leaves/ Plants (#)	Dry Matter (g/plant)	Nodules/ plant (#)	Weight of Nodules/ plant(mg)	Root Dry Weight (g)	Primary Branches (#)	Secondary Branches (#)	Pods/ Plant (#)	Seeds Pod (#)	1000 seed Weight (g)
					FYM (tonnes ha^{-1})						
0	24.4	56.8	8.0	9.0	297.5	1.6	7.0	14.0	23.5	1.1	182
10	26.8	74.8	8.3	9.7	302.9	2.2	9.3	15.0	25.8	1.4	199
CD (P=0.05)	NS	12.5	NS	NS	NS	0.4	1.6	NS	NS	0.12	9
					Sulphur (kg ha^{-1})						
0	22.0	51.4	7.0	8.5	267.7	0.9	6.3	12.8	24.0	1.2	169
20	25.7	72.8	8.5	10.1	328.5	2.4	9.8	15.4	24.0	1.3	212
40	28.8	73.2	9.0	9.5	304.5	2.4	8.7	15.8	25.8	1.2	190
CD (P=0.05)	4.9	15.4	1.2	NS	11.4	0.5	1.9	2.4	NS	NS	11
					Zinc (kg ha^{-1})						
0	23.8	65.7	7.1	9.3	293.3	1.7	7.9	13.6	24.2	1.1	183
5	27.1	65.9	9.2	9.4	3.7	2.1	8.5	15.8	25.2	1.4	197
CD (P=0.05)	NS	NS	1.0	NS	9.7	NS	NS	2.0	NS	0.15	9

However, nodule dry weight was also registered significantly higher under 20 kg S ha^{-1} due to application of sulphur up to 20 kg ha^{-1}. But it was significantly reduced with addition of higher doses of sulphur *i.e.* 40 kg S ha^{-1}. This might be due to adequate supply of S to plant which helps in stimulation the Rhizobium bacteria for nodules formation and their dry weight. These results confirmed the findings of Sirinivasan *et al.* (2001). Application of zinc slightly improved the nodule formation at 50 and 65 days stages, while, nodule dry weight/plant significantly increased due to addition of zinc 5 kg Zn ha^{-1}. Such more nodules and greater their dry weight under zinc addition might be because of activation of various enzymes including which involve in N_2 fixation. Kasturikrishna and Ahlawat (2000) reported that application of 40 kg S + 5 kg Zn ha^{-1} obtained significantly higher root nodules/plant, dry weight of nodules/plant and nitrogen activities at flowering of pea compared with control and 40 kg S ha^{-1}.

Table 18.2: Effect of FYM, S and Zn level on yield and economics of chickpea (Pooled mean of 2 years)

Treatments	Seed yield (kg ha^{-1})	Straw yield (kg ha^{-1})	Harvest Index (%)	Cost of Cultivation (Rs. ha^{-1})	Gross Monetory Return (Rs. ha^{-1})	Net Monetory Return (Rs. ha^{-1})	Return/rupee Invested (Re.)
0	1367	2882	32.2	18832	28171	9339	2.28
10	1570	3267	32.4	19858	32182	12324	2.41
CD(P=0.05)	201	380	NS		2020	2071	
			Sulphur (kg ha^{-1})				
0	1167	3036	27.7	14830	24626	9795	2.91
20	1589	3252	32.8	19346	32648	13302	2.54
40	1640	2937	35.8	23861	33277	9415	1.93
CD(P=0.05)	278	NS	4.2		3217	3281	
			Zinc (kg ha^{-1})				
0	1360	2993	31.3	18140	28325	10184	2.43
5	1562	3152	33.1	20552	3204	11497	2.28
CD(P=0.05)	200	NS	NS		2022	NS	

Yield and Yield Attributes

Application of 10 t FYM hal recorded significantly gave higher seed yield than that of no FYM addition. Such enhancement might be because of FYM addition in soil improves the supply of available nutrient due to the release of alphatic, aromatic hydroxyl acids, humus and legnins and brought about favourable soil environment which ultimately increased nutrient and water holding capacity of soil for longer time that resulted in better growth and significant higher yield attributes *viz;* primary branches/plant, seeds/ pods and 1000-seed weight and gave higher yield of chickpea. The results were confirmed by the findings of Reddy *et al.* (2004) in chickpea crop and Singh *et al.* (2008) in urd bean. Straw yield of chickpea significantly enhanced by 385 kg ha^{-1} due addition of 10 t FYM hal than control owing to balance supply of major and micronutrients through FYM and increased availability of nutrients to the plants. This leads to better growth, higher photosynthetic efficiency resulting in higher biomass production.

Sulphur addition up to 20 kg ha^{-1} significantly increased seed yield of chickpea. Further addition of S did not show the significant improvement in seed yield. This increase in seed yield might have resulted from the favourable influence of S on growth; yield attributes *viz;* like primary branches, secondary branches, 1000-seed weight and efficient and greater partitioning of metabolites and adequate translocation of nutrients to developing reproductive structure. Although straw yield did not vary significantly due to sulphur addition but it was markedly increased with the application of 20 kg S ha^{-1}.

The higher straw yield under sulphur 20 kg S/ha^{-1} was because of higher growth parameters *viz;* plant height, trifoliate leaves and plant dry matter as well as greater nodulation.

Addition of 5 kg ha^{-1} significantly increased seed yield of chickpea and gave 193 kg ha^{-1} higher c than that of no zinc application. This increase in seed yield might be because of zinc takes part in metabolism of plant as an activator of several enzymes and enter directly or indirectly affect the synthesis of carbohydrates. The higher value of growth, nodulation and significant greater yield attributes *i.e.,* secondary branches per plant, seeds/ pod and 1000-seed weight of chickpea due to zinc application were also supported the higher seed yield of chickpea. Sharma and Abrol (2007) reported higher grain yield of chickpea with at 5 kg Zn ha^{-1} application. Straw yield was marginally increased and gave 514 kg hal higher under zinc 5 kg Zn ha^{-1}. This was probably owing to its influence on auxin synthesis, nodulation and N-fixation which promoted plant growth and development their by favourably influencing straw yield. Similar findings were also obtained by Kasturikrishna and Ahlawat (2000) in pea.

Harvest index was little higher under FYM 10 tonnes hal. It might be because of higher proportional seed yield as than that of control. This increased significantly with each increment dose of sulphur owing to greater proportional seed yield as compared with respective straw yield. Application of 5 kg Zn ha^{-1} led to record marginally higher harvest index than that of no zinc because of significantly greater seed yield than straw yield of treatment.

Economics

Net monetary returns of chickpea estimated significantly higher 10 t FYM ha^{-1} as compared with control. Such greater net returns were because of more gross monetary returns as compared to proportional increase in cost of cultivation of respective treatment. Addition of sulphur upto 20 kg ha^{-1} recorded significantly greater net monetary returns of chickpea. Further addition of sulphur *i.e.* 40 kg S ha^{-1} showed significant reduction in net monetary returns. Here, it has been noted that the cost of cultivation was enhanced too high due to greater cost of elemental sulphur. The cost of cultivation may drastically be reduced by addition of other cheap sources of sulphur instead of elemental S. Application of zinc marginally enhanced and gave Rs. 1313 higher net monetary returns than that of no zinc application. Such trend was because of significant greater proportional increase in gross monetary return compared with enhancement in cost of cultivation of the same treatment. The net monetary returns value under 5 kg ha^{-1} were not observed high because zinc had applied as zinc dust, being a costly input (Rs. 470/kg) which cost is too high (Rs. 2350 ha^{-1}) for use in one hectare and it accelerated the cost of cultivation and ultimately decrease the enhancement value of net monetary return. Return per rupee invested of chickpea marginally enhanced with addition of 10 t FYM ha^{-1} (Re. 0.13 ha^{-1}) owing to proportional higher gross monetary returns than that of cost of cultivation of respective treatment. In case sulphur addition, return/rupee invested was noted higher under control treatment (Re. 2,91) and it was subsequently reduced with addition of sulphur. Such trend was because of greater proportional increase in cost of cultivation due to addition of elemental S as compared with enhancement of gross monetary return of respective treatment. Application of no Zn gave little higher return/rupee invested under control (Re. 2.43) than that of zinc application 5 kg Zn ha^{-1}. The marginally lower value of returns per rupee invested under zinc 5 kg Zn ha^{-1} was because of higher cost of cultivation due to addition of zinc as zinc dust. Thus, it may be concluded that application of 10 t FYM ha^{-1} along with the sulphur 20 kg S ha^{-1} and Zinc 5 kg Zn ha^{-1} was found to be most appropriate dose of, FYM, sulphur and zinc for chickpea in rainfed area of Central India.

REFERENCES

Kasturikrishana, S. and Ahlawat, I.P.S. (2000). Effect of Moisture Stress and Phosphorus, Sulphur and Zinc Fertilizers on Growth and Development of Pea (*Pisum sativum*). *Indian Journal of Agronomy* 45: 353-356.

Rao Ch. Srinivasa, Singh K.K. and Ali Masood (2001). Sulphur: A Key Nutrient for Higher Pulse Production. *Fertilizer News* 16: 37-48.

Reddy, S.G., Maruthi, V. and Rekha Sree M. (2004). Assessing the Method of Application of Farm Yard Manure on Dry Land Crops. *Indian Journal of Agronomy* 49: 104-107.

Singh, D. and Singh, Y. (1995). Effect of Potassium, Zinc and Sulphur on Growth Characters, Yield Attributes and Yields of Soybean (*Glycine max.*). *Indian Journal of Agronomy* 40: 223-227.

Srinivasan, K., Sankaran, N. and Prabhakaran, J. (2001). Influence of Sulphur Application on Nodulation and Protein Content of Black Gram. *Madras Agricultural Journal* 87: 456-458.

Sharma, V. and Abrol, V. (2007). Effect of Phosphorus and Zinc Application on Yield and Uptake of P and Zn by Chickpea under Rainfed Condition. *Journal of Food Legumes* 20(1): 49-51.

Singh, V.K., Sharma, B.B. and Sahu, J.P. (2008). Effect of Organic and Inorganic Sources of Nutrients on Urdbean Productivity. *Journal of Food Legumes* 20(3): 173-174.

Index

******